ADVANCE PRAISE

"Every page of William Luers's memoir conveys the impact that a cultivated and principled person can have on life . . . As the title suggests, he has kept "Uncommon Company," and the book provides that same lucid intellectual companionship, as well."

—David Ignatius, Columnist, *The Washington Post*

"Bill Luers played an important role not only in the complex world of geopolitics and foreign policy but also in the intersection of diplomacy, culture and public institutions. Bill's deep insights into the museum world through his exceptional service as President of the Metropolitan Museum of Art make him an internationally versed and profoundly articulate participant and observer in the developments and changes of the world of culture over the past decades."

—Max Hollein, Director of the Metropolitan Museum of Art

"You will enjoy this portrait of a great patriot working around the world for the betterment of his country and mankind."

—Timothy E. Wirth, former US Senator from Colorado and president of the United Nations Foundation

"Bill Luers is a practitioner of strategic empathy—the art of listening without prejudice in order to gain insight into the motivations and intentions of others . . . His focus on artistic and cultural exchange as a powerful . . . diplomatic tool reflects his conviction that literature and art help us know ourselves while also revealing deeper insight into others, even those we consider adversaries. This is an inspiring story."

—Stephen Heintz, President of The Rockefeller Brothers Fund

William H. Luers

UNCOMMON COMPANY

Dissidents and Diplomats, Enemies and Artists

RODIN
BOOKS.

Hardcover ISBN 978-1-957588-30-8

eBook ISBN 978-1-957588-31-5

PUBLISHED BY RODIN BOOKS INC.

666 Old Country Road

Suite 510

Garden City, New York 11530

www.rodinbooks.com

Book and cover design by Barbara Aronica

Manufactured in Canada

To Wendy, without whom nothing works in this family and without whom this book certainly would not have happened. Wendy has been both my inspiration and my partner over this past half century and a major contributor to the words that made it to these pages.

I want to acknowledge my love for our five children—David, William, Amy, Ramsay, and Connor—and their spouses, and also our ten grandchildren—Cedar, Arden, Carl, Erin, Riley, Maya, Sofia, Luis, Mika, and Seiji—who make life such a daily pleasure for Wendy and me. Family first is our banner and motto. I hope that my love for Wendy and our children and grandchildren radiates throughout our lives and keeps us strong.

And to Frank Stella, a close friend and a giant internationalist artist who told his story of Abstract Art.

"Since wars begin in the minds of men, it is in the minds of men that the defenses of peace must be constructed."

—The preamble of the Constitution of UNESCO

CONTENTS

Photo Insert follows page 224

INTRODUCTION

In 1957, I entered the US Foreign Service as one of the thousands of aspiring diplomats who were then responding to a call to serve their country at a time when America and the Soviet Union were entering in the cold war. Little did I know that I would very quickly find my way to an unconventional form of diplomacy dominated by cultural exchanges and enriched by the vitality of the arts.

After the Second World War, there was a palpable sense in the US and Europe that America had come alive culturally. Louis Menand in his book *The Free World* gives flavor of this new world. After World War II, he notes, conditions changed for Americans.

So did art and ideas. The expansion of the university, book publishing, the music business, and the art world, along with new technologies of reproduction and distribution speeded up the rate of innovation. Most striking was the nature of the audience: people cared. Ideas mattered. Painting mattered. Movies mattered. Poetry mattered. The way people judged and interpreted paintings, movies, and poems mattered. People believed in liberty and thought it meant something. They believed in authenticity, and they thought it meant something. They believed in democracy and (with some blind spots) in the common humanity of everyone on the planet. They had lived through a worldwide depression that lasted almost 10 years and a world war that lasted almost six. They were eager for a fresh start.[1]

President Eisenhower, aware of this vitality in American society, proposed the establishment of the USIA, the United States Information Agency. His purpose was to tell the American story of what was happening in the US honestly and fully to the world. His predecessor, Truman, had been reluctant to do so, not wanting to be labeled as propagandistic; but Eisenhower, influenced by his advisors on "psywarfare" during the war, wanted to be as straight and factual as possible.

Eisenhower then went one step further: in 1959, he invited the Soviet Premier, Nikita Khrushchev, to visit him and tour the United States, which he did. During their meetings at Camp David, the two leaders, driven by the urgent need to find effective ways to head off nuclear holocaust and better manage the nuclear standoff, agreed to a series of people-to-people programs of exchange that sought to foster mutual engagement and awareness between the two countries. The exchange programs would eventually bring together millions of Soviets and Americans to learn from each other. These programs would have the effect of opening up, in the era of nuclear weapons, Soviet and American societies to the other.

This spirit of bringing together people of diverse—sometimes antithetical—backgrounds in a celebration of culture appealed to me; it made sense. In the end, it became my crusade.

As a young diplomat, I was tasked with arranging the visits of some of America's cultural luminaries, often escorting those in the program around the Soviet Union. These visits were filled with dinners and drinks and talks—lots of talks—between American painters and writers and playwrights and scholars and their Soviet counterparts.

From my first introduction to this refreshing program, I became a believer. So stark were the differences between the cultures, I believed, that there were bound to be eyes and minds opened.

To the American artists, these exchanges were often the first time they had had the opportunity to converse in person with their Russian, Czech, Hungarian, or Uzbek contemporaries. The Americans often found themselves sitting across a table from men and women whose efforts to create and innovate were harshly policed, whose art had to be sanctioned by the party to be legal, and who faced reprisal, deprivation, and exile if their work was deemed unacceptable. Though it was true that during their visits, the Americans' artistic and political ideas were challenged by party apparatchiki, these same ideas and views were eagerly engaged by their fellow writers and artists and many thousands of students.

To the Soviet writers and artists, these exchanges opened their eyes to the creative freedoms enjoyed by Americans and shone a spotlight on the state-imposed constraints that bound their creativity, inventiveness, and innovation. These interchanges contributed to the mounting dissonance between what they were being told of America and what they were learning from Americans themselves. The exchanges cast into doubt much of what they assumed about America and the West and helped shift the Soviet perspective from a propaganda-fueled fear of and hostility toward America to a recognition of commonality and a shared need to create.

For me professionally, the results of my interactions with these American and Soviet cultural figures were profound. The American writers and artists I hosted increased my insight into American strengths and weaknesses. They opened a window onto the dynamism that is the engine of American culture and introduced me to the seductive power of the arts.

The message of this book—what I worked for throughout my life—is that we must recognize and harness the power of culture to bridge the vast differences between peoples. There are a great many problems the world faces today—far more than when I started as a young Foreign Service Officer in the 1960s. One can point to the Russian invasion of Ukraine, the October 7 attack on Israel, the Iranian missile attacks upon Israel, the growing number of failed states, or the chaotic frontiers of Africa. But most worrisome to me is the static and toxic state of society in America today.

Today, the US is still the economic-political power of the world. Yet, our political system and society do not present to the world the aura of a model nation. Nor can a society struggling to keep itself together be held up as a shining light of competence. My message to the leaders of this country is clear: Diplomacy works. We must talk to the other. However, until we ourselves can learn to talk with the other *who lives next door*, until we learn to listen with civility *to family and friends and strangers alike*, it will be impossible to suggest to other nations that they do the same, but on a global stage. Until we right our own ship, it will be much more difficult for the US to conduct international relations under the auspices of these same principles.

Yet, I do believe the US will eventually return to these values at home. I also believe that the arts and humanities will play an important role in easing relations and tensions among Americans. If we learned anything from the Cold War, it is that the arts and communications can leaven attentions among groups that are ostensibly confrontational.

Though the cultural milieus I was most active in were painting and literature, there is a vast common language shared with the other cultural components of the arts. Music, both classical and popular, played a deeply consequential role in bringing the West into the homes of the citizens of the Soviet Union and the Eastern Bloc. There's no question that jazz played a vital connecting role between the United States and people of Communist countries. As early as the 1920s, jazz had become the metaphor

Duke Ellington and Paul Gonsalves jam session
in Leningrad with Soviet musicians, 1971.

for freedom in the Soviet Union. During the Cold War, it became a vital lifeline for those who listened to the Voice of America's radio program run by Willis Conover, who broadcast a nightly jazz program that was the most popular and beloved program in the entire Voice of America (VOA) repertoire.

Classical music, too, was broadcast to an immense audience for whom the VOA became a lifeline to the outside world. I remember when the New York Philharmonic was visiting Moscow to play with the Moscow Philharmonic. Worried about how the two symphonies would "talk to each other," Ambassador Foy Kohler lamented to me that the Russian and American musicians had no common language. I replied that certainly they have a common language: music. In looking to the future, that is how culture should be perceived: as a common language.

Diplomacy and the arts. So completely do I believe in their collaborative power that I have spent fifty years advocating for them, fighting for them, and celebrating all that has been accomplished in their names. This book is my testament to how the arts can be used to move our nation and our world toward higher levels of cooperation and understanding with each other. It is also a celebration of the human desire to create in the face of the existential threats we face today. As we look around to solve the problems that confront us, it is to diplomacy and to the arts that our society and our world must turn.

UNCOMMON
COMPANY

Bill at six years old.

CHAPTER 1

Beginnings

My earliest instincts to talk with "the other"—people not of my tribe or not of my in-group—are traceable to my upbringing in a small midwestern town. Springfield, Illinois, had no obvious "others." Like most such towns in Illinois and the rest of the middle west, the social breakdown in the 1920s and 1930s in our predominantly white community was based on income differences . . . and religion. In Springfield, the division was among German Protestants and Irish and Italian American Catholics. My mother, who came from an old family of long English heritage, was Scotch Irish Protestant and was particularly bothered by the Catholics. A brilliant bridge player, Mother played several times a week but rarely, if ever, with Catholic lady friends.

I had two older sisters, Gloria and Mary Lynd, both of whom married Irish Catholics from the Boston area. Gloria converted to the Catholic Church and became a true believer as a Catholic. Mary Lynd's husband, Richard Phelps, was an entrepreneur who would have liked to have played professional baseball. He had a high energy level, which saw him through many critical moments. Dick gave me my first exposure to the private sector when he put me on the board of his company—Superior Pet Products. I found the experience exhilarating and instructive. Lynd and Dick had three children, one of whom is named William Luers Phelps. Dick was particularly generous to my

Luers grandparents and uncles in Springfield.
Bill's father, Carl Luers, is on the right.

eldest son, Mark, who had lost his way but was brought back by my nephew Bill. Dick Phelps also made it possible for my son William Luers to attend Andover. My eldest sister, Gloria, had four children, including Trish McCaffrey, who became a soprano at the Metropolitan Opera in New York. She had a large voice and sang in several Wagner productions at the Met and was invited to sing in several opera houses in Europe, in various Wagner roles. She became a voice trainer for the Met after she retired from singing.

I attended Butler Elementary School, a public grade school near my home in the suburbs of Springfield. There was a tradition at Butler wherein the Protestant kids stood at the front of the school in the morning and jeered or shouted anti-Catholic epithets at the Catholic kids, who were walking to the Catholic grade school, Blessed Sacrament, only a few blocks away. We

Mary Lynd, Bill, and Gloria Luers.

would call them "cat likers" and "fish eaters" and other more disagreeable names. The rumor within "our tribe" was that the nuns who taught at Blessed Sacrament were cruel and beat the kids with rulers on their knuckles and taught only religion and the church, and thus the Catholic kids didn't know much. When I was in the eighth grade, a Catholic girl I had come to know at the Illini Country Club told me that our rumors about Blessed Sacrament were ridiculous. She invited me to spend a day going to classes with her at Blessed Sacrament. I thought it an interesting idea but knew my friends at Butler would think it a bad move and might signify a "giving in" to the Catholics, and certainly a weakness on our part. My mother, too, was leery, but not opposed. My father encouraged me. Pops was a banker and well-connected in the community, with friends everywhere of all faiths. He had a beautiful, trained singing voice and sang with choirs all over town. He took me to the First Presbyterian Church every Sunday. Among my fondest memories of childhood are of standing next to my tall straight-standing Pops, beautifully singing elegant hymns in harmony in the church Abraham Lincoln attended as an adult. After church, as we were departing, the congregation would come up to greet him. He would then proudly introduce me as his "Tucker" (the affectionate nickname my father used for me).

I sang in choirs in Springfield and continued to sing in the Navy. Our choir in the Naples command took me all around the Mediterranean, including my first and only visit to Malta. My voice was never comparable to my father's. My pops also greatly enjoyed drawing and was an elegant artist. His ability to draw building and spaces in rooms astounded me. His refined and precise lines seemed like those of a trained architect.

With my parents' agreement, my Irish Catholic pal Marion Nierman and I planned our day with our walking together to Blessed Sacrament, so that my jeering Butler grade school friends would see what I was doing. It was a lovely, sunny spring day and I learned a lot—mostly that none of my tribe's assertions and beliefs were true. The nuns were most kind and excellent teachers, so far as I could judge from one day in class. Their classes seemed more advanced in science than ours at Butler—one of the nuns had given an excellent talk on biology. No one tried to convert me to becoming a Catholic. I had a very good day and rejected any suggestion that the nuns were on good behavior because a Butler spy from the other tribe was in the school.

I walked home that day from Blessed Sacrament and told my friends at Butler that we had it all wrong about the Catholic school. I am not certain that all my male friends believed me, but I believe that all the girls did. Most of them knew Marion from the neighborhood. They also knew her from the country club. At some point, it did occur to me that our considering Catholics as "the other" was based less on ethnicity and religion and more on economics.

Butler had no Catholics as students. Nor were there any Hispanic students. And there were only two Jewish boys—Bobby Lubin and Arnold Stern. Bobby Lubin's father owned the local lumber company and lived only a few blocks from me. He and I began playing chess together, and I would frequently go to his house. His mother was always nice to me. I did sense a different culture in Bobby's house. Arnold Stern was one of the brightest students in our class, and we became good friends. I never went to his house, which was further out of town. Arnold's father owned Stern's Department Store in Springfield. I knew Bobby and Arnold were both from Jewish families, but I was never quite certain what that meant and why they were treated as "the other" by most of my friends. There was one Black student named Bobby White. I never met his parents or visited his house. He was a good athlete, and years later, when we both attended Springfield High School, he encouraged me to join the football team, even though I was already on the basketball team. But I was too lightweight to succeed at football. I had a group of friends who were six feet or over, and we played basketball virtually every day in the spring, summer, and fall. I also began to take golf lessons at the age of seven, and began to play golf frequently. I got to the point where I played golf nearly every day. I was pleased with my progress and particularly liked to play in the early morning when the dew was still on the greens. I found golf courses unusually athletically pleasing. I was captain of my golf team at Springfield High School and Hamilton College, but

I took up tennis when I married Wendy and gave up the game of golf. My first regular flow of income was from my hours working as a caddie on the golf course.

During this period of my childhood, I began to build dream-worlds during the very early morning hours: I imagined my role as a superhero who defeated the bad guys and brought peace. To this day, my most creative period in a day is from 4:00 a.m. to 7:00 a.m., when I organize my thoughts and write essays in my head, or pen op-eds or letters. As a kid, building dreams and fantasies or conceiving a better way to accomplish a task gave me great pleasure.

Many years later, John Cheever spoke to me about his creative morning moments, which were often spent writing. For example, after he was diagnosed with cancer, he shared with me his early morning musings about the stories of amazing cancer survivors. He spoke vividly about the stories he was writing of these survivors. John's daughter, Susan, who wrote his biography, told me she never found a trace of any of those stories among his papers. Perhaps he did not have the energy to write them down in the morning after his creative and hopeful early hour fantasizing. My early morning superhero musings have been the font of many of my most imaginative ideas for decades.

In 1942, we moved to Dayton, Ohio. My father had decided to go back into the Army after the Japanese bombed Pearl Harbor. He did not hesitate in his decision to drop his stature as a senior VP of the Illinois National Bank to go back into public service. This time, he was commissioned as a major in the US Army Air Corps and assigned as commanding officer of a new air base the US had decided to build in Dyersburg, Tennessee. Years later, I learned that, about a year after his assignment to the command, a letter had arrived at the War Department from a disgruntled former bank employee who alleged my father was a Nazi spy. The letter made a series of allegations drawing on the fact that my father's father was a German American immigrant, and that my father—an inveterate world traveler like my mother—had traveled as a tourist to Berlin in the mid-1930s. To my father's horror, he was relieved of his command in Dyersburg and sent to Fort Benning, Georgia, for interrogation and investigation. After a year of painful questioning and the gathering of letters attesting he had not been a Nazi spy during his years of community leadership in Springfield, Illinois, he was fully exonerated and given a new assignment as the budget and fiscal officer at Wright-Patterson Air Force Base in Dayton,

Bill's father Carl U. Luers at Wright Patterson Air Base.

Ohio—the headquarters of the US Army Air Corps which, after World War II became a new branch of the military, the US Air Force. For my father, being accused of being a Nazi spy after having fought in World War I against the Germans, having earned a silver star for bravery and a purple heart for his injury in battle during that war, and then having decided to go back in the military out of his patriotic sense of duty, was truly devastating. He never fully recovered from that disappointment in his government's reaction to a baseless allegation. Many German Americans experienced similar disappointments and degradations. It was my father's experience with questioned loyalty that made me particularly sensitive to the loyalty questions I faced during my career.

After this happened, our family moved to Fairborn, Ohio, the home of Wright Patterson Air Base near Dayton, where I entered ninth grade in Oakwood High School, in the suburbs of Dayton. I went from being the quintessential insider in Springfield to being "the other" in Oakwood. I was bused in from Fairborn with the other kids who lived at Wright-Patterson Air Force Base. I was seen as an Army brat. And all my friends were back in Springfield, hundreds of miles from Oakwood. I did find that my skill at basketball helped me break down the burden of being the outsider. Nevertheless, it was hard work to find a friend group in Oakwood, which seemed even less diverse than my community in Springfield. This transition was another experience that helped me in later life to adapt and adjust to new, unfamiliar situations, and to reach out to those who were considered "the other." From that point on, my other moves were less traumatic and easier for me to navigate. I came to understand that all people, no matter how different, have something to offer.

Young Bill Luers entering Hamilton.

Another major factor that reinforced my instinct to always talk to "the other" was my decision to go to Hamilton College rather than attend West Point. After two years living at Wright-Patterson Air Force Base, I had become friends with other Army brats, many of whom were headed for West Point to continue their father's profession. I chose to try for West Point to relieve my father of the cost of a private university. My father, of course, was not a career military officer. I got the West Point option; surprisingly, my father asked whether I thought that a good idea. I asked what my alternatives were. He did not know because he had never gone to university. He also asked whether I wanted to be a career military officer; he thought that I would get a broader education at a college or university than going to West Point. He said he would ask a friend who had attended Hamilton College. Intrigued by the idea, I applied to Hamilton and was selected quickly as a midwestern A student who attended public school. I have no doubt that the decision to attend college at Hamilton was fundamental to altering my life's trajectory and opened me up to many new worlds, including philosophy and history. Yet, much more was needed to pull me out of my narrow development, particularly the deprivation of not having a rich intellectual and cultural environment when I was growing up. Neither of my parents had attended university. They were highly intelligent and loved world travel and learning. But our conversations around the dinner table were not about books, ideas, or the arts.

My mother paid special attention to me as her youngest child and first boy. She taught me many games, including bridge; she was one of the best bridge players in Springfield. Good dining delighted her and she would take me out to dinner frequently. She was a great reader of American literature and an admirer of Edith Wharton.

When I arrived at Hamilton, I was set on a career in math and science, which ended up as my honors subjects. Even though many close friends and professors steered me toward a more intellectual path, nothing I perused at Hamilton even vaguely suggested a career as an internationalist or diplomat. I studied the French language for four years and hated it. In high school, I enjoyed Latin and treated it as I treated math—as a solvable puzzle. But the idea of learning a living language that would enable me to explain problems and differences to "the other" in their own language seemed a stretch for me.

After Hamilton, and strongly influenced by my father and some senior business leaders in Springfield, I decided to go to graduate school in chemical engineering at Northwestern

University, where I had received a fellowship for room and board at a fraternity house, thanks to my childhood friend Stuart Robinson. I had saved enough money from decades of summer jobs that I could cover the tuition out of savings. Two months of graduate work in chemical engineering convinced me that I was neither psychologically nor intellectually equipped to be a chemical engineer. In addition to taking engineering courses, I also had begun to audit the famous course on James Joyce and William Butler Yeats taught by Richard Ellmann. Riveted, I audited all Ellmann's classes on *Ulysses*. *Ulysses* is built like an indecipherable literary puzzle, not unlike what has always attracted me to math. Ellmann was a compelling speaker, and as the top biographer of Joyce, knew Joyce literature better than almost anyone. The experience with Ellmann moved me in a completely different direction. Also, since I had begun studying philosophy in my last year at Hamilton and found philosophy more compatible than engineering, I took the leap into taking graduate work in philosophy—to my father's astonishment and displeasure. He had questions: How would I make a living? Where would I live? And what happiness (comfort?) could I expect from a profession as a "philosopher"? And what about those companies that had offered me good jobs in Springfield as a chemical engineer?

I did not share with him that during my first few months at Northwestern, I was undergoing an intense period of thinking about a career as an Episcopal priest. A close friend from Springfield had recently committed to becoming a Catholic priest.

In a neat bit of foreshadowing, my first professor of philosophy at Northwestern was a Venezuelan, Eliseo Vivas. Vivas had a deep interest in Russia and had been drawn to Marx as a young man; he was also deeply interested in Russian intellectual history and culture. Later, as he learned more about the practices of the Communist Party in the USSR, he became anti-Communist. On the first day of class, Vivas announced to us that no student could consider himself educated until he had read Dostoevsky's *The Brothers Karamazov*, which became required reading for my first course with him on the British Empiricists—Locke, Berkeley, and Hume—none of whom had even the most vague connection to Dostoevsky.

Since the Korean War had begun during my Northwestern experience, I decided to enter the US Navy as an officer candidate rather than wait to be drafted into the US Army. I did it and dodged two bullets. First, it allowed me to move past the question of whether to enter the church, which I knew by then was not for me (by then I had come to enjoy life's many pleasures). Second, it allowed me to put off seeing the disappointment my father would surely feel when he learned that I would not be following a professional career at which I could make a living. Instead, I went off to war like he had done twice.

I completed the Naval Officer Candidate School in November 1952, and got the assignment I had requested and was posted to an aircraft carrier stationed in New York. Two days after reporting aboard the USS *Tripoli* in the Brooklyn Navy Yard, we sailed for our new destination home port, Alameda, California. Our "jeep" aircraft carrier, which was too small to launch modern day fighters, instead was designated to ferry the fancy new fighter aircraft, such as the F-86, to US forces in Asia and Europe. In my first year on the USS *Tripoli*, I crossed the Pacific half a dozen times, ferrying the F-86 to Japan and South Korea.

In June of 1953, the *Tripoli* was sent to Scotland to deliver several F-86 aircraft to the Royal Air Force. I was the officer of the

Ensign William H. Luers, 1952.

deck charged with taking the ship through the locks and narrow passages up the River Clyde to Glasgow. Guiding us was a professional Scottish river pilot without whom we could not have made this treacherous passage. During the passage, the pilot told me that the next day, the newly crowned Queen Elizabeth would be making her first official visit to Edinburgh as Queen Elizabeth II. He told me how to take a train to Edinburgh to be in position in time to watch the young queen's entry. He recommended I go to a hill overlooking Princess Street. Since I had done a senior thesis at Hamilton on the plots on the life of the first Queen Elizabeth, I planned to go to Edinburgh.

I got up early the next morning, on June 23, 1953, and I took the train to Edinburgh, arriving in time to see the grand entry on Princess Street of the queen surrounded by the guards of the Black Watch, the legendary third battalion of the Royal Regiment of Scotland, with its elegant black royal carriage. Riding in that carriage was the Duke of Edinburgh, the queen's consort, wearing his black uniform. Each horse pulling the black equipage also was black. The only non-black color in the entourage was the queen. She wore a stunning light-blue suit that glowed amid all the black. I can recall that color to this very day. Fifty-six years later, in the fall of 2009, I had an opportunity to meet Queen Elizabeth in Buckingham Palace. I asked her whether she still had the striking light-blue suit that she wore while surrounded by the Black Watch on Princess Street in 1953. She threw her head back in laughter. "Certainly not," she exclaimed. After a good-humored exchange, I told her that I had been so impressed by seeing the event that I swore to myself that I would begin to focus more attention on my own life. After all, the queen was only a couple of years older than I was. It was clear to me that I needed to pay attention to my own profession. As it turned out, the next week I noticed there was an opening for a junior officer (I was then an ensign) to serve as a permanent shore patrol officer in Naples, Italy.

The assignment was to live in Naples, Italy, starting in 1954, for a two-year assignment to NATO's Southern Command headquarters. To commit to completing the assignment in Naples, I would have to extend my three-year commitment to the Navy by one additional year. Naples was a city that our ship had visited several times, and one that I found fascinating. I was accepted for the transfer and extended my duty one more year.

Naples and Italy became a change factor that transformed my life and initiated my lifelong commitment to the arts and beauty.

Those two years opened me up to a new world and forced me to think more deeply about my major interests.

My initial fantasy was that I would find a lovely young Italian woman who would teach me Italian and the Italian way of life. The Italian teacher I finally contracted with was Signora Collucci, a middle-aged Neapolitan grandmother who was simply the finest language teacher I would ever have in my years of learning languages—Russian, Spanish, Czech, and German. From our first meeting, she spoke to me in Italian and encouraged me to reply in Italian, too. She was tolerant of my pronunciation and always encouraging when I tried out new words and new formulations. She was the opposite of the didactic French professor with whom I struggled for four years at Hamilton.

I began to feel comfortable speaking Italian in the same way that I came to know Naples: by walking and talking everywhere. I was much more comfortable at speaking than Italians were at understanding me. I met and befriended members of the Naples police force with whom I worked daily at the Central Police Headquarters (*la Questura Centrale*). Except for the Italian head of the vice squad, who spoke perfect English and who was my counterpart in overseeing the shore patrol, no one in my office spoke English. As such, I had to learn to communicate in Italian fast, which worked for me. The pressure to speak Italian rapidly fit with my plan. To learn the language more thoroughly, I also began to read Dante in Italian with the help of Signora Collucci. I read Dante's *Inferno* slowly, literally sentence by sentence; I still have in my library that small edition of Dante with all my scribblings in English in the margins. I began to study the issues of southern Italy and became particularly smitten by the enlightened leadership of Emperor Frederick the Second (thirteenth century), after whom the University of Naples was named. To learn more, I read, in Italian, Jacob Burckhardt's classic study of the amazing reign of Frederick, who was the king of Sicily and Holy Roman Emperor, and of Frederick's court in Palermo. Frederick surrounded himself with many of the great scholars of the Mediterranean and top scholars from the Middle East. It was not until the year 2000 that my wife, Wendy, and I were able to visit Palermo and learn more directly about the amazing cultural richness that had characterized Frederick's court.

I was quickly sucked into the culture of Naples and became a permanent convert to Italy—I became an unashamed Italophile. I, like many Americans, fell for its music, its art, its humor, the vitality of its people, and the food. And thanks to my tutor, Signora Collucci, I discovered that Italian has a word that characterizes so much of what I had come to believe was vital in my work. *Immedesimarsi* is a complex reflexive verb that represents both the concept of putting yourself in somebody else's shoes and the thought of empathy.

During those years of living in Naples, I read more books in English than in any other period of my life. What I learned is that living abroad stimulated my desire to read about the United States and read American literature, perhaps because I was so frequently asked questions about the US. My American friends in Naples were well-educated men and women and well versed in the arts. They helped guide my education in art. My roommate in Naples was Robert Melson, a graduate of the Yale School of Design. He and his close friend Jack McGregor became my informal tutors on Italian art and architecture. They recommended books and advised on sites and museums to visit during my frequent travels. I later took an apartment with Jack when I moved to New York. Jack was moving to New York after completing his PhD in art at Harvard to assume his new job as a curator of European Decorative Arts at the Metropolitan Museum of Art.

By the time I left to return to New York to study Russian and international relations at Columbia University, I had visited at least once all the major cities of Italy and all the national museums and major works of art. I had made friends with several new Foreign Service Officers (FSOs) on their first assignments as new diplomats at the American Consulate General in Naples. By that time, I had realized that I *was* able to learn a foreign language and had become convinced I should learn Russian and see whether I could become sufficiently knowledgeable about international affairs to pass the demanding Foreign Service exam. Specifically, I had decided to enter the US career diplomatic service to become an expert on the Soviet Union. The pull of the Soviet Union had become a dominant factor in my life because of the growing tensions between the NATO countries and the Warsaw Pact.

I resigned from the US Navy in June of 1956 and went to Harvard for an intensive summer course in Russian. I applied to study at the Center for Russian Studies at Harvard, but they sensibly rejected my application, as nothing in my education suggested that I would succeed in graduate work in Russian studies. I *was* accepted, however, to the master's program at the school of international relations at Columbia University. It was at Columbia, or rather at Columbia's Russian Institute, the other premier academic center for the study of Russian affairs in the US, that I would learn to speak Russian. Columbia was less concerned than Harvard about my lack of academic preparation and took into account my high motivation for changing course and my experience in the world, since my days of concentrating on math and science.

I arrived in New York City and joined up with Jack McGregor at our apartment on the Upper West Side, perfectly located so that I could walk to Columbia and Jack could walk to the Met.

My first months at Columbia were a challenge. I had not been to school since my graduate work at Northwestern University nearly five years earlier and had never studied political science and Russian before. In my initial meeting with Alexander Dallin, the director of the Russian Institute, before my summer school work at Harvard, I asked him whether Columbia offered a course on Marxism, explaining that I hoped to work in Moscow eventually. I was convinced that I would need to become proficient in at least two languages, Russian and Marxism-Leninism. I expressed surprise when Professor Dallin explained at length that Columbia, already perceived as a harbor for left-wing thinking by Senator McCarthy, would not consider having a course on Marxism-Leninism in its curriculum. Then, as I was leaving Dallin's office, his assistant summoned me secretively and told me that the university was offering a course *off campus* that might interest me. He hinted that it might touch on the basics of Marxism and Leninism. Quietly, he signed me up for the course.

The following week I had to travel quite a distance from the campus to the basement of a brownstone apartment building on Broadway, to a class which was listed only by a number. There was no course description or even the name of the professor who was teaching the class. It turned out that that semester's clandestine course on Marxism was being taught by Herbert

Marcuse, the German philosopher who became the darling and intellectual guru of the American radical left movement in the 1960s. The course was just what I wanted—an academic and intellectual romp through Marx. Since Marcuse disliked the Soviet distortion of Marxism and the rigorous power focus of Lenin, I was in no danger of being perverted. The course was invaluable from my perspective of learning the key vocabulary of Marxism, although, quite frankly, it was a bore.

During my studies at the Russian Institute, I looked at other jobs with US government agencies that might send me to work in Moscow. I interviewed with the CIA, the United States Information Agency (USIA), and took the Foreign Service exam. Because of the excellent learning experience at Columbia, I passed the written Foreign Service exam and then passed the oral exam. The panel that was testing my oral skills asked me to describe the history of socialism—as luck would have it, I had just finished reading the definitive intellectual history on that subject, which was *To the Finland Station*, by Edmund Wilson. It was another break of good luck facilitating my move to become a professional diplomat.

In seeking senior recommendations for the Foreign Service, I turned to Philip Jessup. Jessup had taught a course on international law at Columbia that I had taken. He had graduated from Hamilton College, where he had been president of the Senior Honorary Society, a title I also held at Hamilton. Professor Jessup drew a broad smile and told me that the last thing I wanted was a letter of recommendation from him. He explained that he had been hounded by Senator McCarthy for several years because of his close relations with Alger Hiss, because of his refusal to denounce Hiss because of his "unusual affinity for Communist causes," and because of his membership with several organizations with Communist affiliations. McCarthy was never able to prove any of his allegations against Jessup. In 1960, Jessup was elected by the General Assembly of the United Nations to be a judge on the International Court of Justice—a position that did not require Senate confirmation.

My other experience with McCarthy took place in 1986, after my retirement from the Foreign Service. That year, I was presented with the Foreign Service Cup by the head of the career service. The main benefit of receiving the cup was that I was given the opportunity to recommend next year's winner. I decided we should give the honor to John Stewart Service. Service was one of the old "China Hands" who had been accused of being a Communist for his writings as an FSO, when he criticized the nationalist Chinese government and advocated working in some way with the Chinese Communists and Mao. The pressure got so great that then secretary of state Dean Acheson fired Service. This initiated one of the most traumatic periods for the diplomatic service; it meant an end to unvarnished analysis and policy recommendations and raised the ante for one's perceived loyalty to country.

The question of loyalty was always a hard backdrop for me, given my father's extreme disappointment during World War II. The phenomenon haunted me throughout my time with the Foreign Service as I watched colleagues take the risks of dissidents during periods of political turmoil.

I entered the Foreign Service in the fall of 1957 and moved to Washington, DC, with my new wife, Jane Fuller, a painter from New York. My first assignment turned out to be vice consul in Naples, a city the Foreign Service understood I knew well. The assignment to Naples proved propitious because the consul

Bill in Naples with first son Mark.

general at the time was Jim Henderson, who had been the father of one of my girlfriends when I was living in Naples during my time in the Navy. Jim had developed a level of understanding and respect for my Italian language abilities.

In 1959, after four years in the Navy and nearly three more years with the Department of State, I was asked to interpret, from Italian to English, for President Harry Truman. I had never come close to meeting an American president. Truman was to receive a surprise visit from former president Enrico De Nicola, who had been the first postwar Italian president. De Nicola had never been a fascist. As a member of the Italian Liberal Party, he had been asked by the Italian establishment to take the place of Mussolini, who had been killed, and the king, Victor Emmanuel III, who at the time was about to abdicate his throne to make room for Italian democracy. Since I had been interpreting for Jim

Henderson for nearly two years, he evidently thought me up to the task.

During my time translating for President Truman, there were no high politics discussed. He had been that day to Pompeii but wanted to discuss the history of southern Italy, which had been the Kingdom of the Two Sicilies, under Habsburg Spanish rule, before Italy was united into one country in the late nineteenth century. I was deeply impressed by Truman's knowledge of the history of that still underdeveloped and obscure part of Italy. He was traveling with his favorite traveling companion, Judge David Edelstein. Clearly Truman knew Europe and the dynamics of southern Europe. I was not awestruck; I was reassured and impressed by our former president's curiosity and grasp of the issues.

In the summer of 1959, I returned to Washington, DC, for my first assignment back in the State Department. I had the good fortune of being assigned as the first junior officer in the Office of Soviet Union Affairs that was to be headed by a man I knew well from Naples. John McSweeney had been a political advisor to the southern commander of NATO. Working with John in Moscow was the perfect assignment for me, given my career focus on the Soviet Union.

CHAPTER 2

Edward Albee and John Steinbeck as Writers in Official Exchange with the USSR

On the evening of November 22, 1963, the playwright Edward Albee and I were walking back to our hotel from the National Opera House in Odessa, Ukraine, USSR. We had just finished a stirring but depressing rendition of Mussorgsky's *Khovanshchina* in which a large group of Old Believers commit suicide in a burning structure. Even for a Russian opera, the ending was spectacularly cataclysmic. Edward was bothered by the "screeching soprano." As we approached the long, graded stairway toward the entrance of the hotel, I was explaining to Edward the great music history of Odessa, which was almost comparable to that of Vienna. I told him that two of the most in-demand solo violinists in the world at the time were from Odessa: Nathan Milstein and David Oistrakh, and the brilliant pianist Sviatoslav Richter, was a native of Odessa. Also Ira and George Gershwin and Bob Dylan's family were from Odessa.

Entering the hotel, Edward and I saw dozens of hotel staff we saw dozens of hotel staff and guests gathered in front of the entry. Their presence was foreboding; I was certain we were in trouble. As we neared the gathering, the hotel manager said to us in Russian, "President Kennedy has been killed."

My first thought was that I most certainly had misunderstood. My second thought was, *Was this a Soviet provocation?* Regardless, if true, America and the world had suffered a tragic loss. In that moment, I was unable to compute the impact such an event would have upon the world stage and American foreign policy, and upon the two of us, should the Soviet Union have been involved in the assassination.

I don't remember what Edward said, only that the manager led us to the radio in the middle of the cavernous entry hall. Voice of America was transmitting in English the details of the events from Dallas, Texas. Edward and I, like most Americans around the world that day, were disbelieving and struck dumb. But so far as I could tell, we were the only Americans there that night.

Soviet citizens gathered around us. They spoke words of sympathy in Russian. Shock etched shadows in their faces. Many wept, revealing a depth of admiration for the charismatic American president and for the United States that I had not previously seen. I had arrived in Moscow only four months earlier, as a new Foreign Service Officer, assigned to the American Embassy.

Over the next two hours, the sorrow and sympathy emanating from our fellow listeners began turning to uncertainty and then fear. Their questions were my own.

Were the Soviet secret police behind the killing?

What will this mean for the new relationship between Kennedy and Khrushchev?

Was this Soviet retribution for Kennedy's demand, just the year before, that Khrushchev withdraw the nuclear weapons from Cuba?

The guests in the hotel, along with the Odessans who had gathered that evening, were full of remorse at the loss of the young and dynamic American president who contrasted so sharply with the distant septuagenarian bureaucrats who made up the politburo. The shock of the event gave way to anxiety about the impact on their lives.

Edward was hit hard. He thus far had been unimpressed by the charmless and heavy-handed Soviets who were managing him. He was particularly distressed by the drabness of their lives and their cities. Kennedy's death punctuated the grim reality of where he was. He later wrote to a close friend:

> I'm sure [Kennedy's death] doesn't even make any *reality* sense in New York, but it is almost impossible to come to grips with it here. I miss everyone and everything so greatly and have cried like a child or maybe like a grown up.[2]

Of Kennedy's murder, Edward wrote to his producer, Richard Barr:

> The whole experience has been—is being—what they call irreplaceable, or something, but it would be hard for you to imagine the depression and numb panic that sets in for a while each and every day.[3]

That evening, the small radio seemed to grow in size. For several hours, we sat beside our lonely lifeline to the world, its voice echoing in the vast marble hall. We sought to console and be consoled by the dozens of locals also gathered in the hotel. We tried to assure them and ourselves that this terrible act would not lead to war with the Soviet Union. But honestly, we did not know. Nor could we fully grasp the potential impact to

Soviet-American relations. We reminded the Russians around us that because of our constitutional system, a new president had already been installed—there had not been a coup. But we knew nothing more than what VOA was telling us. Throughout that evening, I tried to interpret for Edward the moving, spontaneous, and often irrational sentiments of our companions, who began to feel closer to becoming friends with every moment.

Later, after we had heard everything VOA was broadcasting several times over, Edward and I went up to his room with a bottle of vodka. Together, we sat speculating about what this event could mean. *Might the Soviets have been behind the killing?* the locals had asked. We wondered as well. Late into that night, we worried and wept in the distant corner of an unfamiliar and alien world.

Edward had a particular fascination with death. Many of the settings of his plays, along with the characters and their actions, imbued with a sense of death and darkness.

Death was his muse, but so too was it the muse for many writers. Years later, I asked Philip Roth what *he* had been writing at the time of Kennedy's death.

He replied, "You know me, Bill. The same things I always write about—death and pussy."

For Albee, the thrill he had felt seeing Sergei Eisenstein's legendary three hundred steps (famous from the film *Battleship Potemkin*), just the day before, had been wiped out by Kennedy's assassination. He and I flew back to Moscow from Odessa the following day. As was protocol, the embassy observed three days of mourning.

Edward's official cultural visit was suspended.

———

I had arrived in Moscow a few months earlier, in July 1963. At that time, diplomatic communications between the United States and the Soviet Union at the highest levels were being cautiously and tentatively restored after the Cuban missile crisis in 1962.

With the threat of nuclear war behind them, both leaders had found it easier to change course and resume serious and constructive leader-to-leader communications once again. The exchange of letters between Kennedy and Khrushchev, which had begun when Chairman Khrushchev first reached out to Kennedy when he was president-elect, resumed. A hotline was established between the US president and the Soviet premier on August 30, 1963. The most significant result and far-reaching event of this thaw was the signing of the Limited Test Ban Treaty, also in August 1963.

This treaty, the first of many subsequent agreements to manage the nuclear arms race, was signed in Moscow on August 5, 1963. It had been imagined by both governments for many years, but only after those thirteen worrying days in October 1962 was Averell Harriman, so trusted by the Soviets and one of Kennedy's "Wise Men," instructed to conclude the deal. A new era of diplomacy with America's enemy number one seemed possible.

The signing of the treaty was celebratory and memorable. To my young eyes, the historic treaty illustrated how diplomacy at the highest levels was meant to work. The signing took place in the Kremlin. It was followed by a reception for the two delegations at Spaso House, the residence of the American ambassador to the Soviet Union. Attending the signing were Khrushchev, members of the Politburo, and Andrei Gromyko, the Soviet minister of foreign affairs. The British foreign secretary, Lord Hume, also joined the event since the UK, already a nuclear power, was party to the treaty. The Russians mixed with American secretary of state, Dean Rusk; Senator Hubert Humphrey; and the American ambassador to the United Nations, Adlai Stevenson. Witnessing the sight of these men standing and drinking together left an indelible mark on all who were there, including me. It seemed there *was* a better way to manage the Cold War.

Adlai Stevenson, whom I had known from my hometown of Springfield, Illinois, when he was governor of Illinois, pulled me aside. He noted that Averell Harriman, who had negotiated the treaty, had chosen not to attend the ceremony. The Soviet leadership had always found it easier to deal with Harriman, as he fit into their ideological thinking about the US.

Averell was from the railroads and Wall Street and was at the top of Washington's political power elite—he matched perfectly the Soviet view of how the US worked. Stevenson went on to point out that he himself could probably not have negotiated the agreement. He had never been treated with respect by Soviet leaders because he was seen as unconnected to any of those power worlds and was a two-time loser for the presidency.

After the signing of the Treaty, Ambassador Stevenson and Senator Humphrey decided to show several of the FSOs and interpreters the parks and subway stations of Moscow. On this excursion, the two of them then began to proclaim their message of unity directly to Soviet citizens in the streets. In loud voices, they announced that Soviet and American peace and cooperation was now possible.

Watching two of America's most accomplished, retail, "stump" politicians practicing their trade in English to dozens of befuddled Soviet citizens who had no idea who these two earnest guys were, or what they were talking about, was one of my most amusing memories of that first year in Moscow. Such interaction with political leaders was never seen in the USSR.

After the heady experience of witnessing the signing of the Test Ban Treaty, I was resigned to starting my slightly less impressive first-year job in the embassy as the General Services Officer.

My first real assignment as the new General Services Officer in the embassy was to work with a new security specialist who had come from Washington to find microphones in the embassy office spaces. His name was Mac Musser, and he was particularly talented at discovering listening devices. We'd had quite clear indications that the Soviets were hearing, rather precisely, the conversations we were having in all the embassy offices and rooms in the building on Tchaikovsky Street. Mac made the decision that we should simply strip the rooms to find the microphones. Anxious to rid ourselves of the bugs, we took one of the military attaché rooms of the embassy and stripped it down to the bare concrete floors. But still Mac got a signal for a bug. We sat in the completely empty room one evening, befuddled, when Mac looked at me and said, "It's there behind the radiator." The radiator was under the window, so we proceeded to turn off the heat so we could drain the radiator and remove it. It turned out Mac was right: we discovered that every radiator in the rooms on the facade side of the building was shielding a live microphone. Our experience, however, was not unique.

I had friends who'd served in the American Embassy in Moscow in the 1940s; they informed me that they could recall when

Stalin ordered that the American Embassy should not be sited across Manezh Square from the Kremlin but moved instead to a different location. These same former diplomats said that the preparations for the move into the new embassy building took several months, and they recalled that the facade of the building was covered with scaffolding, which had presumably concealed the installation of microphones in the radiators in every room on the facade of the new embassy.

Mac and his jubilant team took great pleasure in feeding electricity back through the Soviet wire to the receivers and ears at the other end. Surprisingly, ten years later, when the US government built a new embassy behind the one on Tchaikovsky, it did not remember the history of this discovery and, for economic reasons, authorized the Soviets to play a role in the construction of our new embassy, which, of course, was subsequently found to be riddled with microphones and other listening devices—it was a problem that plagued the new embassy for decades.

Beyond hunting for microphones, I was to oversee the work of about 170 Soviet employees who helped run the embassy— drivers, janitors, maids, painters—all of whom were also working in some way for the Soviet secret police. The good news about my job and my position being centered among almost two hundred Muscovites was that my fluency in the Russian language would get better. The bad news was that the job would not allow me the greater contact with the far-flung Russian people I yearned for, nor the opportunity to travel, which I felt I needed in order to grow in my job. As a budding diplomat, I felt it was essential for me to get to know that seemingly endless country that spanned eleven time zones.

However, professional pivots can happen without warning,

and three months into my new position, I was given a surprise assignment. "Rocky" Staples, the head of the information department, asked me to accompany two writers during their upcoming visit to Moscow.

Though little fanfare was made over the assignment, I was about to be introduced to a dimension of traditional diplomacy I had not expected. It was an assignment that would change the trajectory of my career and my vision of diplomacy for the next sixty years.

Almost twenty years earlier, amid a growing Soviet propaganda campaign, President Truman had been reluctant to proclaim the US story too boldly. His successor, however, facing an even greater barrage of Soviet propaganda, chose to shout America's story and creative energy to the world. The premier American warrior in World War II, Eisenhower knew well the value of psywar. In 1953, he established a new entity to work alongside other institutions dealing with US foreign affairs, including the State Department. The USIA was charged with going on the offensive to counter Soviet propaganda efforts, and to do so via a celebration of American culture.

As described by the President's Committee on International Information Activities, which had been formed specifically to conduct a comprehensive review of America's foreign policy:

[The] primary and over-riding purpose of the [program] should be to . . . submit evidence to the peoples of other nations that their own aspirations for freedom, progress, and peace are supported and advanced by the objectives and policies of the United States. The efforts of all media—radio, press and publications, motion pictures, exchanges of persons, and libraries and information centers—should be directed to this end: to show the identity of our goals with those of other peoples. These goals and desires which we hold in common must be explained in ways that will cause others to join with us in achieving them.[4]

Through the USIA, the Eisenhower administration sought to codify as official policy an effort to expand American diplomatic efforts to spotlight the freedoms, advantages, and richness of American culture. This effort would come to be called cultural diplomacy.

Some of America's most creative minds were tapped as the USIA developed the substance and concept of cultural diplomacy into a high art form. Upon its rollout, this new tool of diplomacy allowed FSOs and ambassadors around the world to communicate America's values and successes in an understandable format with local governments and, more importantly, the local citizenry.

As one of its pillars, Eisenhower's strategy of cultural diplomacy was to utilize much more actively the diplomatic corps in reaching the peoples of the Soviet Union. His "means" were to shine a light on America's cultural, intellectual, and artistic freedoms. His "ends," he hoped, were to reach those members of the Communist states most likely to open up their societies.

Though Eisenhower's program of cultural diplomacy came into being over the full course of the 1950s, it took a decidedly personal turn in 1959, when he invited Soviet Premier Nikita Khrushchev to tour the United States and to meet with him at Camp David. Eisenhower's initiation of direct engagement with the Soviet Union was greatly motivated by the threat of nuclear holocaust. But he carried his mission beyond merely meeting with the Soviet leader.

In a series of encounters—both direct and indirect—during Khrushchev's 1959 visit to the US, the Soviet leader and Eisenhower came to an understanding that the great power relationship should be managed as a competition between two political systems to demonstrate which was most successful in satisfying the needs of people. Eisenhower and his team defined the US role in the competition around the evident successes of the booming American economic system that made possible the high American standard of living and the core American ideas of freedom to write, create, speak, and worship in their own way. The Soviets defined their role around the wisdom of a planned economy, the absence of the corrupting consequences of private capital and capitalism, and Communism's promise of wide and equal distribution of goods and services across society.

One might well wonder why Khrushchev would accept such an engagement. It seems that Khrushchev predicated his belief—and that of the Politburo—in the dominance of the Soviet Union in such a competition on the strength and internationalism of Communist ideology in a world that had been shaken by World War II and was undergoing a resurrection and traumatic transformation by the unraveling of the European-dominated colonial system. The Soviet leadership that had kept the Soviet Union from being crushed by the Nazi invasion and had survived Stalinism had a certain confidence that their system was working and could be made to work better for a world in search of development models.

We always wondered what the Soviet leaders really believed with regards to Marx and the long-term viability of government-controlled complex industrial societies. The evidence that we had suggested that Khrushchev, in particular, believed that party and state total control of industry and the economy was the correct path. Khrushchev believed that the inefficiencies in the Soviet system in the late 1950s existed because the economy was still hobbled by the rigid controls and brutal methods of the Stalin era. What was needed, he thought, was a better way to implement and execute the manner in which the state controlled the economy. Khrushchev's personal bias was to determine how the Communist Party could better deploy the government agencies to achieve a more successful and productive society. Thus, he was given to trying out fundamental system reforms of how the Communist Party oversaw the government. Eventually, he was referred to as a "harebrained schemer." For his efforts, he was thrown out in 1964.

Over the years, through intercepts and other indications we had from Soviet leaders, we learned that they continued to be persuaded that the capitalist system was severely weakened by internal contradictions and corruption and was progressively undermined by social and political movements. In addition, Khrushchev retained certain confidence that Russian scientists were potentially equal to American scientists. A major goal for the Soviets in this competition with the US was to mine the American knowledge base and to learn the how-to of American scientists and engineers, and also to discover and transfer scientific innovation and technical know-how into deployable technology that would help the society and the state. This—the belief that if only they could turn their own scientific efforts into working technology, Communism would triumph—was to be a foundational belief shared by other Soviet leaders. We have enough evidence from Gorbachev himself that he continued to believe in the Communist system, and in the idea, shared by Khrushchev, that wiser forms of the execution of Marxism were needed.

Finally, there was an underlying belief by Khrushchev that the corruption and excesses of American capitalism were leading to the collapse of the American system, which would be replaced by a system more compatible to the Soviet Union. For these reasons, therefore, the Soviet leadership accepted the terms of open competition that led to the extensive cultural and intellectual exchanges from which the Soviets hoped to glean wisdom on how better to reform Soviet technology and science.

And so it was in November 1963 that Rocky Staples, in charge of the embassy's Press and Cultural Department, who had gifted me with my new assignment, announced that the American writer John Steinbeck and his wife, Elaine, were to arrive in Moscow as a part of the new writers' exchange program. They were to begin a two-month tour behind the Iron Curtain. Peter Bridges, a fellow FSO and friend, was assigned to accompany Steinbeck and his wife on their travels. I was tasked with accompanying the young playwright Edward Albee, who arrived alongside John and Elaine.

I picked up Albee at the Sheremetyevo Airport in Moscow in early November to start his "travels with Steinbeck." I took him directly to a reception at the embassy given by Rocky. Rocky "was a former US Marine: blunt, smart, and an earnest communicator. On entering the room, Edward and I were greeted enthusiastically by Rocky, who stuck out his hand and said, "Welcome to Moscow. You can call me Rocky, if I can call you Ed."

Albee replied coldly—as only he could do—"No one has ever called me Ed."

During the first two weeks, Albee and Steinbeck met with dozens of official Soviet writers and translators, plus seemingly hundreds of students and young writers in Moscow and Leningrad. Peter Bridges and I often traveled with our writers together, but the programs for each man had been developed differently.

Some of the leading lights of the Soviet literary scene at the time served as ubiquitous hosts, including Yevgeny Yevtushenko, a poet; Andrei Voznesensky, also a prose writer; Vasily Aksyonov, a novelist; the poet Bella Akhmadulina; and the fabulous Anna Akhmatova, one of the most significant Russian poets of the twentieth century. There was much drinking and eating at all events. Edward gradually warmed to the intellectual environment, as he began to sense sparks and creative fire coming from within the seemingly moribund authoritarian culture.

John Steinbeck was the logical first choice for the writers' exchange. He had won the Nobel Prize in Literature in 1962 and was probably the best-known American writer in the Soviet Union. Steinbeck's moving tales of America's social struggle and economic injustice qualified him in their minds as the perfect American progressive writer of the Left. Many had assumed, incorrectly as they would discover, that he was a closet Communist.

The sixty-one-year-old Steinbeck had recommended that Albee accompany him, since, at thirty-five, Albee came from a different generation and worldview. At the time, due mainly to the success of *Who's Afraid of Virginia Woolf?*, Albee was regarded as the most significant avant-garde American playwright in a generation. His off-Broadway productions *The Zoo Story* and *The American Dream* were widely acclaimed. In 1963, *Virginia Woolf* was still playing to packed audiences in New York and London. John and Elaine became close friends with Edward during their shared Russia trip. They were to remain so until John died. Elaine and Edward continued the close relationship that had been locked in place by their common intense, depressing, and exhilarating Soviet experience.

One evening in Moscow, John and Elaine were invited to a reading of a play adapted from the Steinbeck novel *The Winter of Our Discontent*. The book had been published only two years earlier in the US and was already available in Russian. The producers of the dramatic adaptation were from the Moscow Art Theater (MXAT), the most celebrated drama theater in Russia. The novel is about a family that has fallen onto bad times. It describes the desperate and even criminal drive of the characters to acquire money in the capitalist society.

Elaine, a former actor and stage director, listened carefully to the translation of the words spoken by the actors. She had been whispering to me throughout the reading. When the performance ended, she announced, "John, they have turned your story into a Communist propaganda tract."

John frowned, and the two of them walked off the stage, politely but resolutely. That was only the first of many stressed moments of John's clarifications. The Russians learned several times that John supported Kennedy's entry into the Vietnam War and was proud to have his son serving in the military in Vietnam.

A few days later, on a trip to Leningrad, John and Edward were invited to a dinner offered by the officially sanctioned, notoriously conservative Union of Soviet Writers of Leningrad, headed by the notorious Stalinist poet Alexander Prokofiev. We learned afterward that both Edward and John, having drunk extra vodkas, had become rattled by the primitive Stalinist banter of the hosts. When Edward gave his toast, he said that writers were treated worse under Stalin than under Hitler. In the city that had barely survived a nine-hundred-day Nazi siege, that remark did not go down well, particularly for the Stalinist head of the Union of Writers.

Edward's intellectual honesty and direct response to all questions stunned me. I had not met anyone like him before. In his conversations, he answered questions as he saw the truth at that given moment. The next day, in a different environment with different people and feeling differently, he would likely give an equally honest, but completely different answer. He resisted patterns of talking and thinking as if patterns were a disease. When asked about parents—his real parents whom he had not known and his adopted parents whom he knew too well—he would vary his responses and use words that seemed right for the truth at that instance.

His attention to the precise meaning of words and phrasing was intimidating—as it was for many of his associates in the theater. My education had been in mathematics and the sciences; I had always been attracted to facts, numbers, and how to solve problems. I had not read widely in college and certainly not the classics. The language, diction, and idioms used by Albee transfixed me.

Albee was the storm that swept me into a new world of ideas and words. Our friendship lasted until his death. At his memorial service at the August Wilson Theatre in the theater district in Manhattan, we heard from dozens of Broadway's leading actors, directors, playwrights, and friends about the unique and dominating spirit of Albee's presence in the American theater. We attended performances of most of his plays—some multiple times. His work grabbed the imagination of American audiences of all types for over forty years. Europeans, as well, were enthusiastic about every new Albee play, which helped him manage the decade during which the *New York Times* critics rejected him regularly.

While in Moscow, Edward had asked the Union of Soviet Writers whether he might visit Odessa. He wanted to see the grand Potemkin Stairs. Edward, whose plays often include an unseen but talked about baby, recalled vividly the signature Eisenstein scene in which a baby carriage dives wildly down that entire stairway. He had to see those stairs.

Upon receiving permission, we went via train first to Kiev where we were to meet the prominent nonconformist Ukrainian writer Vsevolod Nekrasov. On the eleven-hour train ride from Moscow, we were accompanied by Edward's escort, a man named Georgiy Braitburg. Braitburg was a member of the Union of Soviet Writers and was most certainly closely associated with the KGB. He was smart and spoke English well. Edward distrusted him from the first moment.

Tensions on long train rides are meat for Russian writers. Russian expanses are vast and there is much time for talking and for drinking. On this ride, the vodka flowed freely, thanks to the beneficence of the Union of Soviet Writers and to Albee's thirst for the stuff. Along with the vodka flowed debate about Soviet history. Edward asked Braitburg whether he had ever disagreed with his government's policies. Braitburg said he had

Baby carriage on steps in Odessa from the film
Battleship Potemkin by Sergei Eisenstein.

disagreed on any number of positions, but when asked to clarify
he was unwilling or unable to be specific. The interrogation persisted for hours. Edward asked whether Braitburg, who was Jewish,
had opposed the Hitler-Stalin Pact in 1939. Braitburg wobbled.
Ultimately, he gave the Soviet line that the pact was signed to
gain time for the strengthening of Soviet forces against Germany.
Edward replied that it was a cynical act to divvy up Poland.

Edward then said to Braitburg, "I will kill you." Quite drunk,
Edward did not appear to be joking.

For the rest of the trip, there was quiet but neither tran-
quility nor sleep. On arrival in Kiev, Edward said calmly and
determinedly to our host, who was from the Ukrainian Union
of Writers, that he did not want to continue with Braitburg. He
would prefer not to see him again.

It was Edward's way of "killing" a disagreeable Soviet bureau-
crat.

Over the years I have tried to sort out the reasons for Albee's occasional outbursts during the time we spent together. The mixture of the booze and his displeasure of the Soviet bureaucrats were two obvious causes. But Edward also was lacking a love relationship—which was his muse as a playwright and flowed out of the loveless relationship he had with his adoptive parents. His temperament changed dramatically when he finally met and fell in love with Jonathan Thomas, who gave him the love he had never had.

His threat to "kill" Braitburg seemed straight out of one of his plays. A persistent theme of Albee's plays is that his characters endure the lies they tell themselves. Over the course of the play, the characters face the question of whether they will be able to survive without the lie. In *Who's Afraid of Virginia Woolf?*, George's relentless and cruel verbal attacks on his wife, Martha, are meant to break her dependence on the lie that they have a child. The resolution of the relentless vitriolic exchanges between the two is dependent on whether she can survive without her treasured lie.

Edward's plays set up confrontations in which cruel and shocking verbal attacks force characters to recognize the lie and risk the uncertain future. Edward found in Braitburg a character who was living by a lie he refused to question. Edward's verbal cruelty was to create a shock that might help Braitburg reject the lie and try to survive the consequences.

Albee's flights of anger and confrontation worried me about the future of the writer exchange program. Yet, I came to appreciate over the coming decades that the best "exchanges" were not necessarily always enriched by civil discourse. As in diplomacy, stern confrontation plays an important role. But diplomats generally use anger sparingly. Edward, not so much.

In good spirits in Kyiv, we spent a relaxed time with Ukrainian writers. Following that, we flew to Odessa on the morning of November 22, without Braitburg—or any other escort from the Union of Soviet Writers—to see the Potemkin Stairs.

The stairs thrilled Edward. But the news of Kennedy's assassination later that night defeated our good spirits and left us wondering about the state of the world.

After we had returned to Moscow for the three-day mourning period, I offered to drive Edward to the "Golden Ring" of ancient Russian towns near Moscow. He agreed, and together with my then wife, Jane, we drove into the countryside. Halfway there it began snowing. I considered turning back—Russian snowstorms in November are not for the faint of heart. But foolishly, we decided to push on to Rostov. By the time we were close to Rostov, where we would be spending the night, it was already dark, and we were in a full Russian blizzard.

Though there were virtually no cars on the road. The snow was so thick that I was driving very slowly. Suddenly, out of the blinding whiteness, I saw a flash. There, directly in front of my headlights was a person riding a bicycle in the dark down the middle of the road. I hit the brakes and the car slid sideways. It banged hard against the bike, knocking the man onto the ground.

We quickly stopped and went to the man, who was injured. After a few minutes, Jane was able to flag down the lone car that passed by. The Soviet driver took the injured man to the nearest hospital, and we followed. The hospital would not let me enter but gave me a number I could call the next morning. We drove on to Rostov. I called the embassy and was cautioned not to pursue the issue with Soviet authorities but to return to Moscow the following day.

Both Edward and I were distressed by this event. Would the man live or be permanently disabled? Was there any way I could help him? And what would Soviet authorities do? Would they take retribution against me?

Our discussion that night brought out thoughts in me that I did not know were there. I discussed my thinking about becoming an Episcopal priest and why I had dropped that idea. He talked about his childhood and again, as always, about his parents.

We never talked about his personal life. I had sensed that his occasional calls to New York, presumably to a current partner, left him anxious. In that era, relationships were not discussed easily among men. It would have been misunderstood or offensive to have said anything to him, even though Edward's homosexuality was public knowledge. He had made no effort to conceal his sexual orientation.

Many years later, Mel Gussow, Albee's biographer, revealed that Edward had planned to meet Terrence McNally, another American playwright, in Prague. Albee was to continue his State Department cultural exchange to Communist Central Europe by visiting Poland and then Czechoslovakia after Moscow. Edward's long-term relationship with McNally was breaking up while Edward was in the Soviet Union.

The following morning was one of those sun filled days in Russia that bless the eye after blizzards. The gilded domes of Rostov's ancient churches beckoned, but per the embassy, we were to return directly to Moscow. Edward and I were still deeply shaken by the accident, and hoped the man would survive. I filled out

extensive reports at the embassy on what had happened and made
several calls to the hospital to seek information. I was assured he
did not die.

The embassy strongly advised me to cease trying to reach the
man or his family and nothing more came of the event. One year
later, the Soviet Foreign Ministry requested by diplomatic note
that I provide a sum of money to cover the hospital bill for the
man's injuries. My insurance company miraculously covered the
cost. To this day I am haunted by the memory of the sight of that
man emerging before me in the blinding snow, pedaling home at
night in the middle of the dark road. It is a trauma that endures.

Winters offered my most mesmerizing Russian experiences.
Every morning, I walked from my apartment on Kutuzovsky
Prospect to the American Embassy on Tchaikovsky Street,
roughly a thirty-minute walk from my apartment. During the

Bill with Mark and David in Moscow.

winter, I never ceased to marvel at the babushkas with their straw brooms, sweeping the snow from the streets as it fell. This Sisyphean task spoke to the Russian refusal to allow the snow to control their lives. The beauty of newly fallen snow shielded the drab reality of Soviet Russia: Moscow was never more beautiful than when covered with snow.

After the ill-fated trip to Rostov, Edward wanted to take one last trip to Leningrad before his official exchange visit ended. The opportunity came when Edward ran into William Walton at his hotel. Walton had been one of President Kennedy's closest friends in Washington. Less than a week after the president's burial, he had arrived in Moscow on a special personal mission from the Kennedy family. Walton was a renowned journalist and an abstract expressionist painter. He had been a central actor in Kennedy's presidential campaign; his home was used to house Kennedy's transition office before the inauguration in 1961. At the time he arrived in Moscow, Walton had just overseen for Mrs. Kennedy the ceremonies for JFK's funeral.

The timing of his trip was strange. I could not figure this out. Why would Walton fly that great distance less than a week after the loss of one of his best friends for something so mundane?

Three decades later, in 1997, the opening of the Russian government's archives revealed that Robert Kennedy, only eight days after the assassination, had asked Walton to go to the Soviet Union to convey a secret message to Georgi Bolshakov, a Soviet journalist and spy.

The Walton mission was an unusual breach of diplomatic practice. Tense relations between Robert Kennedy and Lyndon Johnson had long preceded the shock of the assassination.

Nevertheless, for the attorney general to send an emissary to America's number-one adversary without the knowledge, never mind approval, of the president of the United States was a serious violation of national security and diplomacy.

The fact that Edward chose to go back to Leningrad to spend some time with Walton adds an element of intrigue. During their hours eating and drinking at the Astoria Hotel in Leningrad, Walton and Edward hit it off famously. Edward was interested in art and design and in the aura of Walton as a painter, writer, and friend of JFK. From suggestions that Edward passed to me the next day, while we were returning to Moscow, I believe that evening that Walton told Albee much about his secret mission. Years later, I told this story to a close friend of Walton and Robert Kennedy, George Stevens. George seriously doubted the accuracy of the report (which had suggested that Walton was carrying information to the Soviets on behalf of Robert Kennedy). He speculated that it was a Soviet false information release. His strong reaction was that Walton would not think of transmitting such a message to the Soviet leadership in that sensitive moment. George also stated that it was highly unlikely that Robert Kennedy would seek to send such a message to Moscow at that time.

The Albee visit did not change US-Soviet relations—no single visit would. But it did introduce many Russians to the unusually candid, intellectually provocative, and formidable American writer. And the visit deeply changed Edward. Albee became deeply engaged in freedom for writers and was a regular spokesperson for the PEN International. He and I collaborated for years on writers and theater exchanges with the Soviet Union. We worked together with Zelda Fichandler, the legendary director of the Arena Stage in Washington, DC, to bring top Soviet playwrights to the US. He also played an important role in helping cast light on Václav Havel during the mid-1980s when I was ambassador to Czechoslovakia.

In the years following his first trip to the Soviet Union, Edward reduced his heavy drinking but continued to remain intolerant of Soviet bureaucrats. By the time he and Jonathan Thomas began their long relationship, he already had given up drinking entirely. Edward visited us in Caracas when I was ambassador, and later in Prague, at a critical moment, to meet with Havel.

The Albee/Steinbeck visit to the Soviet Union helped me define and shape my diplomatic experience: American culture moved to the forefront for me. When I became ambassador, first to Venezuela and then to Czechoslovakia, I underplayed the public image of the American ambassador as the representative of American commercial and military might. Culture would soften that obvious message.

One of Albee's signal themes during his visit and in his plays sticks with me to this day: the lies we tell ourselves and begin to believe are the sources of our greatest failures in relations with others.

Albee always spoke at an intensely human level. In his plays, there are rarely more than two people on the stage. So it is with nations. We correctly studied the lies the Soviets told themselves about building Communism. *But do Americans tell themselves lies and believe them, as well?* Such a question was a dangerous path to go down as a public servant and diplomat.

But such was the path I chose.

CHAPTER 3

Finding Their Way to the Light: Protean Dissidents

The various forms of Soviet dissidence were inspired by the profound dissatisfaction with the Communist political system in the Soviet Union and Central Europe. Early, violent manifestations of opposition took place in East Germany in 1953, in the Hungarian Uprising in 1956, and in the Prague Spring of 1968. All of these protests were repressed and crushed by an overwhelming Soviet military force. The subsequent "nonviolent dissidence" was fueled by intellectuals, artists, and spiritual leaders in the forms of public statements, literature, and other forms of art, such as music—particularly jazz.

In the Soviet Union, dissidence was first provoked by the widespread reaction to the death of Stalin in 1953. At every level of society, from the Politburo to local communities to individual Soviet citizens, discussions and policies were shaped around the challenges of how to rid the system of the cruel, murderous legacy of Joseph Stalin, who had dominated, beguiled, and terrified Soviet society for thirty years. Such conversations continued to occur throughout the fifteen Soviet republics and the dozens of autonomous "republics" in the USSR I visited during my posting to Moscow.

The precondition for such dissidence is the "absence of fear." Under Stalin, the slightest dissent provoked prisoner exile to

Siberia. During Khrushchev's "de-Stalinization," however, these muffled voices gathered strength. Under looser societal controls, the habit of fear was replaced by a bolder desire to be heard. Eventually some dissidents demanded attention and risked exile to be heard.

The Soviet writers and poets and painters of the early 1960s, who stood up and publicly embraced a new creativity and looked specifically toward the West for their cultural cues, were part of a fragile and protean pro-liberty movement in the USSR. These men and women were not monolithic: within this group, there were keen divisions. Some of the most public dissidents, such as the Soviet poets Yevgeny Yevtushenko, Andrei Voznesensky, Vasily Aksyonov, and Bella Akhmadulina, preferred to remain within "the velvet prison," a term coined by Hungarian dissident writer Miklós Haraszti to describe that large body of writers who chose to retain their international travel and publication privileges by withholding direct criticism of the system, or by offering "tolerable" criticism. Yevtushenko, for example, used his public prominence outside the Soviet Union to urge Khrushchev to move more aggressively against the residue of Stalinism in the Soviet system. Other writers chose to speak out against the system more boldly; these souls paid a deep personal price for doing so. Such vocal dissidents included Joseph Brodsky, Anna Akhmatova, Nadezhda Mandelstam, and Aleksandr Solzhenitsyn. Brodsky died in exile in the United States. Akhmatova and Mandelstam died in Moscow. And Solzhenitsyn chose to return from exile to Russia, where he died in 2008.

The most prominent group of Soviet writers in the 1960s were those writers who served as hosts to visiting Americans under official exchange. Yevgeny Yevtushenko and his wife,

Bella Akhmadulina, along with Andrei Voznesensky and Andrei Aksenov, were ubiquitous hosts for John Steinbeck, Edward Albee, John Updike, and John Cheever.

The flamboyant Yevtushenko spoke some English, as he had already visited the West many times. He was most famous for his poem, "Babi Yar," which condemned the mass slaughter of Ukrainian Jews by the Germans. The slaughter took place over a two-day period in 1941, as more than 33,000 Jews were forced into a ravine called Babi Yar and then shot. The haunting first lines set up the entire poem:

> No monument stands over Babi Yar.
> A steep cliff only, like the rudest headstone.
> I am afraid.
> Today, I am as old
> As the entire Jewish race itself.[5]

A condemnation aimed at Russia for their role in covering up—by refusing to acknowledge—one of the largest massacres of Jews in the war, "Babi Yar" remains Yevtushenko's most famous poem. Yet, it was his poem "The Heirs of Stalin" that placed him in the forefront of writers who were pressing Nikita Khrushchev to take further steps to eliminate Stalin's legacy in the Soviet system. In the poem, he demands that Stalin not be allowed to rise from his grave ever again:

> [Stalin] wished to fix each pallbearer in his memory:
> young recruits from Ryazan and Kursk,
> so that later he might collect enough strength for a sortie,
> rise from the grave, and reach these unreflecting youths.

He was scheming. Had merely dozed off.
And I, appealing to our government, petition them
to double, and treble, the sentries guarding this slab,
and stop Stalin from ever rising again
and, with Stalin, the past.[6]

At the end of the poem in which he described Stalin being laid to rest inside the tomb, there's a telephone in the coffin, by which Stalin is instructing the infamous Stalinist, the Albanian Enver Hoxha. Yevtushenko asks, who else would Stalin call from his tomb? Yevtushenko then states, "No, Stalin has not given up. He thinks he can cheat death." Many today ask whether Putin has that line to Stalin, who may have cheated death in his tomb.

Yevtushenko was first married to the formidable Bella Akhmadulina, a serious and highly respected poet. Yevtushenko had mentioned to me that he and Bella could not have children, and Yevgeny wanted children, which he had with his second wife, Zoya, who had been divorced from his friend Andrei Voznesensky. Yevtushenko had a charming dacha in Peredelkino, the legendary community of writers in the country outside of Moscow, where Boris Pasternak had been buried. He traveled many times to the West, and eventually moved to the United States, where he married again and had several children. He moved to Tulsa, Oklahoma, where he taught at the University of Tulsa.

Yevtushenko had been a promoter of the publication of Solzhenitsyn's short novel *One Day in the Life of Ivan Denisovich*, the first written description of life in one of Joseph Stalin's concentration camps. The translator famously described the difficulty in finding translations for the Russian words in the book. Indeed, the book became a source of a new Russian language originating in the concentration camps, which was found mainly in Solzhenitsyn's novels, including *In the First Circle* and several others.

I first meet Solzhenitsyn in person when he traveled the United States in 1975 as a guest of the AFL-CIO. I heard his groundbreaking talk on human rights and was so deeply moved by his eloquence and by his impact on the audience of thousands that I called Secretary Kissinger's aide Larry Eagleburger to tell him that if President Ford wanted to be reelected, he should go against the recommendation of his secretary of state Henry Kissinger and receive Solzhenitsyn in the White House. I told him it would be seen as a demonstration of American support for human rights in the Soviet Union. Larry's reaction was, "Didn't you get the word that no State Department employee should attend Solzhenitsyn events?"

"No," I said, "I had not heard that instruction."

It came as little surprise that, despite my urging, Henry Kissinger persisted in his recommendation to President Ford against receiving Solzhenitsyn in the White House, lest it offend the Soviet leadership. Ford famously lost the 1976 election to Jimmy Carter. I am still persuaded that Ford, Nixon, and Kissinger's failure to annunciate a coherent policy on American human rights was a major factor in causing President Ford to lose the presidential election in 1976.

Andrei Voznesensky, whose wife Zoya later married Yevgeny Yevtushenko, was considered "one of the Soviet Union's boldest and most celebrated young poets of the 1950s and 1960s [who] helped lift Russian literature out of its state of fear and virtual serfdom under Stalin."[7] While drawing the line at publicly refuting the party or Khrushchev, Voznesensky pushed against the boundaries of the accepted conventions of socialist realism in literature.

He, too, took on Russian and Soviet antisemitism, writing *The Ditch: A Spiritual Trial* about another German massacre that took place in Crimea in 1941. Twelve thousand people were killed, most of them Jewish. Later, in the 1980s, the bodies of the dead were looted by the Russians. In his book, Voznesensky attributes the willingness of the Russians to loot the dead—and the Soviet leadership's willingness to overlook it—to antisemitism.

> Tired from the sun, we walked slowly away from the highway. And suddenly, what is this? On the path through the green field, there is a black rectangle of a freshly dug well. The earth is still damp. Beyond it is another. Around them are heaps of smoke-blackened bones, rotten clothing.[8]

Unlike Yevtushenko, who chose to leave the USSR, Voznesensky defiantly remained in the Soviet Union, saying he "belonged to the people."

The third couple who lived in a "velvet prison" were also frequent hosts to the American writers. Vasily Aksyonov and his wife, Maya Aksenova, were both Jewish. (They often discussed their Jewish heritage with me, believing I was a Jewish American.) Vasily's mother was Yevgenia Ginzburg, who had written *Journey into the Whirlwind*, a story about her life as a prisoner in Stalin's concentration camps.

The liberalization of the Khrushchev Thaw meant that Aksyonov could move away from the monotonous and static socialist realism style most writers were compelled to use and instead turn to the youth culture that Aksyonov was part of— writing poems of modern young men and women listening to

jazz, going out to night clubs, and being hip to the wildly popular American fashions.[9] But when the Thaw ended, Aksyonov's
poetry turned more political and less acceptable to party leadership. "His open pro-Americanism and liberal values eventually
led to problems with the KGB. And his involvement in 1979
with an independent magazine, Metropol, led to an open confrontation with the authorities."[10] Eventually, his reception in the
Soviet Union turned dangerous, and he and his wife, Maya, left
for a trip to the West. While they were away, they were stripped
of their Soviet citizenship and forced into exile.

The "liberalization" of the arts, which began in 1953, following Stalin's death and Khrushchev's ascension to the position of
first secretary of the Communist Party, emboldened painters and
musicians and novelists and poets to reach beyond the narrow,
proscribed confines of the government. The liberal writers and
artists, most of whom long ago had chosen the safer "conspiracy of silence" under Stalin, had since 1953 reemerged and had
actively resumed the game of who can publish what and where.
Even conservatives began standing up for new literature. A certain confidence was in the air in Moscow: the broadcast of the
Voice of America and the BBC, which had been jammed for
over a year, resumed without traditional jamming; the year-old
nuclear test ban treaty, plus the mounting angry exchanges with
the Chinese, pointed to even closer relations with the West in
the coming year; indeed, the atmosphere in Moscow seemed so
hopeful that the visiting Yugoslav dissident Mihajlo Mihajlov,
despite his general pessimistic view of Soviet system, saw the road

ahead for Soviet artistic freedoms. He predicted "a final liberation of literature and arts from all restriction and dogmatism."[11]

But ten years on, by 1963, conservative attacks on the arts
had begun to escalate, led by Khrushchev himself. The general
air of well-being was further ruined by the announcement of
Khrushchev's fall in October 1964. The immediate reactions of
the intellectual community, and probably most Soviet citizens,
were misgivings and uncertainty and concern about what lay
ahead. Such feelings no doubt outweighed the actual changes.
The liberals were the most confused, for they had long felt ambiv-
alent toward Khrushchev. They all knew that Khrushchev was the
instigator who opened the floodgates against Stalin and had personally authorized the publication of *One Day in the Life of Ivan
Denisovich*. Also, he seemed impressed by certain independent
artists like sculptor Ernst Neizvestny and the poet Yevtushenko.
But even as he presided over the Thaw, he was the deepest personification of the system the liberals fought and protested.

In the 1960s, I wrote an article on the labels assigned to
various groups of intellectuals who were working in the Soviet
system at the time. Two of these groups warrant our attention.
The first were the Modern Liberal Conservatives. This group
was composed of the men and women who emerged from the
Khrushchev era fully accepting de-Stalinization, but who were
supportive of developing further criticism of the Stalin era by
pressing for further revelations of the past. This group included
all generations who shared the belief that the party and intellectuals must work hand in hand to change Soviet society. On
the pages of *Pravda,* the official Communist Party newspaper,
this position was represented officially by Aleksei Rumyantsev,
Pravda's editor-in-chief: "Communist criticism must rid itself of

the tone of literary command. The party must in every way eradicate attempts at homebred and incompetent administrative interference in literary affairs," and "Genuine creativeness is possible only through search and experimentation, free expression and clashes of viewpoint."[12] Through artistic style and behavior, this group produced a new vitality in cultural life. They were artists and poets in their thirties and forties, and included Voznesensky, Aksyonov, Bulat Okudzhava, Viktor Nekrasov, and Yevtushenko. This group enjoyed the support of many notable members of the older generation, such as Ilya Ehrenburg, Valentin Kataev, and Korney Chukovsky.

The second group of intellectuals that concerns us are the Slavophiles. This was a subtle and safe way to be a Communist . . . *without being a Communist*. It is how I see Vladimir Putin today; he draws his power through his deep belief in the superiority of the Russian people and couches it within the architecture of the (totalitarian) Communist autocrat. Such Russian-centric Slavophilia was completely contrary to the prevailing view espoused by Khrushchev, yet its advocates skated under the censors' notice.

One extreme form of Slavophilia is represented by the *smogisti*, "who have stated in their manifesto: Contemporary art is in a *cul-de-sac* and it cannot turn back. It is steeped in the fumes of foreign literature and art and has become epigonic. National art is dead, we should and must resurrect it."[13] One of the leaders of Slavophilia of the 1960s whom I knew well, Ilya Glazunov, famously wrote, "As is known, Peter opened just a window not a door on the west so the Russians can look at life in Europe, study it and from students becomes teachers but unfortunately by throwing out their national identity many Russian broke connections with their homeland. Cutting off their beards they lost

Glazunov and Putin.

their Russian individuality."[14] Glazunov would also say, "When looking into the history of Russia and the very fabric of Russian culture we shall not find one single thread that does not lead to its original source of Russia's historical consciousness and the idea of heroic moral strength and military glory. The Russian systems of government, art, architecture, literature and science all flow from this."[15] Glazunov would rise to the top of (Communist) center of government and be considered almost a "court painter" to Communism's elite.

In my reporting on literature and in my conversations in the sixties, I tried to make the point that Slavophilic thinking seemed to be emerging as a powerful ideological force, particularly in the youth movement *Molodaya gvardaiia*, or the Young Guards. It was the fallback of the ideological opposition—the easy way to stay in line was to be a Slavophile . . . while not being Communist.

The Slavophiles were a burgeoning phenomenon, but ran contrary to Soviet ideology. Young people were reading the tea leaves and were realizing that this phenomenon, to be a Slavophile, was an acceptable—and safe—deviation of Communist doctrine. Glazunov was a true believer and captured the spirit of the ideas that Putin would echo later. He painted massive paintings of the heroes of Russia but did not paint Stalin or any of the other Soviet leaders. In this way, he embraced the big truth, while eliding the problematic little truths. As V. Lakshin notes:

> Marxism has always considered truth to be concrete. It has always assumed that absolute truth exists but that historically and practically it is composed of an infinite number of relative, specific, concrete truths that strive toward absolute truth but that never fully exhaust it. The demand that an artist portray the "big truth of the phenomenon" and not the "little truth of the (individual) instance" has introduced a new element into this concept. The "big truth," the "truth of the century," has begun, in some critics' writings, to look like a mysterious absolute, which must be described in far too general, abstract, evasive words …. The Communist approach induces the honest Soviet writer to depict the entire truth without cautiously dividing it into "big" and "little," convenient and inconvenient, permitted and forbidden, truths. Yet in critical articles, the words "big truth" are most often used as a synonym of the happy life, the desired general well-being, while "little truth" is taken to mean the depiction of any shortcomings, difficulties and deprivations.[16]

The big truth is basically the big Communist lie: that the Communist Party was building Communism, which, they said, would result in balancing the wellbeing of Soviet citizens. This big lie is characterized by a Radio Yerevan joke about communism being on the horizon:

Q: What is the horizon?
A: The horizon is an imagined line that can never be reached.

For the Marxists, the big lie of a Communist future that would bring equality of opportunity and goods and the little truth of the Slavophile writers were their ways of seeming to support the big truth of Communism while staying out of jail.

CHAPTER 4

Dissent, Courage, and Repercussions: Andrei Amalrik

At precisely noon on a Thursday in late April 1965, I knocked on the door of the communal apartment of Andrei Amalrik, located near the Inner Circle in Moscow. I had come to know the apartment of this Soviet dissident well over my two years at the American Embassy. The discipline for such meetings was always to be on time. Amalrik was not yet the world-famous author of *Will the Soviet Union Survive until 1984?*, which was written after several years of forced exile in Siberia and his subsequent expulsion from the Soviet Union.

For the first time, I had come to his apartment with someone else: Bud Korengold, *Newsweek*'s Moscow bureau chief. Amalrik

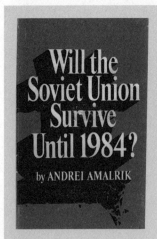

Will the Soviet Union Survive until 1984? by Andre Amalrik, who was sent to the Gulag because of this book.

had agreed to arrange for Bud to interview the Soviet "unofficial" painter Anatoly Zverev for a *Newsweek* cover story on Moscow's growing underground art movement. Unofficial painters were those who were not members of Artists' Union of the USSR. They were not recognized as painters. Though later he would be called "the Russian Van Gogh,"[17] in 1965 he was still a Russian underground artist. I had been urging such a story on Bud for over a year. The more I learned about the stirrings of the intellectual underground, the more I became convinced it was a story that must be told. As Zverev had just opened a well-publicized exhibition of his work in Paris, now was the moment for that story to be written.

Zverev Self Portrait.

The door of the apartment was opened by a woman from one of the three other families in the communal apartment. Hers was not a happy face. Andrei then appeared, in the green turtleneck wool sweater that was his trademark. He showed us into the small set of rooms he shared with his ailing father. Zverev was not there. Dima (Dmitri) Plavinsky, another painter I knew, was present. I whispered to Bud that if Zverev was not there, something had gone wrong, since everyone must be on time. In a few minutes, there was a knock at the door. Thinking it was Zverev, Andrei opened the door. In walked four large men, none of whom were Zverev.

The KGB and local police chose the moment to catch Zverev in the act of . . . *something*. Meeting with foreigners? I might well have given them the opportunity. In setting up that appointment, I followed Amalrik's instructions from two years earlier on meetings with "unofficial" Soviet citizens. He recommended I should "always ring the bell" in meetings with dissidents. He said to call from an official phone and give a clear reason for the meeting. Andrei advised me that being secretive about meetings raises alarms for the officials. He said diplomats all over the city tended to leave the embassy to call from the public phones. Of course, he said, public phones outside embassies were bugged more effectively than the lines from diplomats' own offices. Don't try to conceal what you are doing, since it virtually never works, Andrei told me. I had come to know that Amalrik's instructions to me were on point. I had been following his recommendations in Moscow and other Soviet cities, and my surreptitious meetings had gone unchallenged. Until now. I did not think Andrei would have entrapped me after the years of our relationship and our activities together. I also had come to learn the unpredictability of the Soviet paranoia and system. Andrei had assured me that he knew there was one KGB section that followed him and a separate KGB section tracking me. They often did not share information. The thought had never given me much comfort.

The head man questioned Andrei in his apartment, using the familiar form of address in Russian, as to whether Amalrik was trading in hard currency and making secret deals with foreigners, and why he continued to avoid getting a job. He called him a "parasite" (*tunyadets*). It was certainly an unsettling moment for Amalrik and for Dima Plavinsky. Being convicted of social parasitism was punishable by two-to-five-year terms of exile and hard labor. The interrogation was conducted in an almost jocular way. The large KGB officer who was talking kept addressing Andrei as Andrushka, the diminutive of Andrei.

The moment was stressful but not frightening. Because of my diplomatic immunity, it was unlikely that the police would try to take me into custody. But Bud, as a journalist, was vulnerable. After a short time listening to the dialogue with Andrei, I grabbed Bud by the arm, and we departed. I returned to the embassy to report to security and to my boss, Malcolm Toon, who was then political counselor.

"Mac" Toon was a famously hard-line and accomplished American professional who later became ambassador in Moscow. He distrusted all Soviets and did not like Russians. Mac had long warned me I was playing with fire by seeing so many nonofficial Russians, and particularly intellectuals and dissidents. He was convinced that Amalrik was a KGB provocateur. When I told him about the event in Amalrik's apartment, Mac could not resist: "I told you so," he said. Years later I read a strongly worded negative appraisal that Toon had put in my personnel file because of my continued meeting with Soviet citizens outside of my regular work with the government. He was critical of me for bad judgment and for refusing to follow his instructions. The ambassador, Foy Kohler, told me in person years later that when Mac would complain about me, he always told Mac not to stop what I was doing. Kohler said that I was gaining insights into the Soviet system, which was my job. I was doing it in what I believed was the best way to approach my responsibilities, and any risks I took were my own.

The following morning, I was in my office early, as usual. I received a frightened call from my wife to come home immediately. Andrei had arrived at the apartment and wanted to talk to me urgently. The talk we had that morning in my heavily bugged apartment on Kutuzovsky Prospect, well outside the American Embassy compound, was one of the most revealing of our many conversations.

Andrei wanted to assure me that he had not set me up and to tell me what he thought would happen to him. He was surprised when the police had appeared. I reminded him that, following his early suggestions to me, I had called Andrei from my office phone to set up the meeting between Korengold and Zverev. Andrei understood but was not clear why the KGB had chosen that particular moment to pounce.

Andrei explained that the authorities had been after him for several months because he had been taking foreign diplomats to meet with artists. His reluctance to get a formal job was the typical excuse for the harassment. Andrei always responded that he was a writer of plays, poetry, and essays. Writing was work. He expected that the authorities would bring him to trial and probably convict him of parasitism and exile him to Siberia.

I urged him to get a job to avoid the parasite charge, so he could stay in Moscow. He rejected my repeated recommendations that he get a job in a library or some other institution to avoid going to Siberia. That confrontation with the authorities was to be an action-forcing event that would shape the rest of his life as a thinker and as a Soviet dissident. According to him, his rights as an individual were being violated by being forced to seek government-approved work. I pleaded with him. Andrei absolutely refused to go along. He had entered a new zone in his form of rejecting the Soviet system. He was stoic and resolved.

Over the two years we had been talking, for practical and philosophical reasons, Andrei had become progressively more intolerant of the infractions on the freedoms of individuals. When we first met, Amalrik was twenty-four years old. He was savvy and plugged into the unofficial intellectual and arts community in Moscow. He had just been expelled from Moscow University for his thesis that the Varangians (Vikings) and Greeks, not the Russians, had played the major role in founding the original Russian state. He then wrote a number of plays (several of which he gave me) and essays. Andrei, ten years younger than I, served as my tutor for the other side of the Soviet state.

Amalrik had become acquainted with some of the more radical opposition actors such as Alexander Ginzburg, whom I had also met. I had concluded that Ginzburg was too open in his opposition to the government and party. A relationship with him would be a step too far, even for an American diplomat who was prepared to risk extensive contact with the Soviet "underground." By 1966, Amalrik and Ginzburg had become partners in building a new, more active dissident movement allied with Solzhenitsyn.

In retrospect, that KGB intrusion into his apartment and life provided Andrei the clarity to become more openly part of the opposition. The time had come for him "to sit" in Siberia. Russian dissidents since czarist times established their credentials after having "sat" (*sidel*) in forced exile or labor camps in Siberia. Fortunately, Khrushchev had closed down most of Stalin's labor camps, but forced exile was still used extensively.

His visit to my apartment was the last time I saw Andrei in Moscow. My tour ended in the summer of 1965, and I returned to the Department of State in Washington, DC. The Soviet authorities never took action against me for my role in Andrei's meeting with Bud Korengold. When I returned to Moscow in 1977, as a more senior official in the department, I noticed that I was being trailed closely and offensively. I had assumed that my file had popped up with the Amalrik connection, and that was why they were more aggressively following me. During an official call with the deputy foreign minister Alexander Bessmertnykh (Sasha) immediately after arrival in Moscow, I said, "Sasha, your people are following me so closely; I find it offensive. You know me from our years of working together. Please have them give me some space." The police hung back for the rest of my time dealing with the Soviet Union—but they were always there, somewhere.

After that meeting in my apartment, Andrei *was* found guilty of being a parasite and was exiled to Tomsk, in western Siberia. It was there that he wrote *Involuntary Journey to Siberia*, which was published in English, after he returned from "sitting" in Siberia.

That book established his credentials as an important player in the expanding dissident movement in Soviet Russia.

In the first two chapters of *Involuntary Journey to Siberia*, he retells the basic story of his relationship to a tall American diplomat with glasses and about our talk about art. He carefully and wisely does not mention my name and did not mention the variety of political issues we debated. His memory differs from mine in several details, but that can be expected given the quite distinct positions of each of us. However, the basics of what transpired are all there. For Andrei it marked the beginning of a new, more public role.

Following publication of *Involuntary Journey* in English in the West and his participation in several higher-profile protests in Moscow, Amalrik wrote his most important book: *Will the Soviet Union Survive until 1984?*, in which he predicts its collapse. That book, when published in the United States in 1970, had a large impact and angered Soviet authorities. He was convicted in late 1970 for "defaming the Soviet state" and sentenced to three years in a labor camp in Kolyma, in eastern Siberia.

After serving three years, he was given a second three-year prison term but was released after one more year because of health reasons and strong protests from the West. He returned to Moscow and became an even more prominent opposition leader. The Soviet authorities forced him into exile outside the USSR in 1976. He and his wife went to live in the Netherlands. Andrei was later killed in an automobile accident in 1980, while driving with his wife to an East-West meeting in Madrid to review the work of the 1975 Helsinki Accords. The tragic irony was that Amalrik had spent much of his last five years defending the work of the Helsinki agreement in protecting the human rights of individuals living in the Communist world.

Much has been written in more detail about Amalrik's role. I add here certain impressions and conclusions about him. His youthful innocence and intensity were compelling. He was in the great tradition of Russian intellectuals going back to prerevolutionary Russia. But Andrei was not a Slavophile and was not attracted by the Orthodox Church and its lore. He also seemed to harbor no particular belief in the wisdom of the Russian people, whom he considered passive—almost inert. He had already developed a point of view which at no point did I imagine he could become a Navalny—a leading opposition figure who spoke for the many varieties of dissidents throughout the USSR. Like Alexei Navalny, though, he was torn between dedication to his principles and his love of his country. I cannot imagine Andrei seeking or walking into martyrdom like Navalny—even though it is a very Russian thing. Andrei was a hearty debater, quite certain in his evolving attitudes that the Soviet system could not be reformed. He talked more about the individual, not the system. He was Russian to the core and found little to draw him to the West or to capitalism. Having tried to find a way to coexist in the system, his struggle for individual freedom began to take precedence. Amalrik was also not a joiner. He became an important player in the movement but usually as a loner. The same was true of Alexander Solzhenitsyn, Andrei Sakharov, Natan Sharansky, Zhores Medvedev, and so many others. Over his years as a Russian dissident, he developed his own direction. He was authentic and honest to himself—and with me. Still, my belief that the Russian or Soviet system would inevitably change went contrary to his belief that it simply could not.

The Amalrik connection helped open doors to the worlds of many of the artists and collectors in Moscow during that explosive blossoming of the intellectual world after 1963. Because of the good fortune of my assignments to accompany Edward Albee (with John Steinbeck), John Updike, and John Cheever around Moscow and the Soviet Union, I had gotten to know many figures of the literary world. The world of artists was at least as compelling.

As the Russian curator, author, museum director, and my friend Joseph Backstein wrote:

> The quality of life in which the official perception of everyday reality is independent of the reality of the imagination leads to a situation where art plays a special role in society. In any culture, art is a special reality, but in the Soviet Union, art was doubly real precisely because it had no relation to reality. It was a higher reality. . . . The goal of non-conformism in art was to challenge the status of official artistic reality, to question it, to treat it with irony. Yet that was the one unacceptable thing. All of Soviet society rested on orthodoxy, and non-conformism was its enemy. That is why even the conditional and partial legalization of non-conformism in the mid-1970s was the beginning of the end of the Soviet regime.[18]

Nonconformist art was well along in the early 1960s. Vladimir Weisberg, perhaps the most intriguing of the artists I came to know, used an unusual device to become "officially" nonconformist. Barred from painting and teaching nonofficial and abstract art, Weisberg decided to declare himself insane. In that way, the authorities would not deny his interest in modern painting because he was an "invalid of the second category" (the official euphemism for a form of insanity). He put himself in a sanatorium for one month, took the treatment of drugs they required, and returned home officially "insane" with papers to prove it. He was thus free from the Stalinist Union of Artists and able to paint what interested him. He even taught some courses on modern art at the slightly more open Moscow Union of Writers.

This was a decade before Zhores and Roy Medvedev's book *A Question of Madness*, published in the US in 1979, which tracks the nineteen days that Zhores was forcibly detained in an asylum and his twin brother's attempts to save him. Upon publication, it revealed the details of the regular punishment of dissidents in the Soviet Union in which authorities declared them insane and retained them in asylums. But for Weisberg, his "madness" liberated him as an artist.

I came to know Weisberg's young brother, S. Yudin, who, with his friend, B. Kaligin, told me of their trips to villages to the far north of Russia. The two were sociologists who recorded the hundred-year-old traditional wails of the women of the villages. At major communal events, such as weddings and funerals and holidays, the women of the village would sing traditional songs or wails. Young Weisberg and his friend sat one afternoon in my apartment and gave me a rendition of the wedding wails from one village that they had memorized. Weddings for the young women were sad events because the bride was about to accept the servitude of being a wife. I bought from Weisberg a large modernist portrait of those two young men. It has always hung in a prominent spot among our paintings. The two boys disappeared

Vladimir Weisberg's painting of dissidents Yudin and Kaligin.

a few years after I left Moscow during one of their trips to the far north. They were both Russian Jews. I always suspected they were checking out Soviet prison camps in the far north as part of their sociological research.

Most of the other non-conformist artists I knew lived in Moscow. The Lianozovo Group lived near each other on the out-skirts of Moscow and formed the basis of the nonconformist art movement there. The leader was Oscar Rabin, whom I came to know rather well, along with his wife, Marianna Kropyvnytskyi, and artist Lydia Masterkova. Rabin's dissidence was the gloom of his cityscapes, Russian churches, and life. He painted a large painting of his internal Soviet passport with a large word identifying him as a Jew. Rabin became ever more active and was a key organizer of the Bulldozer Exhibition of nonconformist art in 1974, which the authorities literally bulldozed away.

Ilya Glazunov was a Slavophile and a prolific patriotic painter who churned out small and giant paintings on the themes of Russian legends, villages, and heroes. He was by no means interested in Western art, was favored by many key figures in the Soviet establishment, and was unabashedly antidemocratic and anti-Western. I got to know him well precisely because he was so plugged into Soviet politics. He persuaded me that he would be part of the future in Russia, whatever that might be. One characteristic citation of Glazunov from 1965, from the Soviet journal, *Molodaya Gvardiya* should help explain the worldview of the Putin government today.

> When looking into history of Russia, one shall not find a single thread that does not lead to this [Russian Orthodox Church] source of the Russian historical consciousness, to the idea of heroic moral strength, and military glory.[19]

After the collapse of Communism in 1991, Glazunov was encouraged and financed by the government to establish the Russian Academy of Painting, Sculpture and Architecture, which essentially taught art in a perceived Russian tradition—neither Western nor socialist realism. He was repeatedly honored by the government until his death in 2017.

Two of the leading art collectors in Moscow during that era were George Costakis and Nina Stevens. Costakis was raised in Moscow in a wealthy Greek merchant family. After his parents died, he began working in the Canadian Embassy. In 1946, he began to collect the great Russian artists since the 1920s. By 1963, when I first met him, he had amassed an immense, diverse, and priceless collection of Russian paintings dating back to1917. They were stuffed under beds, were stacked against walls, and occupied all the closets in his modest Soviet apartment. I would occasionally carry tubes of drawings and paintings back to the US for him. A Canadian friend of George would come to Washington, DC, to pick them up and presumably to sell them so that George would have money to acquire more paintings.

He and I remained in touch over the next two decades. When I became president of the Metropolitan Museum of Art in 1986, I began discussing with him the possibility that the Met might buy a large part of his collection. The collection would have provided the Met with a unique and transformative collection unequaled by any other Western museum. The curators had little interest in this opportunity, and we never reached an agreement on the price of the acquisition. He eventually left much of it to the MOMus–Museum of Modern Art, Thessaloniki, Greece. He was required to leave a large part of his collection to the Tretyakov Gallery as "payment" to allow him to export the major part of his collection. The Costakis collection hanging in the Tretyakov was never designated as a gift of George Costakis. Those paintings, as far as I can determine, were never labeled as agreed to.

Over my two years living in Moscow, I became increasingly intrigued by the willingness of so many Soviet citizens in my neighborhood to gather regularly to march to Red Square for a celebration of one type or another. May 1 was always one of the most well-attended marches in Moscow. On May 1, 1965, on the eve of my departure for DC and my new State Department assignment, I decided to join the marchers.

Mind you, this was not instigated by personal support for the May 1 celebrations or the efforts to develop pride in the proletariat's work. It was my insatiable curiosity about the nature of Soviet society that drove me to enter the crowd gathering on Kutuzovsky Prospekt. I wore a very proletarian-looking shirt and began to mill about with the crowd outside my apartment building at 9 a.m. A local leader with a loudspeaker called us together to begin our walk to Red Square, which was roughly two miles away. I had some misgivings about marching with the crowd past the gathering of the Politburo, with Leonid Brezhnev, among others, standing on Lenin's tomb reviewing the mass of Soviet citizens walking through the square. Nevertheless, I marched with the crowd and made it to Red Square in good time. On our long walk to the square, my neighbors obviously knew I was not a native Russian speaker; they were curious about who I was. We gathered again in Manezh Square, which was very close to Red Square.

When it was time for our group to go forward and actually into Red Square, we were summoned to a narrow entrance located between the Museum of Marxism and Leninism and the History Museum. In that narrow entrance was a large loudspeaker instructing us to look happy: the world would be watching.

There were indeed television cameras, which were always

present at such parades. We were told not to break ranks when walking through Red Square. Security guards on both sides lined the passageway. As we were about to head into the square, I became increasingly uneasy about what I was doing—walking past the Politburo on one of the most honored Soviet holidays. I certainly did not want to imply in any way that I supported the Politburo or the parade, but I was swept up in what I, out of curiosity, had already committed to.

Just before we passed Lenin's tomb on the right, I moved to the left and broke through the guards that guided our march through the narrow entry. They were frankly astounded at my pushing past them. Once free, I ran across half of Red Square, past the Gum department store, and straight into a KGB officer who, in effect, said, "What the hell are you doing?"

I said I was leaving Red Square, and I had diplomatic immunity. I darted away from him, ran behind the Gum, and caught a taxi, which took me back to my apartment in Kutuzovsky Prospekt. Amazingly, I was not followed or approached after the fact. I informed the security guard at the embassy of what I had just done. By then, they had had sufficient surprises from me and my behavior in Moscow so that they seemed to pay no attention. It's fair to say that my pride in the United States surged to one of its highest points as I broke out of that dreadful file of obsequious Soviet citizens demonstrating their support for Lenin, the Politburo, and the Soviet military.

I had planned my final trip in the Soviet Union to Grozny, the capital of the Chechen-Ingush Republic in the Northern Caucuses, before returning to DC for my assignment in the State Department.

It was a trip of respect for my favorite teacher of Soviet Politics at the Russian language total immersion training program I took in Bavaria. The school was called Detachment R. My trip to Grozny was late on the day of May 1. I stayed the evening in Grozny and all of the next day. The professor's name was Kunta, which was his name when he was doing clandestine work in Chechnya under Stalin. His Chechen name was Abdurakhman Avtorkhanov. He was a prominent historian of the Soviet political system which he knew well since he was head of the Chechen Communist Party under Stalin. His scholarship later led him to the dissection of the way the communist party exercised power. I got to know Avtorkhanov well, and he shared with me many insights about the Stalinist system. He also told me at great length about the hostile Russian-Chechen relationship which dated back to the eighteenth century, and later included the forced exile of half a million Chechens from their republic in 1944 during the Second World War, essentially emptying Grozny of its population. Stalin dispatched more than 100,000 troops to move the Muslim Chechens and Ingusheti to Siberia during the crucial battle of Stalingrad against the incoming Nazi army, not far from Chechnya in the Northern Caucasus.

At the time of my visit, I knew from Soviet media that the Soviets had decided to allow hundreds of thousands of Chechens to return to Grozny from Siberia in 1964. Avtorkhanov had told me I should visit Grozny during the May 1, 1965, celebration to find out how many Chechens had been allowed to return home and what their attitude was like. I had visited many Republics where the local population was hostile to the Russian state, but that visit to Grozny on May 1 and 2, 1965, was an eye opener about the hostility between this ethnic minority and the

Russians. I stayed only one afternoon and evening, and was able to have many conversations with Chechens who had returned. The anger toward the Russians was verbalized more by that local population than I had heard from any before, even by the population of Estonia. Their animus toward Russia was rooted in religion and a century of hostility, based on the fact that their region is heavily Muslim.

The Chechen Republic changed its name to Chechnya after the breakup of the Soviet Union, when the wars between Yeltsin's Russia and Chechnya became brutal and bloody. Yeltsin fought two wars against tiny Chechnya, and Putin established his role as President of the Russian Federation after crushing Chechnya in 1999. The Chechens continue to be a Muslim population and a powerful dissident force in post-communist Russia. Influenced by conservative Sunnis and the Wahabi strain of Islam. The Northern Caucasus region, and Chechnya in particular, which is populated by Sunni Muslims, are likely to present challenges to Russia in the future, as they are influenced heavily by Sunni Wahabis. However, Putin has managed to establish an important alliance with the family that are now the autocratic rulers of Chechnya, the Kadyrovs. Ramzan Kadyrov and his militias have been helpful to Putin in the Ukraine War.

CHAPTER 5

Diebenkorn, Khrushchev, Lenin, and Einstein

Great nations write their autobiographies in three manuscripts, the book of their deeds, the book of their words and the book of their art. Not one of these books can be understood unless we read the two others, but of three the only trustworthy one is the last.

—John Ruskin

My first year in Moscow had been given a great boost by the signing of the Test Ban Treaty in the late summer of 1963 and by my assignment to participate in the visit of John Steinbeck and Edward Albee, only months later, in the fall of 1963. The diplomatically groundbreaking Test Ban Treaty set a new, more positive tone for American diplomats in Moscow, and the travels with Steinbeck and Albee opened doors to Soviet intellectuals and dissidents and real Russians I might otherwise never have known. Also, during that first year, I had my first real encounters with the KGB and the secret police and their efforts to penetrate and harass American officials serving in the embassy in Moscow.

As the junior FSO in the US Embassy, I worked as the General Services Officer (GSO) for my first year, after which I would move to the political section to cover and report on

Soviet internal politics. As the GSO, I was to oversee the nearly 150 Soviet citizens who were employed by the embassy to do the heavy lifting on keeping the building in condition by supervising the work being done on the plumbing and electrical needs. Also, I was expected to drive and maintain the pool of official cars in the embassy carpool. I also had to find ways to get repairs from the official diplomatic service agency (UPDK) that provided services and workers for all diplomatic missions in Moscow. Since the US had by far the largest diplomatic facility of any of the other nations maintaining diplomatic relations with the Soviets, the American need for services was on a much higher order. My first experience was with decisions managing the "Marine House," the separate facility the embassy leased to house the US Marine Corps detail which provided security for the embassy (and embassies around the world).

The next year, 1964, the cultural office of the embassy learned that the home office of the USIA had finally selected the first American painter to visit the USSR under the official exchange agreement between the two principal adversaries of the Cold War. They had chosen Richard Diebenkorn, who was a painter who had been part of the dynamic and dominant American abstract expressionist movement centered in New York City and led by Mark Rothko, Jackson Pollock, and Willem de Kooning. The USIA selectors who had decided on Diebenkorn knew that he had left New York and was moving away from abstract expressionism, a style offensive to the Soviet hosts. Abstract expressionism was held up as a cultural triumph of the West, one that celebrated artistic freedom and an artist's individuality. This was in contrast to the static, utopian, propagandistic style of socialist realism that was favored by Soviet leadership.

Diebenkorn had returned to Berkeley and to his origins as a California painter, with roots in figurative painting and drawing in the Bay Area. Dick was much admired as the best of the California painters (a patronizing put-down by national art critics). He had begun a series of cityscapes of San Francisco in a style that was representational but also preserved his fascination with the opportunities of Abstract Expressionism. By his 1964 visit to the Soviet Union, already he had made a name for himself on the national stage. By the end of his life, he would be considered one of the great masters of twentieth century American painting.

The representative of the USIA office in Moscow was a cultured, perceptive, and intelligent retired Marine officer named Rocky Staples, who had initially selected me as the junior officer to accompany Edward Albee the year before, on the first exchange of writers. Rocky asked me to accompany Diebenkorn, perhaps because my wife, Jane, was an accomplished painter, or perhaps because I had established a reputation as a competent Russian-language officer who had met with a number of the unofficial painters in Moscow. Rocky had already asked me to accompany John Updike and John Cheever, who would be visiting the USSR in the second writers-exchange that same fall. Rocky and the ambassador had come to respect my work with writers and thought that because of my interest in and knowledge of the visual arts, I would be a good match with the visiting painter, Diebenkorn.

As agreed, I went to Sheremetyevo Airport in early October 1964 to greet Richard Diebenkorn and his wife, Phyllis, along with representatives of the conservative Moscow Union of Painters who were to act as the official hosts of the Diebenkorns during their visit to the USSR. Such official bureaucratic oversight was the valuable link that made the Soviet government take the visit seriously and provide the visiting artist serious access to Soviet artists.

Two additional dimensions are needed to understand the enormity of the Diebenkorn visit. First, Russian avant-garde art, which evolved at the time of the Russian Revolution, was probably one of the most enduring phenomena of that violent and creative period of the late teens and early 1920s. In that period, the suprematists were headed by Kazimir Malevich. From Ukraine came Vladimir Tatlin, who would help found the movement known as constructivism, which spawned a group of other artists groups who called themselves symbolists, Cubo-futurists, rayonists, productivists, concretists, and even engineerists. This crazy array of artists was all lined up against the czarist legacy of the Academy, which sought to channel all the visual arts in one direction. But of course, the czar had been deposed and the visual artists continued to fight their own revolutions. Those artistic revolutions probably contributed more to the style of abstract expressionism and to the work of Richard Diebenkorn than the impressionists and Matisse. Malevich and Kandinsky were seminal modernists—as influential as Picasso and Braque on today's trends in art.

Just as the artists were churning to find new ways of expression, the emerging Stalinist system sought and found effective means of crushing independent creativity. The far-reaching consequences of the imposition of socialist realism upon all creative artists became clearer once Stalin assigned Andrei Zhdanov to set defined limits for all art forms. Those who dared step outside the approved style of socialist realism found themselves exiled or killed. The purges, killings, and punishments carried out against

artists who violated Zhdanov's rules or doctrine were called the
Zhdanovshchina.

Zhdanovism essentially held that the cultural world is divided
into two worlds: the imperialist world headed by the US and the
democratic world, as it was known in this context, headed by the
USSR. Zhdanov denounced "cosmopolitanism," or the mimick-
ing or following of artistic trends drawn from other countries. He
was on constant lookout for writing and writers he deemed to
be dangerous or pernicious. In this, he distinguished himself by
leading the charge against the poet Anna Akhmatova (calling her
half harlot and half nun), who was arguably one of the greatest
Russian artists of the twentieth century. She was condemned after
Isaiah Berlin's visit to her Leningrad apartment followed by his ill-
advised report of the encounter. Berlin wrote on her death in 1966:

> The widespread worship of her memory in the Soviet
> Union today, both as an artist and as an unsurrender-
> ing human being, has, so far as I know, no parallel. The
> legend of her life and unyielding passive resistance to
> what she regarded as unworthy of her country and her-
> self, transformed her into a figure . . . not merely in Rus-
> sian literature, but in Russian history in [the twentieth]
> century.[20]

The final historical piece to understanding this environment was
the role of Khrushchev, who had succeeded Stalin after his death
in 1953. Khrushchev had tried to be a reformer of the Soviet
system during his tenure. He saw the reform of the Communist Party as a key component of reform of the Soviet system.
Many Soviet intellectuals, including Sakharov and many writers,

convinced Khrushchev that ridding the party of the Stalinist legacy was an essential precondition for reform.

Khrushchev's groundbreaking "Secret Speech"—"On the Cult of Personality and Its Consequences"—at the Twentieth Party Congress in 1956, began laying the groundwork toward strengthening his own stature as a reformer, and started the process by suggesting that Stalinism was not an integral part of the system of Soviet rule. That idea formed the crux of Khrushchev's challenge and the political problems such a challenge created for him as a leader and reformer. The question was, how far could he take the Communist Party toward wiping its hands clean of Stalin without arousing the ire and opposition of Stalin's heirs (as poet Yevtushenko warned)?

On the morning of October 16, 1964, Richard and Phyllis Diebenkorn and I were being driven to the Hermitage Museum in Leningrad. That morning, as usual, I had glanced at the early edition of *Pravda*. The lead was a bombshell: Nikita Khrushchev had stepped down as chairman of the Council of Ministers and first secretary of the Communist Party for "reasons of health."[21]

With a chuckle, I told Dick and Phyllis that his "retirement" probably *was* for reasons of health—his political health.

Khrushchev had led the USSR since Stalin's death ten years earlier. He'd had a stormy and erratic run, including almost bringing the US and the Soviet Union to a nuclear war only two years earlier, during the Cuban Missile Crisis. In his autocratic way, he had tried to reform the stagnant Soviet political system and rid it of the worst of Stalin's legacy. But in doing so, he offended those on the Left *and* the Right. For those on the Left, he didn't go far enough to erase Stalin's murderous legacy and to move the USSR into a newer, less censorious era. For those on the

Right, they saw his actions as undermining the party and moving the USSR away from its ideological underpinnings. Moreover, Khrushchev's actions deprived them of Stalin's tools. When these negatives were added to his domestic and international political bumbling and his very questionable policy schemes, they proved too much for Khrushchev to survive.

As I described how I perceived the situation, Dick, who had little interest in politics but a great interest in exploring the Hermitage, immediately asked whether the surprise turn of the announcement of Khrushchev's abrupt departure might cause him to have to cancel his visit to the museum. An important personal objective in agreeing to be the first American painter to make an "official" visit to the USSR was to see the sixty-six Matisse paintings and drawings in the museum. Matisse was his favorite artist. Up until then, he had seen only photos of the Hermitage-housed Matisse canvases. In response to his question, I told him I didn't know, but since we were almost there, we should carry on.

At the Hermitage, we were taken to the office of the director, Boris Piotrovsky, who is the father of Mikhail Piotrovsky, the current director, whom I already knew. We met in the Piotrovsky's spacious suite overlooking the Neva River. He greeted me nervously and was uncharacteristically abrupt in greeting the American painter and his wife on their historic first visit to the museum. I began to worry that things were not going to go as planned. It turned out to be political nerves.

Piotrovsky immediately asked what I thought of the announcement about Khrushchev. I was only a junior American diplomat, and I was being asked a political question by the leader of the institutional pinnacle of the Soviet artistic world. The distance between our positions struck me as infinite. I thought, *You're asking me?*

Nevertheless, with Dick and Phyllis looking at me anxiously, I did venture some thoughts. As my job at the embassy in 1964 was to follow Soviet internal developments, I said that Khrushchev had most certainly been replaced for political reasons. There had been indicators for the past year that some Communist Party leaders were losing patience with his increasingly erratic behavior and the excessive time he spent on foreign travels while the Soviet economy was tanking. Piotrovsky listened intently. He asked for specifics.

He wondered what might happen to the Soviet-American cultural exchanges. Would the thaw in bilateral relations begin to freeze over again? In the past year, he had already experienced the benefits of improved relations with American and European museum directors and professionals.

While Piotrovsky pondered, I could feel Dick's anxiety level rising. His face was telling me that seeing the Hermitage, and particularly their collection of Matisse paintings, was the task of the day. Was he about to miss the opportunity of a lifetime?

I asked the director whether we might begin the tour since Dick and his wife had come a long way to visit one of the greatest collections in the world. Piotrovsky nodded, and we were soon joined by the curator of Modern Western Art who was to act as our guide to the collection. Over the next three hours, we covered the high points of the Hermitage collection, including the extraordinary collection of Old Masters, many of which had been brought to St. Petersburg by Catherine the Great. In the late seventeenth and early eighteenth centuries, Peter the Great had built St. Petersburg to "open a window on the West," in

Pushkin's words. Fifty years later, Catherine set out to westernize Russia through that St. Petersburg window.

After two hours exploring the Hermitage, we got to the end of the rainbow: the museum's staggering collection of impressionist and postimpressionist paintings, which had originally been owned by wealthy Russian businessman Sergei Shchukin. Shchukin, who had been born in Moscow in 1854, made his money in world industry and trade. His taste, however, came from Paris. Lenin expropriated the Shchukin collection in 1918, along with the collection of Ivan Morozov. Shchukin's assemblage of art, which would be worth more than $3 billion today, included fifty Picasso paintings, thirty-seven paintings by Matisse, sixteen by Gauguin, sixteen by Derain, and thirteen by Monet, as well as works by Cézanne, Degas, Marquet, and van Gogh.[22] They were taken by Lenin without reimbursement and distributed primarily to the Hermitage and the Pushkin Museum in Moscow.

The Matisse collection was unmatched, but that day only a few were on display. Dick said not a word as he walked up to each painting. He seemed particularly attracted by the powerful blue Matisse painting *The Conversation* (1908–1912). The large canvas, which shows the artist in conversation with his wife, Amélie, is painted with the rich, lush cobalt blue that Matisse used again and again. The artist has situated the two characters on either side of a prominent center window overlooking a minimalist garden with ponds. The painting suggests future fields of color and embraces Matisse's play with dimensionality.

Diebenkorn was also shown dozens of Matisse's Moroccan paintings, along with many of the artist's drawings. During the Soviet era, the postimpressionists were considered by the masters of Soviet culture to be dangerously far removed from the approved art form: socialist realism.

During this glorious day looking at art with one of the most stirring American artists, I was mesmerized by Diebenkorn. He never spoke. Yet, through his intent examinations of each canvas, almost each brushstroke, you could vividly sense his focus and his intense joy. He was processing Matisse's use of the figure and color and space. I was transfixed, not by the paintings, but by watching Dick categorize and process how the artist put paint on each canvas.

Yet I was getting anxious to return to Moscow to see what I might learn in my limited way about what had happened to Khrushchev. We flew back to the capital that afternoon, Dick thinking about Matisse, I about that other guy.

The next morning, *Pravda*'s lead story confirmed my suspicion: Khrushchev had been thrown out. The editorial condemned "subjectivism and drift in communist construction, harebrained scheming from half backed conclusions, hasty decisions and actions divorced from reality, bragging and bluster, attracted to rule by fiat and unwillingness to take into account what science and practical experience had already worked out."[23] That was the party leadership's view of Khrushchev in a nutshell, without once mentioning his name.

Reassured that my analysis had been sound, I began a round of visits to the most important history museums in Moscow that told stories about history from the current political perspective. The party controls that history. My suspicions were correct. In forty-eight hours, Khrushchev's name, face, and mention had completely disappeared from Moscow. This "clean up" demonstrated an efficiency and determination worthy of the launch of Sputnik.

The Institute of Marxism-Leninism had had a special exhibition of Khrushchev's recent visit to Cairo to open the Aswan Dam with Egyptian president Gamal Abdel Nasser. I had visited that museum only two weeks earlier. The institute was now closed. Other museums, including the State Historical Museum on Red Square, were open but without a picture or reference to Khrushchev anywhere. Mind you, there was never a "cult of personality" around Khrushchev; busts and photos of him did not clutter streets and public squares. But only days earlier, his name and face were ubiquitous in the media and current events. The Institute of Marxism-Leninism, was completely clean of the man's name or picture.

I went to the Exhibition of Soviet Economic Achievements, a large fairgrounds park outside of Moscow where there were dozens of pavilions dedicated to the major aspects of the Soviet economy. All but one was open and all of them were pristine of the fallen leader.

As I had anticipated, the one pavilion at the exhibition that was shut tight was the Corn Pavilion. One of Khrushchev's most notorious "harebrained schemes" was his obsession with corn. During his 1959 visit to the US, Khrushchev had visited Iowa farmer Roswell Garst in Coon Falls, Iowa, to discuss hybrid corn. Khrushchev became sold on the expansion of corn cultivation as a new solution to the chronic problems of Soviet agriculture and food supply. Garst was invited to instruct Khrushchev on how corn would solve the USSR's chronic food and meat problem. Despite the skepticism of Soviet scientists about the length of Russia's growing season, Khrushchev remained loony over corn. His Russian nickname on the street was *kukuruznik*—"cornball" in English. Yet, despite Khrushchev's emphasis on advancing agriculture, I knew that food stores in 1963–64 were emptier than they had been in a decade. Black bread was all that was available in the towns outside of Moscow, though we were told it was made mostly from grasses with only small amounts of wheat.

The most outrageous example of Khrushchev's excessive scheming was his rehabilitation of the faux geneticist Trofim Lysenko, who since the 1920s had been the director of the Soviet Union's Lenin All-Union Academy of Agricultural Sciences, but who, by 1964, was detested by the Academy of Sciences. In 1949, Lysenko, who rejected Mendelian genetics, had begun a campaign denouncing theoretical geneticists—and all biologists—who disagreed with his claims. Because of his sway, genetics was declared a pseudoscience, and all geneticists lost their jobs. Many were arrested; others were sentenced to death and executed. Lysenko was a charlatan—but one who enjoyed great support, from Lenin to Stalin to Khrushchev. Promising an end to the chronic hunger that haunted the USSR, Lysenko managed to convince Khrushchev that he had developed new genetic strains of grain that would grow in Russia's severe climate. Khrushchev's personal addiction to Lysenko ruined his declining reputation, even within his own family.

In 1962, at the exhibition "The New Reality" at Manezh Hall near the Kremlin, Khrushchev's buffoonery and vulgarity reached a new peak. Amid the comforting examples of socialist realism had been dispersed the work of a number of contemporary artists. The quasi-official organizers had wanted to test the tolerance of the cultural watchdogs for new art.

On seeing the unsanctioned art, Khrushchev attacked the artists in his most colorful peasant expressions, the most benign of which named them as "filth, decadence and sexual deviations."[24] His rages at Manezh were recorded: "Are you men or damned pederasts? How can you paint like that? Do you have a conscience? I am telling you as the Chairman of the Council of Ministers, the Soviet people don't need all this. Forbid! Prohibit everything! Stop this mess! I order! I say! And check everything! On the radio, on television, and in print, uproot all sympathizers. of this!"[25]

A major target of Khrushchev's crude abuse was Ernst Neizvestny, a young sculptor who was a star of the Moscow artistic underground. I came to know him well and saw him frequently during my years in Moscow, and later after the fall of Communism when he moved to New York. After dinner in Moscow one night, Ernst showed me a book with a large name written in Cyrillic letters that I could not read. It was Montesquieu, whom he admired and thought was the "greatest political philosopher" because "Montesquieu wrote that 'checks and balances' are the most dependable devices to control the autocrats. That's what we need in this country—checks and balances."[26] While Khrushchev was touring Manezh Hall, he had picked out Neizvestny specifically to heap derision on. Pointing to one of Neizvestny's sculptures, he said loudly, "Dog shit."

In an act of poetic justice, after Khrushchev's death, his children invited Neizvestny to design Khrushchev's Tomb in Novodevichy Cemetery in Moscow. It is refreshingly modern and measured—neither filthy nor decadent. Of sculpture as an art form, Neizvestny said, "I think of sculpture not as a person, animal or other natural or geometrical form situated in space: the sculpture contains within itself a dialogue between spirit and flesh."[27]

Arthur Miller would call Neizvestny an "artist of the East" regarded by Russians as an "expression of the country, of its soul, language, and spirit" and as a "prophet of the future" who represented the "philosophical conscience of his country." But it was Alexander Calder who paid him perhaps the ultimate compliment: "All my life I create the work of children, and you create the work of man."[28]

Khrushchev's rants at the Manezh were more than just an indication of his taste in art. They belied the harsh strictures the Soviet Union put upon artists . . . even during the Khrushchev Thaw. As cultural doctrine, socialist realism reigned. A style of art, and particularly painting, that heralded the "Soviet hero"— "the brave, steadfast, selfless, and allegorical personification of Bolshevik ideals, the embodiment of history's 'forward' trajectory"[29]—Socialist realism was praised by those who were fierce believers in the Communist utopia. Sergei Dinamov, a worker and lithographer would serve in the Red Army from 1919 to 1926 (during Russia's transformation into a radical Socialist state) and eventually become a literary critic, as well as the 1935 head of the Arts Section, Culture and Propaganda Department, Central Committee, All-Union Communist Party (Bolsheviks) was nothing if not a true believer. Of socialist realism, he said:

The proletariat keeps away from those gloomy and tedious personalities who fear laughter, joking, gaiety, and *joie de vivre*. For the beauty of Socialist art is the beauty of the fight which millions and again millions are waging under the leadership of the genius Stalin. It is a strong and heroic beauty which pictures the stormy course of events, yet does not sweep the artist away, but uplifts his ideas and brings strength to his arm and courage to his heart.[30]

To many, though, socialist realism was a nationalistic and propagandistic art that held no interest. The art form held little interest for me. I wanted to meet the artists who were pushing back *against* socialist realism, those who dared defy doctrine and create on their own terms. The opportunities I had to meet dozens of nonconventional artists were far more compelling for the insights they had on Soviet society and politics. Many of the artists I looked to for innovation were those who had showed in the 1962 Manezh exhibit where Khrushchev exhibited his disgust for the new art.

The iconography of Soviet leaders, however, *did* grab my interest. Lenin's image was the most intriguing. Across fifteen Soviet republics, I took photos of Lenin statues and busts and broadsides posted in the local squares dedicated to Lenin. Unsurprisingly, the face of Lenin seemed more Asian the further east one traveled.

In part because I was raised in Abraham Lincoln's hometown (Springfield, Illinois), Lenin's hometown called to me. Vladimir Ilyich Ulyanov, aka Lenin, was born in Simbirsk, a town on the Volga. (Simbirsk was renamed Ulyanovsk after his death.) He was born of a middle-class family of decidedly mixed ethnic origins, like most citizens of the Russian empire—predominantly Russian, but with a good deal of Tatar and other Asian roots. The tall, pedestaled Lenin in Ulyanovsk had an outstretched arm pointing due east, across the Volga River. The statue had a clearly Asian visage.

Raised with Lincoln's iconography all around me as a child in Springfield, I am still today struck by the incredible variety of his faces. There are almost as many sizes and shapes of Lincoln in images as there are written perceptions of that complex man who is arguably the best-known—throughout the world—and most revered American president. As Lincoln's persona has been analyzed—and evolved—over the past century, his image has become more varied. Lenin's image has also evolved, although in a different direction. As Lenin's history has become locked into the ideology of his nation, his image became stale and repetitive even as the reach of the Lenin icons were expanding exponentially. This phenomenon says something about their distinct persona. But also, it suggests how we and the Russians think about our leaders.

The changing story of Lenin, the person, as told in the Institute of Marxism-Leninism near Red Square always drew me back. During the Gorbachev era, whenever I was in Moscow, I would check in with the same female guard in the Lenin rooms at the institute. In 1989, I asked her what was new on the Lenin front. She secretively took me to a room which contained photos of an ailing Lenin in the hospital in his final year. I was shocked. The display of a Lenin frailty would never have been tolerated before. The guide took care to assure me that the photos did *not* show Lenin dying of syphilis, despite the rumors.

Only a few months before that 1989 visit, I had lunched in my office at the Metropolitan Museum of Art in New York with Chingiz Aitmatov, the prize-winning Kyrgyz writer/diplomat whom I had gotten to know over the years of Soviet-American writers' exchanges. He proudly assured me that Gorbachev's changes were strengthening the Soviet Union, and that glasnost was bringing about a more humane Communist Party. Glasnost was a Gorbachev-endorsed commitment to more transparency in the government. Aitmatov was a strong supporter of Gorbachev's reforms. I said it seemed that glasnost, according to the media, was allowing questions to be asked about Lenin's role and Lenin as a person. I opined that the entire house of cards would collapse should Lenin and his vision be doubted. Aitmatov was not pleased. He did not agree, and my statement shook him. His reaction was just one indicator, even in the final moments of the USSR, of the blind belief of the Communist establishment in Lenin's infallibility.

In my wanderings in 1965, I once came across a ruined and shut monastery on the Moskva River. It had been converted into a Lenin statue factory. Through the flimsy gates, I could see hundreds of Lenin parts—busts, heads, bodies, outstretched arms. Covering all of the Lenin torsos was the suit he is always shown wearing. I found this paradoxical. The leader of "the workers of the world unite," was invariably dressed as a typical bourgeoisie man of business—a capitalist? In this statue factory, at least, all of the Lenin heads had been manufactured from an identical mold. No Asian visages on these Lenin heads.

Yet, despite my fascination with Lenin, it was Stalin's icon that was the defining portrait of Soviet history by any measure. No other image was more ubiquitous in the Communist world in the twentieth century, except perhaps for Mao. But by 1963, most of the monumental statues and images of Stalin had been destroyed. Khrushchev, after his bold 1956 speech, had led the charge to eliminate Stalin's image and demolish parts of his horrific legacy. Khrushchev's speech revealing some of Stalin's crimes shook the Communist world, sparked the Hungarian revolution, and initiated the monumental task of removing the Stalin statues, busts, faces, and names from cities, towns, buildings, and monuments throughout the Soviet Union, Eastern Bloc, and beyond.

It is an ironic measure of the relative significance of Stalin in the Soviet iconography that it took Khrushchev nearly five years to scrub out Stalin's image. (It took Khrushchev's heirs less than forty-eight hours to make Khrushchev disappear.) Still standing was the one giant (twenty feet tall) ominous bronze Stalin still in the central square in his hometown Gori, Georgia. I had to go; what I found is that Stalin still evokes awe from his final pedestal.

Indeed, the once overpowering presence of Stalin over the former Communist lands still casts a shadow. Putin knows.

Stalin's image, surprisingly, remained a looming presence in Khrushchev's own life, even as he ordered Stalin's busts and statues destroyed across the USSR. That awareness was uncovered by a number of American diplomats at a dinner with Khrushchev following his 1959 trip to America and his meeting with President Eisenhower at Camp David.

As a gesture of gratitude for the welcome he received from the people of the United States, Khrushchev had invited then American Ambassador "Tommy" Thompson and his wife to spend a weekend at his large country house. Thompson was accompanied by his deputy chief of mission, FSO Boris Klosson. According to Klosson, with whom I carpooled after I returned to Washington, DC, the dinner at Khrushchev's dacha that Saturday night was elaborate, with several other members of the Presidium (formerly the Politburo) present. At every place setting were three full bottles—one each of vodka, red wine, and cognac. Anastas Mikoyan was the *tamada* (toastmaster) for the ceremonies at dinner. When the guests moved into the grand hall for dinner, the Americans were surprised—shocked?—to see that behind Khrushchev's chair were three giant portraits: Marx, Lenin, and, right in the center, a much larger portrait of Stalin. Icons of the twentieth century. In the house of the man who had tried to make the world forget Stalin's very existence, was a portrait of the Soviet leader who directly oversaw the deaths of more than six million people.[31]

In the eighth century, the Iconoclasts of Byzantium had forbidden the pervasive worship of icons. Icons had become such powerful images that Orthodox believers had become conditioned to worshipping the saints on the icons themselves in the place of worshipping God. In Soviet Russia, a similar destruction of icons followed the October Revolution (1917). The icons during that time, however, were not all destroyed; it proved impossible to obliterate their legacy or the deep penetration of the Orthodox soul. So the Soviet government created new icons: those of Lenin and Marx and Stalin. The new Soviet belief system derived essentially from the leader and not from a higher deity. As Lenin's and Stalin's rule grew, their icons became the substitute for the higher power.

Only days after Khrushchev's fall, the Diebenkorns traveled to Kyiv in Ukraine, and then to Yerevan and Tbilisi in the Caucasus. I continued to send them whatever insight I could gather from Moscow on Khrushchev. On their return to Moscow, I resumed shepherding them through the city. I insisted we see works by the Lenin Prize–winning sculptor Sergey Konenkov, a titan of socialist realism. I described to them the curious relationship that Konenkov's wife, Margarita Konenkova, had had with Einstein during World War II. Einstein had carried on a long affair— presumably a love affair—with Margarita. This had been relayed to me by my former mother-in-law and her closest friend, the painter Marjorie Bishop, who had come to know the Konenkovs when they lived in New York City in the years between 1924 and 1945. Marjorie, my eldest son's godmother, became an intimate friend of Margarita, who was also a painter.

Konenkov, who had supported the Bolshevik Revolution in 1923, had gone to New York to participate in an exhibition of Russian art. He and his new wife Margarita decided to remain in the US, where they lived for twenty-two years. While in New York, this artist, who already was a sculptor of Soviet heroes, began to portray biblical figures in the US. His main interest was figures from the Apocalypse, and he completed several images of Jesus Christ.

In 1935, he was invited to the Institute for Advanced Study in Princeton to do a sculpture of Einstein. It is unclear why he was selected. It does seem that in that period Einstein and Margarita had started up a relationship that became a love affair.

It is one of the quirks of my personal story that while I was spending a year at the Institute for Advanced Study at Princeton in 1982–83, my office was next to where Einstein's had been. One time while writing in my office, I heard loud noises next door. Several Israeli academics were packing up Einstein's papers to ship them to Israel as determined by Einstein's will. The institute had been making copies to retain for their own archives. I pondered whether there might be some trace of Margarita Konenkova in the archives now headed for Israel.

What we do know is that in the 1940s, Einstein had begun to spend more time with Margarita. Marjorie Bishop had put together a weekend away for Einstein and Margarita at the home of my former father- and mother-in-law, near Setauket, Long Island. Einstein stayed in the bedroom of my former wife. Jane received a thank you note from Einstein for letting him stay there. The family has pictures of Einstein and Margarita sailing my father-in-law's boat.

In the late 1940s, Margarita asked Marjorie to protect a box of letters that Einstein had sent her, presumably over several years. Konenkova asked Marjorie to promise that she would burn the letters before Marjorie died. She claimed to want no written evidence of the relationship, as the Americans would conclude that Einstein had been contacted by her to seek secret information about the atomic bomb. Konenkova claimed not to want a blot on Einstein's reputation or, worse, to cause a scandal. Marjorie believed Konenkova and was determined to burn the letters. She showed me the box, but never the letters. Over the years, we discussed what she should do about those letters dozens of times. Konenkov returned to Moscow at Stalin's personal request after the war in 1945. Margarita returned a year later. She continued seeing Einstein until she departed for Moscow.

In 1963, shortly after arriving in Moscow to work in the embassy, I read in the Moscow press of a grand opening in a Moscow of an exhibition of the Lenin Prize–winning sculptor Konenkov. I went to the opening. He was not there, but Margarita was. I introduced myself and asked whether I could call on her because I knew of her close relationship with my friend Marjorie Bishop. Surprised and possibly frightened, she walked away.

The Konenkov exhibit was intriguing. The main gallery displayed a large collection of his art of brave heroic scholars, scientists, workers, and many others who were generic, without distinctive facial features. There were no sculptures of political leaders. Not even a small Lenin bust. But I also wandered into a second smaller room that was filled with imaginative wooden sculptures from branches of birches and other trees. They were authentic and refreshing works of Russian art. I found no images of the Apocalypse and certainly none of Jesus or Einstein.

Marjorie, years later, assured me that she had or intended to burn all of Einstein's letters soon. After her death, I assumed that the secret trove was gone. Years later, however, seven of the letters were sold on the market. As a result, part of the story was revealed. They were not so damaging or revealing as to create a scandal from long ago. Walter Isaacson's definitive and brilliant biography *Einstein* devotes only a couple of paragraphs to the Konenkova affair. Isaacson concluded that Margarita had been a KGB agent. A few of the letters achieved public notice, I assume, because Marjorie's nephew, who knew of the letters, may have understood the financial value of the letters. What would Marjorie say?

Sergey Konenkov died in 1971; Margarita Konenkova died in 1980.

The Department of State had wisely chosen Richard Diebenkorn as the first American painter to participate in the cultural exchange program.

During my time with him in Moscow and Leningrad visiting artists' studios, Dick demonstrated his deep interest in painters as people and as artists. Simply put, he honored artists: their predicaments, skills, and search for the creative. He disliked conflict of any type, but he became engaged by his mission even as he and Phyllis became wary and even fearful of Soviet society. The political pressure and distrust of the accompanying Soviet officials became more distressing than the visual and aesthetic blandness—or even ugliness—of the surroundings. The longer they remained in the Soviet Union, the more tolerant Dick became of the many artists who were working in their trade— and the Socialist Realism milieu—and putting out painting after painting of happy workers and students, heroic military figures, and party leaders building a new Soviet society. The paintings were boring but technically competent.

Additionally, Dick enjoyed his visits to the "unofficial" artists I was able to organize outside of the official visits organized by the Leningrad or Moscow Union of Artists. He was taken by their earnest efforts to break free of official constraints on art but rarely established rapport with their political statements or their artistic challenges. Dick was a painter to his core. He did not relate to political art in any aspect.

I cling to the belief that the jolt Dick received from his encounter with Soviet Russia and most particularly his Matisse experience in Leningrad profoundly influenced his trajectory as an artist. Dick and Phyllis were put off by the crudeness of the people and the repression of artistic freedom but charmed by the high attention and admiration that greeted them wherever they went. He began to sense that Soviet artists welcomed the opportunity to talk with him even though they had no sense of his paintings—except through the few catalogues we were able to distribute. Having looked at much socialist realism, he returned to the US probably even more convinced that he should move on from figurative painting. The Diebenkorns, while treasuring the experience, were relieved that the visit was over.

His time spent with the Matisse paintings in Leningrad pushed Dick to take his own new path. From many hours of conversations, I could tell that he was not satisfied with his current work. He had traveled those cityscapes too long. The Matisse Moroccan paintings at the Hermitage fed his preference for cool tones and color. While he was dazzled by the Hermitage's classic Matisse, *The Red Room*, the expressionistic bright red space covered with design elements was not his instinct. Rather, it was Matisse's *The Conversation*, with its large unbroken spaces of blues and references to other colors and shapes, that caught and held his attention.

The year after he returned to his home in Berkeley, he and Phyllis moved to Los Angeles to live in Santa Monica. He perhaps wanted better light and certainly a different environment from which he could start anew. There he began his Ocean Park series of paintings, which the brilliant art critic Robert Hughes described in his *Time* magazine review:

Diebenkorn's retrospective of more than 130 works . . . is as masterly a demonstration of a sensibility in growth as any living painter could set forth. He is not, as the condescending tag once read, a California artist, but a world figure. He is not an avant-gardist either, and his work keeps alluding to its sources: the color to Bonnard and Matisse, the strong, fractionally unstable drawing to Mondrian and Matisse again. Diebenkorn's best paintings mediate between the moral duty to acknowledge the ancestor and the desire to claim one's own experience as unique, unrepeatable. In short, he is a thoroughly traditional artist, for whose work the words "high seriousness" might have been invented . . . [The paintings in the Ocean Park series] are certainly among the most beautiful declamations in the language of the brush to have been uttered anywhere in the past 20 years . . . They are the medium for one of the most exhilarating meditations on structure—the tradition being that of pre-1914 Matisse and post-1918 Mondrian—ever conducted by an American artist . . . There are perhaps a dozen living painters who vindicate painting's claim to be still a major art. Richard Diebenkorn is one of them.[32]

Diebenkorn's extraordinary Ocean Park paintings grew out of his encounter with the more abstract and peaceful spaces of Matisse. More importantly, Matisse's work engaged Dick's own character and painterly instincts—reserved, concentrated, ambitious, refined, and intensely creative, but neither explosive nor unhinged. He was an artist who struggled with every painting, having to prove in everyone that he was true to himself. Matisse and Diebenkorn, separated by a generation, made a unique pair in instinct for color and design. After the Leningrad trip, Dick was ready to design freely, in luscious color, grand spaces uncluttered by the figure.

Over the next three decades, my wife, Wendy, and I became close friends of the Diebenkorns. Dick grew as a painter and became a prominent figure in the art world. They visited us twice in Caracas and once in Prague while I was ambassador. We saw them frequently in New York and Los Angeles. In 2016, we went to the opening of the magnificent exhibition of Matisse and Diebenkorn in Baltimore, and then again in 2017 at the San Francisco Museum of Modern Art. Many Ocean Park paintings were in the exhibition, which also included some of the paintings that immediately preceded the series. His main work was

Recollections of a Visit to Leningrad (see color insert). The paintings were dedicated as an *Homage to Leningrad*, with a design reference from *The Conversation* in the center of one of his breathtaking canvasses.

With adroit language, the writer and philosopher John Ruskin described his grand philosophical proposition:

> Great nations write their autobiographies in three manuscripts, the book of their deeds, the book of their words and the book of their art. Not one of these books can be understood unless we read the two others, but of three the only trustworthy one is the last.[33]

The seeds of this same philosophy were planted in me in my early years spent with writers and artists as an FSO in Moscow. Looking back, I have tried to integrate Ruskin's thoughts on deeds, words, and art into this volume of personal stories. During much of my life I have been attracted to Russian entanglements with revolution, Communism, and art since the Bolsheviks. Those years after World War I were turbulent, exciting, and transformational at many levels in Russia and beyond. The conflicts and big questions of the 1920s proved to be defining for the world in the twentieth century. *Would the marginalized individual really become the new focus of governance? Would empires cease to dominate national cultures? Would artists and writers be free to create outside the limits of authority and government?*

Russian art of the twentieth century—the suprematists and constructivists and others described earlier—could have perhaps made an even greater contribution to Western culture than Russian literature of the nineteenth century. Lenin and Stalin crushed that possibility. In John Ruskin's imagined manuscript on Russian civilization, the books on deeds, words, and art were permanently changed by the Communist revolution.

The artists of socialist realism that Richard Diebenkorn and I met were not the Russian heirs to those 1920s pioneers of modern art. Diebenkorn, I believe, was very definitely an heir of Malevich, perhaps even more than of Matisse. He had the good fortune to flourish freely as an independent nonobjective painter. His large canvasses invite the viewer in to explore and take quiet pleasure from his colorful spaces. He will be a prominent figure in the volume on art in the manuscript of American civilization.

A year after their visit to Leningrad, Dick and Phyllis Diebenkorn moved their home to Los Angeles to a house in Santa Monica in pursuit of new light and new muses.

Richard Diebenkorn died in 1993 in California.

Khrushchev's campaign to rid the USSR of the Stalin legacy was left unfinished and he was the first Soviet leader not to be buried in the Kremlin Wall. Upon his death, his family assigned the commission for his gravestone to Ernst Neizvestny, who was also one of the founders of the Russian memorial movement pressing for the rehabilitation and recognition of all the victims of Stalin's terror.

Khrushchev died in 1971.

CHAPTER 6

The Open Forum Panel

For a Foreign Service family, the return to Washington, DC, from a foreign assignment is always a challenge—sometimes a traumatic one. After having lived in a foreign community, children always feel uprooted and confused about their identity when they find themselves "home." Returning from Moscow was particularly tough for my two young boys, both of whom had been born in a US Navy hospital in Naples, Italy. They each had lived in four different residences, with vastly diverse environments: Italy; Washington, DC; Germany; and Moscow. Upon our return from Moscow, the boys were once again introduced to a new residence, in a new neighborhood. Neither of them had yet had a close relationship with other American children. Both were already showing signs of having a learning disability, which no school was willing or able to help us address. Not until my eldest son, Mark, was fourteen years old was dyslexia even diagnosed. The understanding of learning disabilities was woefully underdeveloped during my children's early years. The consequences for my Mark would be severe.

My wife, who shared neither my fascination with foreign cultures nor my compulsion about learning languages, spoke no language other than English, though she unsuccessfully tried to learn Italian. She made no effort to learn Russian. She had hated Moscow and the whole experience. While there, she left me for several months, taking my two boys with her.

Stresses on Foreign Service families are typical of the peripatetic. Returning "home" to DC was a test of how well the family had succeeded in working together to keep itself solid and whole. The cost of failure can be high. Marriages break up and families can shatter under deep stress. So my return to DC in 1965 to work in the State Department involved a great deal of family time. I was particularly focused on helping my children become familiar with their country, including the music, the food, and the sports, after Moscow. As it turned out, I needed to familiarize myself with America, as well.

America in 1965 was a very different place from the nation I had left in 1962 to prepare for my Moscow assignment. Determined to understand the noise that had developed in my country, I threw myself into learning America's changing culture with even more gusto than I had in my approach to learning about the USSR. The difference was striking for me. Since I had lived in New York as had my wife, Jane, we were both unfamiliar with Washington, DC. We were able to buy a new, small house in Georgetown on P Street but did not have the income to lead the life of Georgetowners. My wife began to teach painting to a group of friends, including two men, who liked art.

The Civil Rights Act of 1964 had recently been passed by the House and the Senate and signed into law by President Johnson. As a way to play a role in bridging the divide between Blacks and whites, I undertook to develop a program with a group of friends and FSOs to exchange views with some of the radical movements involved in planning the "revolution," which many believed was about to happen. One evening, in early 1967, I invited a group of my friends and associates from the State Department to join me in a conversation in our home with the leaders of the DC branch of SDS—Students for a Democratic Society—which arguably was the most extreme organization working for change. At one point in the evening, the discussion got so heated that I invited some of the group to join me for a beer in the kitchen. There, I stood next to the SDS leader, who was a very smart Black woman about twenty-five years old, already tough and experienced—and also extremely bright and charismatic. Turning to her, I asked what she thought the revolution would do with people like me. She looked me straight in the eye and without hesitation or lament said, "We will probably have to kill you."

I suppose the reason I asked the question was because I had anticipated the answer she gave me. I was, therefore, not shocked. I asked her how many people like me would have to be sacrificed for the revolution to succeed; she said many, but we moved on. I began to review the history of the slaughter that consumed the French Revolution and finally only ended with the rule of an autocrat, Napoleon. My group of colleagues did not hear my exchange in the kitchen with the leader of the group, but I told them after the SDS group had gone home. Most of us decided against further efforts to continue to chat with the SDS group— the enemy.

It is fair to say that most people did not know how seriously certain people believed that the revolution was coming. We saw that approaching the issue with SDS like diplomats would not work.

In my continuing quest to develop new ways to understand and relate to the new America that was emerging from the Vietnam War and the civil rights movement, I had been attending, with my family, the Sunday masses offered by a good friend, Father Bill Wendt, who was the pastor of St. Stephen and the

Incarnation, an Episcopal church on Sixteenth Street. Sixteenth Street was one of the historic divides between Whites and blacks in DC, and St. Stephen was one of the very few churches in DC with a fully biracial congregation. The church was a powerful religious—and political—symbol for those promoting multiracial thinking.

Because of my interest in religion (my earlier brush with the seminary) and my ongoing study of America, along with a passionate conviction about the need to talk to the other, Wendt had asked me to take part in a number of projects in the parish. He also recommended that I become the drafter of a plan modeled after the Los Angeles churches' experience after the Watts riots of 1965, which created such damage to the inner city and destroyed many of the shops and centers for food. The Los Angeles churches took an innovative role and gathered food contributions and organized convoys, which traveled, with security protection from the police, to deliver food to the inner city. Wendt was suggesting that Washington, DC needed a similar program in case the worst happened. In any case, our group, composed of a Presbyterian minister, a rabbi, and the Black leader of a Baptist church, worked together to learn from the Watts experience and to prepare a plan for Washington, DC.

On April 4, 1968, only months after we completed our plan, Martin Luther King, Jr. was assassinated, and riots broke out in DC; the inner city burned, stores were closed or locked up, and food needed to be sent by police caravan into the inner city. Our plan worked: the religious leaders were directly engaged in moving food to the people.

At the same time, I was beginning a new job at the State Department. I had been assigned as the top analyst on Soviet

Averell and Pamela Harriman in Washington, DC.

internal affairs in the State Department's Bureau of Intelligence and Research (INR). I had hoped for a policy office, but I was told, seductively, that because my reporting from Moscow had been so unusually rich due to my extensive contacts with Soviet intellectuals and citizens, and because of my extensive travels (I had gotten to every Soviet republic), that I was needed in the intelligence division. The State Department's Bureau of Intelligence and Research wanted to draw on my intimate knowledge of the USSR. In fact, it turned out to be a perfect transition for me—I was able to improve my writing and briefing style and achieve the high quality that professional analysts in the US government intelligence communities who dealt with the USSR were expected to have.

I was in my office when I got a report from a meeting that

had been held in the office of the director of Policy Planning and had been attended by Secretary of State Dean Rusk. In this meeting, Rusk had charged that *there were no new ideas in foreign policy.* Mind you, this was 1966, during the ramp up to the Vietnam War, which already was dominating the thinking of most Foreign Service Officers. David Owen, who was the director of Policy Planning at the time, challenged Rusk, saying, "Yes, there *are* new ideas. We will go out and ask our State Department officials for their new ideas on US foreign policy."

Gauntlet thrown and challenge accepted.

What would grow out of Owen's meeting was groundbreaking. From its fledgling beginning, a separate *institution* within the State Department would emerge. The Open Forum Panel was built from the ground up from what happened next.

Owen first sent out a query to all embassies asking all of the diplomats, from ambassador on down to the newest Foreign Service Officer, to propose new ideas in American foreign policy. He then set out to gather a group of Foreign Service Officers who would be interested in helping Policy Planning vet the replies that would come from around the world. Sam Lewis, a creative and open colleague of mine who was close with Owen, had already been tapped to participate. Knowing of my outspoken belief in openness and in communication as being the bedrock of diplomacy, Lewis approached me about being a part of the new group. I expressed high interest, and Owen invited me to be one of the first members of the group. In addition to Sam and me, eight more junior and middle grade officers would join our informal group. Also, Owen had assigned Lee Stull, one of his top writers and thinkers in Policy Planning, to help support our work. Lee turned out to be the perfect colleague to collaborate with in Policy Planning: he was open to new ideas; didn't have a closed mind; supported the younger, energetic crowd that I was a part of; and most of all, Lee had a good relationship with the secretary of state.

That was in May 1967. In August of that same year, Secretary Rusk formally announced the formation of his Open Forum Panel.

We began meeting regularly during the week to review the ideas that already were beginning to come in. Our goal was to review the proposals and then discuss them with Secretary Rusk to determine whether the proposal was worth being developed further in Policy Planning.

The ideas that came in varied wildly. Some were worthwhile; others less so. One interesting pattern began to emerge: we received a number of proposals from individuals who had recently been assigned to a new duty station. Their proposals often spoke to an initiative in their old station. Their proposal usually indicated a disagreement with a policy that had been formulated over their objections or criticisms.

Not surprisingly, many of the new ideas called for an end to the Vietnam War. As early as 1965, the undersecretary for political affairs, George Ball, who had opposed the war from the outset, argued for a diplomatic approach to the North Vietnamese. He developed a proposal that was opposed by his boss, Secretary of State Rusk, and the White House. In our deliberations in the Open Forum Panel, we spent a great deal of time trying to determine how best to deal with the Vietnam War, which was beginning to sap the energy from US foreign policy elsewhere.

Nevertheless, we decided that we should first have our

preliminary meeting with Secretary Rusk to see how he reacted to some of the interesting ideas we already had received, before we dove into the issue of Vietnam, knowing the strong commitment he had to the war.

Lee Stull helped arrange our first meeting with Rusk, which happened after we had formally organized as a group. Our first meeting was reported in the weekly department magazine, along with a photo. In the first meeting, we covered a number of the new ideas, including one proposal that suggested that the United States should discontinue its policy of recognition of the Baltic state governments-in-exile. The author of this proposal believed that doing so would have a positive impact on American relations with the USSR. In 1968, the United States did not recognize Soviet rule of any of the Baltic states (Estonia, Latvia, and Lithuania) and maintained relationships with the Baltics through their governments-in-exile or through their diplomats. Rusk wisely thought that such a policy change would be a mistake and have serious domestic political implications. There were also a number of ideas on South Asia, many on better ways of dealing with India. All of which we put to Rusk. Vietnam did come up in a large number of proposals we had received, but we refrained from taking them forward in that first meeting.

One consequence of our first meeting with Rusk was that I was asked to meet privately with the secretary about the speeches he was giving at universities in an attempt to quell the unrest. At the time, I was teaching a course at Johns Hopkins University-SAIS. I had mentioned to one of Rusk's staffers that after spending real time at a university, my instinct was that Rusk's use of the Munich metaphor to justify US policy in Vietnam did not compute for an eighteen-year-old student who would most likely associate the name Munich more broadly with beer gardens or, if really sophisticated, might think of Bavaria or southern Germany. I said that virtually no student would associate Munich with the appeasement of Hitler. He asked me to talk to the secretary directly about my point. The meeting was scheduled within hours. But to no one's surprise, the meeting was eventually postponed indefinitely.

Six months later, after the 1968 election, we all gathered to attend a large Foreign Service farewell lunch for Secretary Rusk. Rusk's final caution to us all was that, when we think of Vietnam, none of us should ever forget Munich.

Looking for a greater understanding of the issues involved in the war and hoping to cast a wide net, the Open Forum Panel began holding policy discussion lunches in a large, secluded dining room of the State Department. In these luncheons, we would invite people from other departments, or other parts of departments, to debate with journalists and members of Congress and, particularly, senior staff members of the Senate and House Foreign Affairs Committees. We were concerned that the new and unconventional policies we were putting forward not be seen as fostering dissent on the Vietnam War. Nor did we want to be seen as creating problems with other foreign policy issues: the Open Forum Panel was there to solve problems, not cause them. We would occasionally have twenty to thirty attendees, but at times there were close to one hundred specialists who would join us at lunch and discuss their concerns about foreign policy.

At that time, early 1968, it was evident from the buzz in

the department that a lot of people were thinking about how to begin negotiations with the North Vietnamese to end the war. Tom Hughes, the director of the Bureau of Intelligence and Research during the Kennedy and Johnson administrations and the head of the bureau while I was in Washington, was active in a number of those efforts. After the elections in 1968, Lee Stull of Policy Planning arranged for the Open Forum Panel group to have a meeting with Elliot Richardson, the deputy secretary designate of the State Department, who was coming in to serve under William Rogers, who had been named as secretary of state by Nixon.

At his invitation, we met with Richardson at his house to discuss what we had learned about the Vietnam War. By then, our Open Forum Panel had representatives throughout the government. Additionally, we were able to glean from other ongoing projects that many of the agencies tended to have quite different takes on the progress of the war. Our experiences at the State Department and as part of the Open Forum Panel—seeing differing POVs from other intelligence branches, policymakers, and legislative staff—tended to make us more objective. Prior to that December evening with Richardson at his house, we had been able to gather together the reports of the various governments agencies who annually would submit their analysis of how the war was going and whether it would require more forces to defeat the North Vietnamese. The office that oversees the assembling of the National Intelligence Estimate (NIE) and the Systems Analysis side of the Pentagon were far more skeptical of US chances of winning the war. We found that the reports by the Vietnam Task Force, run by Bill Bundy in the State Department and the embassy in Saigon under Ambassador Bunker were bullish about

America's chances of winning the war. Those that had the greatest stake in winning were the chairman of the joint chiefs of staff and the staff of the joint chiefs of staff. Those groups gave the rosiest picture of how we were doing in the war. This was the Luers principle in action: how to predict career support for bad policies, as it were; those with an ownership in policy formulation and the execution of that policy are going to be the least likely to recommend changes. From all of these groups and more, we pulled together for Richardson an aggregate report and also made presentations on the differences of each of the reports we had gathered together. This was still several years before the Pentagon Papers were leaked to the *New York Times*.

Richardson seemed impressed by the information and analysis we gave him. But as far as we knew, he never pursued any of the insights we provided to him that evening with the White House. The White House then was dominated by the new national security advisor, Henry Kissinger, who was working with President Nixon to determine the basic strategy for dealing with the Vietnam War.

———

During the late 1960s, observing the faltering role of traditional diplomacy, a group of Foreign Service Officers prepared a book of recommendations, which we then published. We called this somewhat transformative report *Toward a Modern Diplomacy*. This book became the basis for ongoing discussions within the State Department and beyond.

In preparing our recommendations, we worked closely with the Senate Foreign Relations Committee staff. They encouraged us to complete the report, as they foresaw using it as a means of attracting Senate support for the recommendations they had had a hand in writing. Our recommendations included support for the work and approach of the Open Forum Panel. I wrote one of the chapters on the need for openness. Over time, *Toward a Modern Diplomacy* became a center for discussion on how to *encourage and manage* dissent within the State Department and was a strong voice in establishing the need for a dissent channel, which would encourage diplomats to register their concerns about diplomatic policy and recommend alternative courses. There is now a functioning dissent channel, which does not generally exist in the US government.

To recognize the courage it takes to publicly register your concerns about a policy or to recommend new policies, awards are now given to those who speak out.

The Open Forum Panel and *Toward a Modern Diplomacy* both reflected the need to introduce significant changes in how the State Department operated and how they formed diplomatic missions and internal communications.

CODA

The extent of the success of the Open Forum Panel can be seen through the actions of my boss in the Bureau of Intelligence and Research, Tom Hughes. Hughes, who had been selected to head the Carnegie Endowment for International Peace after Nixon's election, had learned of the success of the Open Forum Panel. Seeing opportunity in the structure and format and mission of our group, he hired the Foreign Service Officer from the State Department who was likely to replace me as chairman of the panel to launch a program resembling the Open Forum Panel at the Carnegie Endowment. This program was set up to facilitate conversations between critics of the Vietnam War and US government officials and policymakers. This practice has now become standard practice in Washington with think tanks, which bring together State Department officials, CIA, Defense Department officials, critics, journalists, and members of Congress to debate. Hughes sought to do this by offering stimulating and even provocative sessions to Foreign Service Officers and others from within the government. Tom was able to invest money in this new program he called "Face-to-Face," which became a groundbreaking new initiative at the Carnegie Endowment and for Tom Hughes, its new head. Tom continued to work behind the scenes to find a way out of Vietnam.

CHAPTER 7

Looking South and Speaking Spanish: Venezuela, Part I

After nearly a decade of dealing with the Soviet Union as an FSO, in 1967, I chose to focus my career development more broadly. To be relieved from the obsessive issues of the Cold War—nuclear weapons and arms control—I asked for an assignment to Latin America. I sought to realign my career to focus on North-South issues, which emphasized human and economic development, particularly in Kennedy's Alliance for Progress in Latin America.

The decision proved to be a wise one. I had hoped to find the development issues in the North-South environment to be more attuned to what I had come to expect of diplomacy. My experience in Latin America reinforced my growing belief in the high value of the arts in facilitating diplomacy, but it also lifted the veil for me as to the serious nature of Latin American geopolitics: the cold war being fought over these North-South issues and over the types of government that the US would tolerate in the development of the new states in the southern hemisphere was ongoing . . . and hot. From my position first as political officer and then as ambassador, I was a witness to the US proclivity toward interventionist polices that undermined democracy. I feared that American policies designed to make certain that no Fidel Castro would come to dominate the politics of any country in Latin America were driving US international relations in the wrong direction.

As a result of my career decision, I was assigned, in 1967 to the Bureau of Inter-American Affairs, which dealt with the Western Hemisphere, mainly Latin America and the Caribbean nation-states. My first assignment was to serve as desk officer for Guyana, the former British Guiana. Serving as the desk officer for Guyana involved working with the embassy team, particularly the ambassador, to enhance their voice in the State Department and on issues of concern to other English-speaking states in the region. Guyana, one of the smallest independent nations of the Western Hemisphere, had achieved independence in 1966 from the UK; it had a democratic government headed then by Prime Minister Forbes Burnham, the leader of the People's National Congress (PNC), a party dominated by the Black population of Guyana. Most important for the US and the UK was to retain this status quo. Burnham was a strong leader against the main opposition leader, Cheddi Jagan, who was believed to be a Marxist. The UK and US intelligence agencies had an agreement to keep Burnham in power and make certain Jagan remained outside of the government.

As the desk officer of Guyana, I worked at the State Department in Washington, DC. However, I was anxious to take an embassy position in Latin America. To do so, especially as a political officer, which was going to be my next assignment, I needed to learn how to speak Spanish, which was a core requirement for a chief of the political section. So, I was sent to language training. There, I had an amazing group of Spanish teachers who converted my fluent Italian to a tolerable Spanish in six months. Speaking and caring about the Spanish language is vital to being accepted and welcomed in a Latin American nation. The

Spanish language is at the core of Latin American culture. They take their language far more seriously than North Americans take English. For many US speakers, language is a tool for communication. For Latinos, Spanish is the fabric of their culture and their dignity. The longer I served in Venezuela and elsewhere in Latin America, the more I became convinced of that reality. Much later, after I was named the ambassador to Venezuela, John Updike made several trips to visit us. During that time, he learned of the high regard Latinos have for their language. John, who was not a linguist but a master of the English language, after observing the honor given to the Spanish language, decided to learn Spanish himself. He even wrote me several letters in Spanish, one of which contained a fourteen-page interview of himself with an imagined Venezuelan journalist.

John Updike in Caracas.

When I arrived in Venezuela in 1969 with my wife, Jane, and our four small children, to assume my duty as political counselor of the American Embassy, I was thrilled to be in the Latin world and in the capital of Venezuela. I was soon disappointed to learn that because I was not an experienced Latin hand, the ambassador had persuaded the incumbent political counselor to remain in charge for a year.

Rather than return to Washington, as the ambassador evidently would have preferred, I decided to remain at the post under strained circumstances. My strategy was to get to know the leaders of the political opposition—people not normally seen by the political counselor. This proved to be helpful in the long run, since I became known as the person in the American Embassy who was open to talking to anyone, no matter their political affiliation or the power of their position. The environment in Venezuela was perfect for such an approach, since the administration that had just come to power was headed by Rafael Caldera, the head of the political party COPEI, the Social Christian Democratic Party of Venezuela, which was the second largest political party and shared national leadership with the AD Party, Acción Democrática, another center-left party.

As a social democratic party, AD had close affiliations to the social democratic parties in Europe and throughout Latin America. AD's first strong leader had been Rómulo Betancourt, the first democratically elected president of Venezuela. Betancourt was elected after the fall of Pérez Jiménez, the last dictator to rule. Betancourt, who is often called the "father of his country," developed as a restless young political leader who had risen to the top of the Venezuelan Communist Party in Costa Rica after he was expelled from Venezuela in the late 1930s for his radical views. He

President Carlos Andrés Pérez and President Betancourt.

matured quickly and returned to Venezuela in 1937 and founded the political party that became Acción Democrática. He became president of Venezuela in 1945. As president, he led the country through a series of reforms until Venezuela held its first democratic elections that brought Rómulo Gallegos to the presidency. The former dictator, Pérez Jiménez, returned to power because of another military coup that overthrew the sputtering democracy. The intrepid Betancourt undermined the Jiménez junta and pressed forward toward the elections of 1958, in which he was elected president of the country. Betancourt served a first term as president until the second round of elections came. (When Betancourt died in 1981, I recommended that a senior US government official attend the funeral to represent the United States. American president Ronald Reagan sent Vice President George

H. W. Bush for the event. The vice president and Mrs. Bush stayed at the residence with us during the visit, and we established a relationship with the Bushes that endured until President Bush died in 2018.)

After Betancourt's first term as president, AD won again, which set the course for the democratic evolution of Venezuela. In the third set of presidential elections, four years later, the Christian Democrats won, giving the opportunity for Venezuela to demonstrate that democracy in Latin America can function via free and open elections, and that power can pass from one political party to another as a routine matter.

It was into that environment that I arrived in Caracas in 1969 for my first ever tour of duty in a Latin American country. Like most of my fellow citizens I had never been "south of the border."

My first job was to get to know the country: I was lucky in that regard. The Venezuelans were incredibly open, friendly, and ready to talk about their politics. They are also passionate about their art and their music. I learned much from my travels across Venezuela and came to believe that it was probably the most beautiful and varied country in the Western Hemisphere from the standpoint of its landscape and the dramatic, visual geography it offers. Between the Andes and the Llanos (lowlands) flows one of the great river systems (the Orinoco); the world's highest waterfall (Angel Falls) astounds with its beauty; and the rich jungles of Venezuela defy description. During my eight years living in Venezuela, I became familiar with many of the phenomenal natural Venezuelan settings. To travel in Venezuela is to experience the rich vitality of the New World as revealed by Columbus and studied by Alexander von Humboldt and Charles Darwin.

Gustavo Cisneros and Bill in Amazonas.

As I settled into my quasi-position in Caracas, I learned several important issues and faced several serious questions. First, as
I've mentioned, Venezuelans, like most citizens of Latin America,
place the knowledge and respect of the Spanish language at the
center of the culture. I found that Spanish language speakers in
Venezuela do not open with a joke or an anecdote, like Americans
tend to do. Well-educated Spanish speakers in Latin America will
often open their talk by demonstrating their knowledge of and
respect for Spanish. North Americans are often impatient with

the long preambles in the oration of a Latino political leader or person of business, not realizing that the Spanish speaker is paying his respect to the language. My Spanish was never as elegant or refined as I knew it should be, but I never lost sight of the fact that it is the core of the culture of Latin America.

Besides the primacy of the language, the next universal I learned was that virtually all of Venezuela's intellectuals, journalists, and artists had a leftist bias, which often translated into one of admiration for Castro and the radical Left. I found this subliminal truth about writers and journalists useful in preparing visitors from the US for their press interviews.

A third issue was a question I had to ask myself: How I could explain the low level of interest most North Americans showed in the arts of South America? At times, Americans' interest in Latin American art seemed not so much as a lack of interest, but occasionally downright negative. I was shocked to find that many Americans seemed dismissive, even contemptuous of Latin culture. One good friend, Patty Phelps de Cisneros, who was from Venezuela, was persuaded that the low level of interest in the rich tradition of the visual arts of Latin America was simply ignorance of the artistic movements and trends in Venezuela and Brazil and the Río de la Plata valley around Argentina and Uruguay. Patty and her husband, Gustavo, were particularly attuned to and understanding of the relationship between the appreciation of visual arts and the appreciation of Latin America itself, and the understating of Latin culture in general, particularly by North Americans and Europeans. I wondered if perhaps the lack of appreciation was because American citizens are biased—many make their first international travels to Europe, finding pleasure and comfort in the familiar art found in Paris, Rome, London, and Vienna. Such a grand tour, taken by the wealthy in the eighteenth and nineteenth centuries, and about which American literature flourished, had caused entire generations of Americans in the twentieth century to think of sophisticated travel as being only to Europe. Nevertheless, as I began to learn of the culture of Latin America, and specifically that of Venezuela, I grew deeply impressed by the ties the people had to the arts, music, and literature of their nation. If ever culture could be a bridge between countries, it was in the culturally rich and engaged Venezuela.

With the arrival of Ambassador Robert McClintock to the embassy in Caracas in 1970, I was formally made the political councilor in Caracas. At this point, I set out to get to know the leaders from *all* the political parties and factions, including, once

Ambassador Robert McClintock, Caracas, 1970.

again, the vocal leaders of the Left. One of those political activists
was Teodoro Petkoff, who, along with his brother, Luben, had
been put in a boat by Castro himself, just after the Cuban Revolution (1953–1959), and sent to bring down the new democratic
government of Rómulo Betancourt. (This was told to me twenty
years later by Fidel Castro, during an hours-long conversation
in the back of his heavily guarded limousine.) Petkoff and his
brother had been fighting in the mountains of Venezuela against
the government until the elections, which brought COPEI (the
Christian Democrats) to power that same year. When the new
Christian Democratic leader, Rafael Caldera, came to office, he
encouraged the *guerrilleros*, like the Petkoffs, to come down from
the mountains and become integrated into the regular political
system, including the elections. Not long after Teodoro Petkoff
made public his agreement to be "pacified," I read a review of
his new book, in Spanish, *Checoeslovaquia: El Socialismo como
problema* (*Czechoslovakia: Socialism as a Problem*). I bought and
read the book immediately, given my interest in Soviet Communism. The book was an almost impassioned treatment by a
former true believer in the Communist Party on the decadence
and ineffectiveness of Soviet Communism. I realized that Petkoff
had become a passionate anti–Soviet Communist. He was a particularly knowledgeable insider who was contemptuous of the
Soviet system. I informed the Department of State and the intelligence community about the book and suggested it be promoted
throughout the world. I later wrote a long article on the Petkoff phenomenon under my then pseudonym Benedict Cross,
after my favorite Italian philosopher Benedetto Croce, who had
written an early devastating critique of Marx in the late nineteenth century. The article was titled "Marxism in Venezuela." It

concluded talking about the upcoming 1973 elections in
Venezuela and predicting the Marxists would not reach 10–15
percent of the vote. Certainly, they would not achieve victory.
I concluded with a note of hope:

> If the AD and COPEI parties were mobilized by the
> challenge from the Left to move quickly toward a new
> and energetic phase of social reform and economic diver-
> sification, Venezuela's resilient political democracy might
> point the way toward a new alternative to extremism in
> Latin America.[34]

Sadly, AD and COPEI were *not* mobilized by the challenge from
Petkoff in 1999, and Hugo Chávez became the face of the new
and energetic economic diversification. Venezuela was consumed

Pat Nixon, Ambassador McClintock greeting
Bill in the Ambassador's Residence.

by "Chavismo" and populism, setting the pattern of extremism that has spread throughout the region.

Over the next several years, Petkoff and I would keep in touch. Much to my dismay, my relationship with Petkoff would become a quasi-embarrassment to me and to the embassy after I was named ambassador. But that story will have to wait.

One of my important discoveries during the first year of so-called training to be the political counselor was the realization of the size and reach of the intelligence community. The head of the intelligence team seemed to have separate and close working relations with the former ambassador, Bernbaum. The head of intelligence and the political counselor did not work as a team, on the contrary the ambassador seemed to encourage competition.

Let me be clear: I strongly favor a robust American intelligence capacity. And I believe that CIA operators abroad are loyal public servants who occasionally risk their lives for their country. But they are not diplomats by instinct or training; the role they play in a US embassy is not a diplomatic role, and that ambiguity can often become a source of confusion for the host country and for other states with embassies in the country. Yet "working at the embassy" is often the cover role for CIA agents. In fact, I had worked closely with the head of the intelligence community in Moscow, and on my travels in the Soviet Union, I frequently partnered with the head, who was extremely well informed on Soviet politics and alert to suspicious activities around us. My concern as political officer in Venezuela in the late 1960s and early 1970s was that American presidents and the national security system seemed to be relegating to intelligence clearance in Latin American a particularly preeminent role in US policy. I believe that the decisions that resulted in this policy were driven by fear. I believed that the national security establishment had become fixated on the growing influence of Castro and the Soviet Union.

In the course of diplomacy, it is hard to make a judgment as to the degree to which CIA money contributed to a culture of corruption in Latin America when relationships took on a financial dimension. I also have no way of knowing whether wise judgment prevailed in making decisions of how to spend money in search of information. What I do know is that policy decisions and "diplomacy" decisions seemed to be made by intelligence agents. My impression from my experience in Venezuela was that those decisions were being made without consideration of the long-term implication for US diplomatic objectives in the country.

As it turned out, the fears I had about the covert operations while I was a political officer would only grow larger with my experience with Operation Condor during the mid-1970s. I never questioned the loyalty and dedication of intelligence officers, despite my concern about their freewheeling access to political leaders in Venezuela. At the time I was nominated as the ambassador to Venezuela, I did not know whether the intelligence community had tried to discourage my nomination (as they had in 1975), but I do know they made a special effort to assign one of their top agents to be head of the intelligence community during my tenure. Jack Devine, the assigned head of the intelligence community, was a true professional. I believe that Jack understood my belief that intelligence officers are not diplomats by instinct or training and the role they play is not a diplomatic role. Many foreign governments and government officials agree with that proposition. He and I agreed early on that I would not accept any action by the intelligence community that could embarrass me or the American government if found out. I believe that Jack kept his word to me, for at one point he brought a questionable matter to me for my approval. I proceeded to check with National Security Advisor Zbigniew Brzezinski and with the undersecretary of state who would have to approve that action. I never got any reply, presumedly because both Brzezinski and the undersecretary wanted to retain "credible deniability."

During my early years in Venezuela (1969–1973), my concerns about American covert involvement in Latin America were only just beginning to gestate. Instead, I spent my time falling in love with Venezuela and her people and her extraordinary culture.

During my first tour in Venezuela, I began to visit Amazonas, a state in Venezuela that juts out on the south end of that country into Brazil. It is bordered on the south by Brazil and to the west by Colombia. The border between Venezuela and Brazil is marked by the headwaters of the Amazon and Orinoco rivers, where the waters flow north to become the Orinoco River, or flow to the south as the Amazon River. It is a border defined by nature and not by politics. Amazonas is a separate political entity within Venezuela. Located in a remote and wild part of the country, the only real city in the territory is the capital of that state of Amazonas, Puerto Ayacucho, which is located on the Orinoco. It is an area almost entirely composed of jungle and the wide Orinoco and its tributaries.

I had become a visitor to Amazonas when a friend, Napoleon "Nap" Chagnon, visited me in Caracas. Nap was a well-known and controversial anthropologist who invited me and Ambassador McClintock to visit the Yanomami tribe that occupies much of the Amazonas region. At that point, the embassy's air attaché had a DC-3 American aircraft available for trips in Venezuela. Ambassador McClintock was always interested in new adventures and learning experiences. He welcomed the opportunity to fly to Amazonas—which was a new part of Venezuela, and which he had not visited before—to get to know the Yanomami culture, probably the most unusually primitive, Indigenous tribe in the Western Hemisphere. Chagnon already had done a series of documentary films on the profession of anthropology (based on his work with filmmaker Tim Asch among the Yanomami tribes in Venezuela), which had already become extremely

Yanomami tribe.

popular in classrooms across the country. Nap and another friend—a first-rate photographer—had already mastered the Yanomami language. They opened doors for us that otherwise would have been closed. Nap's book on the Yanomami is called *Yanomamö: The Fierce People*.

On our first visit, we called on the governor of the state of Amazonas in the capital of Puerto Ayacucho and traveled by boat to the nearby Catholic missionary encampment, where we spent the night and had our first opportunity to meet the Yanomami tribe. Napoleon's mastery of the language and culture was dazzling: he described to us how the Yanomami did not have a vocabulary for counting—they have the numbers one, two, and many. He said that the language is strong on nouns and weak on verbs, so that a bird can have one noun for the bird itself, and another noun for the same bird in movement. Nap was fond of saying that the Yanomami males had a far richer vocabulary than I had, precisely because of the number of nouns that were required to replace the absence of the verb structure.

We learned from our experience staying in the jungle with the Catholic and Protestant missionaries. The tension that exists between the anthropologists and the missionaries and their approach to the Indigenous peoples is one of long standing. The missionaries argue that since their discourse with Indigenous people is based on the spiritual and not the material, they are closer to the spiritual belief system of Indigenous tribes. They also maintain that through their work translating the Bible into the local language and their teaching of the Bible to the Yanomami, they are contributing to the education of the Indigenous peoples. The anthropologists, on the other hand, complain that the missionaries are entirely dedicated to the development of

Christian communities and converting large numbers of pagans to Christianity.

McClintock's curiosity about this part of the world and his energy matched my own. It was our first trip to Amazonas, but it would not be our last. Such was our fascination with this extraordinary part of the world.

In 1973, I transitioned back to the United States, where I took a job as the deputy executive secretary of the secretariat of the Department of State. My next job was as deputy assistant secretary of state for the Western Hemisphere (the Latin American Bureau), where I remained to the end of the Ford Administration in January 1977.

CHAPTER 8

When a Friend Acts like an Enemy: Pinochet's Chile and Operation Condor

By the summer of 1976, Augusto Pinochet had become a domestic and international albatross around the neck of the US government. The Nixon administration worked closely with General Pinochet, whom it had welcomed as the president of Chile after his 1973 coup against President Allende (achieved with US help), as a friendly leader and even as an ally in the struggle against the insurgency in the Southern Cone and against the spread of Castro's and Soviet influence in Latin America. Yet the American public's condemnation of presumed American government's support for Pinochet's repression of his left-wing opposition—including secret detention, torture, and the "disappearing" of prisoners—had infected US stature throughout the world and cast a shadow over Gerald Ford's candidacy for president in the 1976 elections. Former president Nixon and then secretary of state Henry Kissinger were at the center of that controversy. In the fall of 1976, the burden of the Pinochet relationship crashed down on Washington, DC, with the bloody assassination of the former foreign minister of Chile under Allende, Orlando Letelier, only months before the US presidential elections.

From the time of the Bay of Pigs in 1960, American presidents

Pinochet and Kissinger, 1976.

had placed Latin America at the top of US national security concerns. President Kennedy wrote to the British Prime Minister
Harold Macmillan: "Macmillan: Latin America [is] the most
dangerous area in the world. The effect of having a Communist
state in British Guiana . . . would be to create irresistible pressures
in the United States to strike militarily against Cuba."[35] After the
failed invasion of Cuba and the Bay of Pigs, President Kennedy
put his brother Bobby Kennedy, then attorney general, in charge
of all covert operations. In November '61, in the greatest secrecy,
John and Bobby Kennedy created a new planning cell for covert
action, the Special Group (augmented). It was RFK's outfit and
had one mission: eliminating Castro.[36] President Kennedy had
twice ordered the intelligence community to kill Castro. The
challenge of the Berlin Wall, which was built that summer,
paled before Kennedy's desire to avenge the loss of the family

honor at the Bay of Pigs. The overthrow of Castro was the top priority in the United States government, Bobby Kennedy told John McCone in January of 1962. In pursuit of that mission, the US established covert operations in Bolivia, Colombia, the Dominican Republic, Ecuador, Guatemala, and Venezuela.[37]

On July 30, 1976, as deputy assistant secretary for inter-American affairs, I learned, at the regular Friday intelligence briefing in our State Department offices, of a new and disturbing twist in the plans of the Southern Cone states against the radical-left movements in their region. The security services of Chile, Brazil, Argentina, Paraguay, Uruguay, and Bolivia had decided to change the direction of Condor. Established with the encouragement of the head of the intelligence community on Chile, Operation Condor, at first, was a communications system and data bank meant to facilitate defense against regional revolutionary movements. But by July 1976, according to an intelligence report, Condor was conducting an active program of identifying, locating, and "hitting" guerilla leaders. This intelligence report revealed, for the first time, that the heads of the regional intelligence agencies had decided to up the ante and coordinate assassinations. It was under this new Condor action plan that the Chilean security service DINA would plan and carry out the execution in Washington DC of former president Allende's foreign minister, Orlando Letelier, and his American friend, Ronni Moffitt. Since that event, I have tried to piece together—from declassified documents, conversations with others, and deep dives into memory—what flawed bureaucratic and personal decisions were taken or not taken over the six weeks between the first realization of the Condor decision to assassinate select individuals and the deaths of Letelier and Moffitt. This troubling series of events has been pondered by dozens of historians and several books have burrowed for elements of the truth. My own personal involvement as one of the players in one of the great scandals of US foreign policy during that period has given me anxiety for decades. Like most of us, I would like to believe that my role was above reproach, while others failed. Yet, looking back, I have puzzled what I could or should have done differently, particularly when pressed by individual scholars who forced the US government through the Freedom of Information Act to declassify thousands of documents.

The intelligence report that Condor was planning assassinations shocked me and disturbed other colleagues from both the State Department and the intelligence community. We pondered what action to take. I told my boss, Harry Shlaudeman, who was then assistant secretary for inter-American affairs, that we must inform Secretary Kissinger at once and recommend that he take action to stop the escalation in Condor actions. I then spent the next two days drafting a memorandum to Kissinger from Shlaudeman alerting him to the embattled "Third World War" mentality emerging among Southern Cone states, and warning of the unacceptable consequences for the US if the escalation of Operation Condor was allowed to happen. Anyone who knows my preferred drafting style will recognize the bulleted and bolded sentences that characterize my way of achieving emphasis and clarity. My name is down as drafter.

Then Bob Zimmerman, the very capable country director of Brazil, and I drafted an action cable that we proposed, to the secretary, should be sent to all the American ambassadors in the Southern Cone states. Our cable instructed them to speak directly to their chiefs of state about this new twist to Condor. The secretary's message, drafted in diplomatic language, instructed the ambassadors to alert their chiefs of state that rumors had been heard that the regional security services were planning to coordinate "assassinations of subversives, politicians, and prominent figures." The ambassadors were instructed to say that such actions "would create a most serious moral and political problem" for the US. That telegram was approved by Secretary Kissinger and sent by a special channel for sensitive intelligence communications that gave it even more clout, as it emphasized Kissinger's personal attention.

The series of missteps and failures that followed the dispatch of that by now well-known cable has been documented and published in several different books. The reactions of the US ambassadors to those Southern Cone states were varied: several ambassadors stated that it was not necessary or smart for them to bring such a matter directly to their host country's president. Ambassador David Popper in Chile was particularly adamant that he would not take the démarche to President Pinochet, and preferred to send the message via the head of the intelligence community in Chile to Manuel Contreras, the infamous chief of the Chilean security forces (DINA)—who was probably the mastermind of this new plan to kill prominent critics. Popper explained in his reply to Kissinger that, "given Pinochet's sensitivity regarding pressures from the US government, he might take as an insult any inference that he was connected to such assassination plots." He asked for authority to go ahead with his plan to have the head of intelligence in Chile talk to Contreras.

Popper's language vividly illustrates one of the flaws often inherent in the dual roles of an ambassador to a friendly government: an ambassador must support the American president while, at the same time, trying to maintain good relations with the president of their host country. The diplomat often tries to avoid challenging the president of a friendly country on hot issues or offending him, since he has to live in that nation's capital and deal regularly with its president.

The approach that senior American diplomats choose often depends "on where you sit." Virtually all foreign policy challenges appear differently depending on whether you are sitting: in Washington, DC, or in a capital thousands of miles away. I recall when I was deputy to Jack Matlock in the Office of Soviet Union Affairs during the 1973 Nixon/Brezhnev summit in Washington. The two of us were dumbfounded by how the embassy in Moscow was incorrectly reading the preparations for and issues of the summit. Shortly after the summit, Matlock, an experienced and highly intelligent professional diplomat, left Washington to be deputy chief of mission in Moscow, and within weeks he was sending in messages reflecting the same disconnect that he and I had seen earlier between Moscow and Washington. It was because of that reality that my rule as chief of mission was always to get back to DC at least every six months to make certain I was up to date on the new thinking.

Another personal experience reinforced the problem of ambassadors who do not want to offend chiefs of state of friendly nations. In November of 1968, when I was the State Department desk officer for Guyana, we were given an intelligence report that the outgoing president of Venezuela, Raúl Leoni, had approved a clandestine plan by the then minister of interior Leandro Mora to seize the Essequibo territory of Guyana long claimed by Venezuela. Leoni's plan was to arrange for the Indigenous inhabitants of the vast Essequibo area of Guyana along the eastern border of Venezuela to organize an uprising against the government in Georgetown, Guyana. The leaders of the Amerindian tribes, presumably well compensated, would then invite the Venezuelan army to invade the territory to protect the Amerindians, occupy the entire disputed area, and remain to take control over a territory that was roughly one-third of the country of Guyana. This was planned to be executed in the interregnum between the outgoing Social Democratic (AD) president and incoming Christian Democratic (COPEI) president, Rafael Caldera. These two ruling political parties shared in the same political objective of restoring the Essequibo to Venezuela, which was a dubious, irredentist claim that Venezuela had harbored for decades against the British Empire since before Guyana become independent.

Learning of the Leoni and Mora plan, my boss and I sent a message to Ambassador Maurice Bernbaum in Caracas instructing him to go immediately to see President Leoni and warn him that we knew of this military plot and strongly opposed such an action. The ambassador used almost exactly the same language as Popper did from Santiago almost a decade later: he refused to carry out the instructions because Leoni would be offended by such a démarche and, besides, the information was just another intelligence report that had little chance of being true. Frustrated and still determined to call off the Venezuelans, we sought and were able to secure higher-level State Department instructions to demand that Bernbaum make the démarche at once. Ambassador Bernbaum did so and immediately realized from the face of President Leoni that his government had been caught red-handed by the Americans. The plot to take over the Essequibo was called off and it still remains a part of Guyana, while the irredentist claims remain a regular political bluster in Venezuela.

During that summer of 1976, my outspoken and negative views of covert operations in Latin America played an important role in the reactions of other players toward me and the actions I took during the crucial two months prior to the assassination of Orlando Letelier. I had already had positive and negative experiences with the intelligence community. I had a high respect for the objectivity of intelligence analysts during my two years working in the State Department Bureau of Intelligence and Research (INR), where I was the principal analyst on domestic politics in the USSR. In that role, I had close working relations with intelligence analysts and participated in two lengthy National Intelligence Estimates (NIE) on the Soviet Union. I had also known from my work in founding the Open Forum Panel during the late 1960s, that the National Intelligence Estimates run by the intelligence community were often the most thoughtful and accurate in evaluating the prospects for US military success in Vietnam. That same positive impression continues up to this day in my contacts with intelligence analysts regarding Russia, Iran, and other issues in the Middle East.

My experience with the operations side of the intelligence community, however, were decidedly mixed. I had worked closely and constructively in Moscow and in other Communist states with the covert side of the intelligence community. The European and American operatives were heirs of that creative and intelligent generation that grew out of the Office of Strategic Services (OSS). But in Latin America, the FBI had been playing that intelligence role. So the intelligence community operatives in Latin America were heirs of the FBI, not the OSS, and while they were highly patriotic and intelligent, they also were a rougher bunch, with different experiences, attitudes, and mandates.

My first learning experience with the covert operations of the intelligence community came after I had become the desk officer for Guyana, Trinidad and Tobago, and Suriname. The major work in Guyana was to ensure that Cheddi Jagan would not become prime minister, as he was considered a potential Castro ally. The mandate to the State Department and, as well, I supposed, to the intelligence community, was to retain Forbes Burnham as prime minister as long as possible and ensure that, in the upcoming elections, Burnham would have enough votes from the Guyanese diaspora in the UK and the US. I found Burnham a charismatic and highly intelligent but increasingly autocratic leader. He invited me often during my trips to join him in his morning gulping down of raw eggs and port wine. My two-year collaboration with the intelligence communities including the British intelligence communities' covert efforts to keep Jagan out of power left a bad taste in my mouth that lasted throughout the rest of my life in the foreign service.

When I became the desk officer for Guyana, I became aware of the actions taken against Cheddi Jagan who was to become the Prime Minister of Guyana.

Some background of my difficulty with the covert side of the intelligence community in is worth reviewing. In 1975, while serving in Washington, DC, I had been proposed by Secretary Kissinger to be the assistant secretary for Latin America. I was to replace Bill Rogers, who had been moved upstairs to be undersecretary of state. Both Rogers and Kissinger had assured me that the assistant secretary position was mine. But many weeks passed, and my name still had not yet been submitted to the Senate for confirmation. The secretary then unexpectedly asked Harry Shlaudeman, an old Latin America hand who was then

ambassador to Venezuela (and who would become my boss), to
become assistant secretary instead of me. I learned during this
uncertain period from a close friend, who was working in the
office of Secretary Kissinger, that then national security advisor
Brent Scowcroft had told the secretary by phone that the intelligence community would not be able to work with me if I were to
become assistant secretary. (Secretary Kissinger often asked staff
to listen to official phone calls from people like Brent to keep
a solid record of what had transpired. Brent was well aware of
this practice.) They recommended that the secretary find another
candidate. Decades later, when I had come to know Brent Scowcroft better, he confirmed to me that the intelligence community
had suggested that it could not work with me were I to become
assistant secretary.

That legacy of my troubles with the covert side of the intelligence community in Latin America played an outsized role in the
summer of 1976. My first awareness of Operation Condor was
almost an accident, since I was not generally asked to attend the
weekly Friday briefing sessions with the intelligence community,
for reasons already described. Yet on this one occasion, the intelligence community had to include me in the briefing because I was
the acting assistant secretary on that day. Throughout that crucial
summer, the intelligence community had been reluctant to coordinate with me; they generally dealt directly with Shlaudeman,
who was traveling or on vacation during much of August. I was
heartened and encouraged by the fact that the intelligence community had agreed to disseminate the report about Condor's new
ambitions and concluded that was a good sign that the head of
intelligence in Chile was alerting the US government to a looming problem and not trying to conceal it.

The intelligence communities' mounting of Operation Mongoose to assassinate Fidel Castro is well covered in other books. It was an effort that continued through the presidency of John Kennedy and beyond.

Finally, perhaps my major shortcoming as a decider that summer was that I knew little about the Southern Cone and had never visited any of those countries. My Latin American experience had been in Venezuela, the Caribbean, and Mexico. I had little knowledge of the major players of the far southern South American countries, their professional diplomats, or the tortured history of US relations with Pinochet. Since I had served in Venezuela when it was virtually the only democracy in South America, I was infected by the Venezuelan contempt for Pinochet. Skeptical of the US-Chile relationship, I was still professional enough to try to learn and do what was right for the US.

With this background of my personal limitations as a player, I want to turn to whether I could and should have been able to play a more aggressive role in heading off the tragedy of the Letelier assassination. The critical objective, as I and others saw, was to tell each president in the Southern Cone what we knew about Condor's assassination plans, and to tell them that they should cease such operations. I drafted a strong cable that became diplomatically watered down by the time it was sent out by Secretary Kissinger. However, the action paragraph remained clear: "While we cannot substantiate the assassination rumors, we feel compelled to bring to your attention our deep concern: if these rumors were to have any shred of truth they would create a most serious moral and political problem." The message did not say "stop these plans immediately," but the fact that the message that was sent came directly from Secretary Kissinger should have had impact and should have opened the door to further discussions, if what we were hearing about Operation Condor turned out to be true.

Ambassador Popper in Chile did not carry out his instructions. His deputy, Tom Boyatt, an excellent career diplomat, argued against going to Pinochet, who, he believed, would probably refuse future requests from Popper for actions the US wanted him to take, and Pinochet might decide for his own reasons not to pass the message to DINA chief Contreras. So, Popper's conclusion was to leave the task to the head of intelligence to take directly to Contreras, who had certainly been part of the original planning for Condor's new role. That August, I was the acting assistant secretary, since Shlaudeman was traveling and the other deputy, Hugh Ryan, who was an expert on Chile, was retiring that summer. I spent the entire month of August trying to get responses to the secretary's message, but heard nothing from Santiago. I suspected that there was a lot of back-channel or personal communications about which I hadn't been informed. It seemed that the Condor issue was being managed between the State Department and the intelligence community secretly and at a high level, and the discussions did not include me. On Friday, August 27, Shlaudeman held the regular meeting with the intelligence community. It was clear that the embassy in Santiago had still taken no action, since they had been waiting for approval to deliver the message to Contreras directly, instead of to Pinochet. Shlaudeman, in a heavily redacted declassified memorandum of the meeting, noted that "we are not making a representation to Pinochet because it would be futile to do so." Up to that point, I had believed that we were still pressing Popper to act with Pinochet. Moreover, since the State Department had not formally responded yet to Popper's proposal to have the head of intelligence in Chile talk to Contreras, there had been no formal effort by the embassy to blow the whistle on Condor. In mid-September, I sent a message to Shlaudeman asking how we should proceed to get Ambassador Popper and the other ambassadors to act directly with the presidents of their host countries. On September 20, declassified messages indicate that Shlaudeman sent me a message instructing me to "simply instruct Ambassadors to take no further action," since there had been no further reports on Condor's intended operations.

On Tuesday morning, September 21, 1976, Orlando Letelier was driving his car to work on Massachusetts Avenue in Washington, DC. Just as he was entering Sheridan Circle, a bomb exploded in the car, killing Letelier and Ronni Moffitt, who was riding in the front seat. Michael Moffitt, an American who had been working with Letelier, was injured but survived the explosion.

The vicious killing was an unprecedented act of aggression by a foreign power in our nation, never mind in our nation's capital. The act was not carried out by an enemy. There was no trace of Soviet or even Cuban involvement. The CIA and other US agencies immediately presumed that Pinochet or at least Contreras had ordered the assassination. After years of investigation, the plot was identified as an act of the DINA, Chile's intelligence service. At the time of the bombing, Chile had a friendly government that the US had helped install, so US counterintelligence had no reason to question the activities of the DINA within US borders. This was similar to US counterintelligence's lack of tracking of the shah of Iran's aggressive intelligence service, SAVAK, while it was operating in the US. In those days, the FBI and other national security agencies had a laser focus on the enemy: the Soviet Union and other Communist states. The revelation to the media of the Shlaudeman message to me on the veritable eve of the assassination created a widely reported media attack on the State Department's failure to act on time. The Shlaudeman cable seemed to give proof to some who had followed this story carefully that the State Department was culpable . . . or at least negligent.

Decades later, when I was president of the United Nations Association, I was invited to breakfast by William D. Rogers, who had been a mentor and close friend during my years in Latin America. During breakfast, Bill was reviewing the events leading up to publication of the declassified cable instructions that Shlaudeman had sent to me. Bill was very familiar with the facts in the Condor story and the proof that had been assembled that landed DINA chief Contreras in jail for many hundreds of years, in part for his role in planning the assassination of Letelier. Bill asked whether I might write an op-ed laying out the case why Pinochet would not have listened to the advice Popper had been instructed to give to Pinochet. Bill said to me, "You know perfectly well that there is nothing the US government could have said that would have changed his mind."

I said, "Bill, I know nothing of the sort. I never met Pinochet and know virtually nothing about his relationship with the US government." I then shared with him my concerns about why Popper did not carry out his instructions from the secretary of state.

That breakfast conversation with Bill Rogers was the last one I had with him, a close friend and mentor who had played a major and positive role in my career. Bill died in 2007 in an accident while fox hunting in Virginia riding his beloved horse.

As this distressing story has been filled in over the past thirty years, I have continued to be troubled by the response of the US government to the warning we had received on July 30, 1976, from the intelligence community. My conclusions, which I hope are balanced, are the following:

1. The intelligence community disseminated to the State Department the report that Condor was planning assassinations and did share in the discussion the actions necessary to stop their execution. Their bringing the issue suggests strongly that this new direction had not been initiated by intelligence community operatives.

2. The Bureau of Inter-American Affairs in the State Department acted in short order (less than a week) to persuade the secretary of state to instruct ambassadors in the Southern Cone states to inform chiefs of state directly that the US was aware of the rumors of Condor's new intentions and actions and to express concern about the moral and political implications of such an operation. I personally wrote the memorandum to the secretary of state and the cable that we asked Secretary Kissinger to send to the Southern Cone ambassadors. The instructions could have been more forceful, but since the message came directly from the secretary of state, who had strong relations with the Chilean government in particular, the cable would have resonated with Pinochet.

3. Ambassador Popper, who had a strong sense of the importance of Pinochet to US strategy in the region, chose not to go to Pinochet directly. I recommended to the State Department that the State Department insist that Ambassador Popper follow Secretary Kissinger's instructions and talk directly with Pinochet. But they did not, and Ambassador Popper did not. Contreras, the DINA chief, said in his trial that Pinochet personally approved of the Letelier assassination.

4. In the month of August, the State Department bureaucracy debated Popper's proposal, but no evident action was taken. There are no documents suggesting contact through other channels had been made, nor are there documents that would confirm or refute whether Popper was told informally about dealing with Pinochet.

5. In late August and early September 1976, since no additional information on Condor plans had been disseminated, there seemed to be no urgency to press ambassadors to take action. However, despite this, several ambassadors did agree to act, or took the matter directly to the president of their host country. The State Department did not provide further instructions to Popper, and Shlaudeman instructed the department to discontinue pressing ambassadors, including Popper, to take the requested action.

6. The day after Shlaudeman's message, Letelier was assassinated.

7. There is also the question of Popper recommending that Contreras be given the responsibility to pass the secretary of state's message to Pinochet; Contreras was widely known to have supervised the crimes against humanity committed under Pinochet. From the time of the Pinochet coup, Contreras was a notorious leader of violence and organized disappearances of Chileans. Under his authority, over forty thousand Chileans were imprisoned, tortured, or slain. Yet, through the late 1970s, the intelligence community was still authorizing official relations with Contreras.

The US government could have headed off the assassination had there been an immediate and forceful presentation to Pinochet, or possibly even to Contreras, within weeks after the earliest intelligence report. Others do not agree. They argue that Pinochet's action could not have been stopped even by a direct démarche to him personally. Since I had very little experience with Pinochet; I am going only on instincts. But the US government's relationship with Pinochet since he came to power argues that the US had leverage that it should have used, particularly in view of what happened on September 21.

Larger questions relate to the nature of the US-Chilean relationship since the coup, and particularly in 1976, and the political environment in Washington at that time. During the years 1973–76, when I returned to the State Department in Washington from four years in Venezuela, I sensed a new and more troubling defensiveness on the part of US national security officials. This new psychological environment at the State Department and within the national security structure seemed to flow out of a fear that US influence was in decline, and that it was necessary to strengthen alliances and relations with friendly states against ever more powerful enemies who were expanding their world role. The many causes of this hunker-down environment were palpable:

- President Nixon had left office in 1974 under a cloud of shame and the obstruction of justice. Nixon had been the driving force behind US foreign policy for seven years and now his main advisor, Henry Kissinger, was essentially in charge, but without a political base in the country. Gerald Ford did not have a developed sense of global strategy and no real experience in Latin America or with Pinochet.

- The US had needed to execute a humiliating withdrawal from Saigon in April 1975, which brought to an end what had been the longest and most demoralizing foreign war in American history.

- Cuban forces entered Angola in 1975 to support the Communist MPLA radical group that had taken over much of the country with the help of the Soviet Union. The Cubans quickly put twenty-five thousand troops on the ground in Angola, signaling for the first time that Soviets and Cubans were capable and prepared to work together in the "third world," far outside of the Soviet periphery.

- Following the multiple détente agreements signed in 1972 and 1973, the Soviet Union felt more confident with regard to the foreign policy affairs with the United States. In addition, the US Congress was developing strong opposition to the Nixon/Kissinger ways of dealing with the Soviet "enemy."

- Popular American opposition to human rights violations, particularly in nations that had close ties with the US, had become a major point in the 1976 elections. President Ford decided not to change course, and Secretary Kissinger was determined to stay with policies and relationships that had been successful since Nixon took office.

- The intelligence activities of so-called friendly states, such as Chile and Iran, had almost free reign in the US. The shah of Iran's SAVAK and Pinochet's DINA were not watched or restricted by the intelligence communities, unlike the KGB, which was the intelligence agency of the major US enemy. Even years later, during the Gorbachev era, the KGB was far more subject to US counterintelligence activities than were Iran's SAVAK and Chile's DINA.

- Finally, the slow pace of change in US-Chile relations, even after the murder of Letelier at the hands of the DINA, and even after the electoral victory of Jimmy Carter in November of 1976, illuminated how slowly those invested in the US-Chile relationship came to realize that some significant Chilean practices were in direct violation of US law and undermined Chile's crucial friendship with the US. During this period, the US embassy in Santiago continued to work to increase cooperation with the Pinochet government.

In January 1977, before the Carter inauguration, a Chilean former military officer, Colonel Jaime Lavin Farina, arrived on a Chilean tall ship into a New York harbor. He had come to celebrate the two-hundredth anniversary of the American Revolution. Lavin Farina had been promoted to deputy foreign minister of Chile, and the embassy in Santiago had invited him on a US-sponsored "leader grant." But, shortly after his arrival in the US, he was accused by Amnesty International of having been in charge of the major center of torture in Santiago and having been an active participant in torture. I was acting assistant secretary for several months during the presidential transition, and I questioned by cable and by phone the embassy's wisdom of selecting such a controversial person to visit the US, particularly after all that had transpired that past summer. The ambassador repeatedly assured me that Lavin Farina was not the head of the center of torture in Chile and not guilty of any of the charges against him. He and others in the embassy argued that former Chilean prisoners now living in the US were leveling baseless accusations. In late January, I passed a message via the Chilean desk officer, Robert Driscoll, to tell Lavin Farina, who was by then visiting San Francisco, that he should cut short his visit to the US, so as not to exacerbate the US-Chilean relationship further.

Subsequently, over the next three decades, it was confirmed to me by a former official in the US Embassy in Santiago and by many Chileans whom I interviewed there, that there was widespread knowledge of Lavin Farina's role as a lead torturer when he was the head of Chile's air force academy in the early to mid-1970s. Lavin Farina, at the time of the last interview I held in Santiago with Isabella Letelier, the widow of the deceased

Orlando Letelier, had never been brought to justice and was still seen regularly at the local marketplace.

President Carter first met with Pinochet in 1977, after having begun a new era of placing human rights at the center of his foreign policy. In that meeting, he assured Pinochet of the US desire to continue to have a close relationship with Chile.

US diplomacy has been marred over the past decades by the inability of American officials to break their habits of not wanting to complicate relations with friendly states in the face of decidedly unfriendly acts. The business of diplomacy, largely, should be to maintain dispassionate communications and mutually beneficial agreements. The US should always talk to adversaries and friends with candor and clarity. The US should be ready to head off unfriendly acts of any state—friend or foe. Diplomatic relations should never be confused with friendly relations.

CODA

Regarding my particular interest in Chile, I feel some clarification might be helpful. First, my wife, Wendy, had been a Spanish-speaking staff member of Amnesty International USA from 1975–1979 and had been active in developing and executing the US government's special asylum parole program for Chileans fleeing Pinochet. Also, our daughter Ramsay married a prominent Chilean writer, Sergio Missana, who, along with his friend Pepe Zalaquett, was the editor of the Rettig Report (officially the National Commission for Truth and Reconciliation Report) published in 1991 in Chile. Our son-in-law was present at a number of interviews in Chile with Isabel Letelier, the widow of Orlando and also a friend of Wendy. He and I discussed in one of those interviews the phenomenon of Chilean officials who were involved in torturing fellow Chilean citizens. These officials are still walking freely on the streets in Santiago. We also have three Chilean-American grandchildren who were raised in Santiago.

In addition to this personal note, I must pay a special tribute to some of the investigative reporters who doggedly pursued the dark trail of US foreign policies that played an oversized role in the dirty war that was perpetrated by the national governments in the Southern Cone of the Western Hemisphere. That war was waged so as to avoid the creation of another Fidel Castro allied to the Soviet Union. It turned into a clandestine hot war against the people of Latin America.

One of my special heroes is John Dinges, who wrote *The Condor Years: How Pinochet and His Allies Brought Terrorism to Three Continents*, and who followed and uncovered true stories about the horrors of Operation Condor. John was never satisfied; he continued to dig to make available to the public, and to me, tales

The Condor Years: How Pinochet and His Allies Brought Terrorism to Three Continents by John Dinges.

of the crimes of Pinochet and his chief of DINA. Until his death in August 2015 of multiple organ failure, Manuel Contreras was serving fifty-eight sentences totaling 498 years in prison for kidnapping, forced disappearance, and assassination. It is painful to imagine how US foreign policy might have evolved differently had the muse for American foreign policy in South America not been the likes of Contreras but, instead, someone more akin to the Mexican poet-philosopher Octavio Paz or the Argentine writer Jorge Luis Borges. It is highly unlikely that a dissident like Václav Havel could have appeared in Latin America in the 1970s, given the dominance of US policy aimed at preventing another Fidel Castro in the hemisphere, and the presence and the ambitions of Fidel Castro and his Soviet patrons.

Another hero of this era was Peter Kornbluh, who wrote the groundbreaking book on Pinochet, *The Pinochet File: A Declassified Dossier on Atrocity and Accountability*, which drew on thousands of pages of declassified US government documents that his organization accessed by the Freedom of Information Act of the

The Pinochet File: A Declassified Dossier on Atrocity and Accountability. A National Security Archive Book by Peter Kornbluh.

US government in a major effort to make its foreign policy more transparent. Peter Kornbluh is a senior analyst at the National Security Archive.

I cannot leave out the National Security Archive, housed at George Washington University in DC, which is a not-for-profit research library of declassified US government documents, and its intrepid executive director Thomas S. Blanton, who pursued the declassifications of official government messages that opened the door to much of what we know about US government policy in Chile with Pinochet and Condor, and so many other activities worldwide.

CHAPTER 9

US Ambassador: Venezuela, Part II

In October 1978, I arrived in Caracas to assume my new responsibilities as ambassador to Venezuela, which seemed at the time to be my dream job, since I had become so fond of the country, its people, and its culture. This was a strange sensation for a career officer who had long set Moscow as his goal.

Looking over Caracas.

(right to left) Connor, Tomales, Ramsay arrival in Caracas.

My time in Caracas was particularly refreshing. I married my new wife, Wendy, the second year I was there. Jane, who had never loved being a diplomat's wife, and I had divorced in 1979. Wendy spoke elegant Spanish with a Castilian accent from her time as a student in Spain, long before I knew her. She arrived with her two daughters, who technically became my stepdaughters, a term I never used with them. They were, in this family's tight environment, the daughters of Wendy and me. Ramsay and Connor lived with us at the ambassador's residence for the three years I was ambassador. Their father lived in San Francisco, and they visited him from time to time. I never asserted myself as a disciplinarian over the two girls, as I felt that that role was completely inappropriate, nor did I try to substitute myself for their dad, for whom they still had great affection. Ramsay and Connor, who were seven and five at the time, were raised by me and Wendy as our children and became good friends with my four children—Mark, David, Amy, and William—who continued to live with their mother.

Bill with Connor and Wendy.

Wendy perked up the embassy substantially, as she became a full partner in everything I did or tried to achieve as ambassador. She had the political instincts, charm, and language ability of a professional diplomat. In fact, I recall saying to her only a few weeks after she had arrived in Venezuela, after a particularly active discussion when she was sitting next to the foreign minister and I next to the foreign minister's wife, "Wendy, you must remember that President Carter appointed me as his ambassador to Venezuela and not you." We subsequently laughed about that exchange, but the fact is, our relationship was so close in everything we did that both friends and officials would very often say things to Wendy they had planned to say to me.

On May 19, 1980, Wendy and I held a vernissage—a private viewing—at the ambassador's residence of the works of contemporary American art that would adorn the walls of the embassy during my time as ambassador. It had been my job to find the painters and dealers and ask permission to borrow a work of art for several years. The Department of State and its office Art in Embassies would cover the cost of shipping the works of art to the embassy. I had been on the phone with artists and dealers and collectors for months putting together one of the best such collections I had seen in any embassy—with the exception of embassies in which the politically appointed ambassadors had their own collections of art.

I decided to invite a group of American artists and dealers to Caracas for the opening, so as to expose Venezuela and its robust community of artists to their American peers. I was equally determined, as part of my mission, to expose American artists and writers to their Venezuelan peers. The array of people from the arts who accepted my invitation to this event gave me great encouragement that a program of visiting American artists and writers could work.

The list of artists who came to Caracas was impressive: Frank Stella, Richard Diebenkorn, Ilya Bolotowsky, Richard Anusz-kiewicz, and Sally Avery, the widow of Milton Avery, all came. Sally Avery lent a fine painting from her husband's legacy. We also had André Emmerich, the noted art dealer, whose gallery lent us a lovely painting by Joan Mitchell, which was a hit. The star of the collection, however, was *Ocean Park #94* by Rich-ard Diebenkorn, lent by Phyllis Diebenkorn out of her private collection.

The press coverage of the vernissage was fantastic. Venezu-elan president Luis Herrera Campíns arrived with most of his cabinet and made several appropriate remarks on the exhibition, including expressing his pleasure that so many important Ameri-can artists were visiting Venezuela. Many left-leaning Venezuelan journalists, artists, and writers also attended. Making the point of the high value of an investment in cultural diplomacy, the lead journalist from *El Nacional*, Venezuela's leading newspaper, pulled me aside and said, in Spanish, "Mr. Ambassador, after this evening's event, we will publish anything you have to say about the price of petroleum." (My single mandate from Washington, DC, was to get the Venezuelans to lead an effort to increase their petroleum exports to the US—hopefully to reduce the price.)

The following day, President Herrera Campíns offered to arrange to have the Venezuelan air force fly the artists, the art dealers, and their spouses to Canaima to see Angel Falls, one

President Herrera Campíns, Bill, Frank and
Harriet Stella in front of a Stella painting.

of the must-see sites in Venezuela. On the way to Canaima, we
made a stop to visit the Jesús Soto Museum of Modern Art in
Ciudad Bolívar. Soto was one of Venezuela's leading artists, who
was little known in the US but greatly admired by the international art community. All of the Americans enjoyed the visit to
the Soto museum, which housed many of his masterworks and
also significant works by Soto's fellow Venezuelan kinetic artists,
including Carlos Cruz-Diez, whose art had decorated the pow-
erhouse of the nearby Guri Dam, which, at that time, was the
largest hydroelectric dam complex in the world.

Following the stop at the Jesús Soto Museum of Modern
Art, we reboarded the plane to head for Canaima. Storm clouds
were beginning to gather, as they often do in tropical climates.
As we headed toward Canaima, I realized we were flying over a

territory I had never seen before and I was concerned that the pilots did not know where Canaima was. Canaima was a small airport without radar or landing lights and was difficult to locate in the dark. I asked the pilots if they had ever landed in Canaima, they all agreed no, this was a new destination for them. I asked how they were navigating to get there; their answer was unsatisfactory. I suggested we return to Ciudad Guayana, where there was ample technology and a relatively modern airport. The pilot said, "No, Ambassador. On the ground you may have seniority but we are in charge of this plane and were ordered to go to Canaima. I returned to my seat to think about the strategy as the skies grew darker and the storm more threatening. Ten minutes later, I went back to the cockpit and said that not one of the passengers in the plane wanted to go to Canaima anymore and they all requested that the aircraft return to Ciudad Guayana. The pilots thought about my strong appeal. I was determined not to show any anger or anxiety so as not to provoke the young pilots, given my awareness of the stubbornness of some pilots when their plane is set on a course. After a long five-minute wait, I felt the plane turning around. Wendy took out some bottles of wine and opened a few of them as we celebrated not going to Canaima. Frank Stella was disappointed, because he was already designing a series of works of art with the name Canaima. We arrived in Ciudad Guayana safely, and then continued on back to Caracas that evening. I subsequently thanked the commander of the air force for the provision of the aircraft and the good judgment of the pilots when faced by bad weather.

I have often thought that were it not for the calm judgment of two young Venezuelan pilots, my aspirations for a greatly enlarged cultural initiative in Venezuela could have been extinguished in the jungles of southeast Venezuela, along with the lives of some elites of the American visual arts community.

———————

During my years in Venezuela, we had many writers and artists who visited us, none more frequently or more enjoyably than the novelist William Styron and his poet wife, Rose Styron. Our friendship was deep and long. They were the first couple who knew of my romance with Wendy. Ultimately, we bought a summer house near them on Martha's Vineyard, where we met most of the writers who would come to Venezuela. And we bought our Connecticut house, in the small town of Washington Depot,

Bill and Rose
Styron in Venezuela.

to be near the Styrons, who lived down the road in Roxbury, as did Arthur Miller and his wife. It would be difficult to exaggerate their roles in shaping our thinking about cultural diplomacy. Indeed, the first trip that Bill and Rose Styron took to Venezuela was in January of 1979, when my future wife Wendy accompanied them as their Spanish language interpreter.

During that visit, Bill Styron gave a number of readings from his novel *Sophie's Choice*, and Rose did poetry readings with a number of English-speaking Venezuelans. I took the Styrons to the city of Maracaibo, which sits on a Venezuelan lake (or lagoon) that holds vast oil reserves. On arriving in Maracaibo, Wendy, taking her role as interpreter very seriously, moved quickly to be close to the Styrons as the governor of the state of Maracaibo was greeting them. She was so earnest in haste that she fell flat on her face at the feet of the oncoming governor. Fortunately, she and the governor were more amused than shocked by the event. It certainly launched Wendy as a presence in Venezuela.

Over the years, the Styrons became a unique pair in our world of diplomacy: they became the hub of a stellar group of artists and writers in the US and abroad. I remember spending one Christmas Eve at the Styrons' Roxbury home listening to Leonard Bernstein play Christmas carols sung by him and his family in Yiddish, courtesy of Lennie's translation. I also remember an evening on Martha's Vineyard when Bill was trying to help Philip Roth deal with his depression.

Rose and Bill visited us virtually every year we were in Caracas, often with other writers and friends of theirs. My relationship with Bill was as a diplomat-bureaucrat to a creative writer. I used to say the only thing we had in common was the fact that our parents chose to call us Billy as young boys. Bill grew up

Peter Matthiessen, Wendy, Rose Styron, Bill,
and Bill Styron bird-watching.

in Virginia, in a storytelling environment. I grew up in Springfield, Illinois, playing sports with little contact with the arts.
Our attitudes were formed in the closing years of World War II,
during which he served in the US Marine Corps. In his book *My
Generation*, Bill quotes F. Scott Fitzgerald, who claimed that after
World War I, America and Americans were left intact. By contrast, Styron said:

> Our war [WWII] despite the nervous overlay of the
> usual frivolity was brutally businesslike and anti-
> romantic, a hard-boil matter of stamping out the very real
> and nasty tolerationism to get along with the business of
> the American way of life whatever that is. Our genera-
> tion was not only not intact, it had been in many places
> cut to pieces. The class just ahead of me in college was

virtually wiped-out. Beautiful fellows who had won basketball championships and Phi Betta Kappa keys died
like ants in the Normandy invasion. Others slightly older
than I, like myself, young Marine Corps platoon commanders, primest cannon fodder of the Pacific war—
stormed ashore at Tarawa and Iwo Jima and met ugly
and horrible deaths on the hot coral sands.

I was lucky and saw no battle, but I had the wits
scared out of me more times than I could count, and so
by the time the bomb dropped on Hiroshima, thus cir-
cumventing my future plans (I was on my way: "You can
figure that four out of five of you will get your asses shot
off," I can recall some colonel telling us, as he embroi-
dered dreamily about the coming invasion of the Japanese mainland), an enormous sense of relief stole over
my spirit, along with a kind of dull weariness that others
of that period have recalled and which, to a certain off-
shoot of my generation, later came to be characterized as
"beat."[38]

Bill and I, over the years, vowed to visit all the "discotheques" on
the Orinoco River (as couples, we climbed through the wilder-
ness, streams, and waterfalls of the headwaters of the Orinoco).
Wendy and I spent endless hours with the Styrons at parties at
their house and on the lawn with literally dozens of their enormous community of writers and friends that gathered around
them. We drank and shouted and laughed until early in the
mornings at their house in Roxbury, to the annoyance of the
Styron children—Al, Tommy, Susanna, and Polly. It is virtually
impossible to imagine the Styron environment without those

children who were so central to their existence. Many years later, we would share in Václav Havel's delight at a dinner the Styrons gave for him in 1995, in their home in Roxbury, Connecticut. That evening all who attended were lit by the golden light of celebration. Havel was surrounded by writers and friends including Arthur Miller, Francine Gray, Phillip Roth, Pete Gurney, and Mia Farrow. That evening, the president of the Czech Republic appeared almost as a child at play—he was in his element, being at the Styrons' home among his fellow writers.

One of my earliest acts as ambassador in Caracas was marked by a political gaffe that threatened to remain with me for years and probably still clouds the attitudes of many Venezuelans and Americans toward my tenure as ambassador.

During my first tour in Venezuela as political officer, I had set out to get to know leaders from all political parties and factions, including the vocal leaders of the Left. One of those leaders was political activist Teodoro Petkoff, who had been sent by Fidel Castro in the sixties, just after the Cuban Revolution (1953–1959), to "continue the revolution," this time in Venezuela against the new democratic government of Rómulo Betancourt. After several years fighting the Betancourt government as a guerilla, Petkoff joined the Communist Party. Yet, after the Warsaw Pact invaded Czechoslovakia, Petkoff pivoted sharply politically and left the Communist Party. In 1969, the newly elected Christian Democrat president of Venezuela, Rafael Caldera, had immediately offered pacification to all former *guerrilleros* and gave them the opportunity to become integrated into the regular political system, including participation in Venezuela's elections. Petkoff had taken up Caldera's offer to enter Venezuela's political system and had determined to run for political office.

And so it was, very early in my new position as ambassador, that Teodoro Petkoff reached out to me on the phone and asked that I attend his press conference to announce his candidacy for the Senate in the upcoming elections in Venezuela. This was a man I had watched move from guerilla fighter to writer and scholar, and now to legitimate candidate for office. I was also impressed by his complete renunciation of Communism. I attended his press conference at the Hotel Tamanaco—the preferred location in Caracas for such announcements. He greeted me with an elaborate *abrazo* (hug), such as Venezuelans are known for, which I returned with genuine warmth. The next morning that picture of Ambassador Luers being *embraced* by the former guerrillero appeared on the front page of nearly every newspaper in Venezuela. I started receiving calls of outrage during my breakfast coffee from friends and officials, generally with the comment "What the hell were you doing?"

In my mind, I was embracing a man I knew well and liked, who was genuine in his efforts to make Venezuela a better place. He was no longer a guerrillero, nor a Communist. But that was not something anyone wanted to hear. I tried over the coming months to explain to my colleagues in the embassy and in my private conversations with others that I knew that Petkoff had become outraged at the Communist Party and was particularly incensed by Stalinism and the Soviet system of government. He had seen the Soviet decision to crush the Prague Spring in 1968 as the tipping point. This betrayal of values led him to vent his anger broadly at Soviet Communism and at Communist parties everywhere. His book was a withering and heartfelt critique of the Soviet system by a Communist insider. In his second-edition introduction to Petkoff's increasingly famous book, the establishment Venezuelan intellectual Arturo Uslar Pietri noted:

> Not without justified pride, Teodoro Petkoff reminds us of his brave and early awakening from the "communist dream." In the wake of the brutal extermination of the hopeful and fresh Prague Spring by Soviet tanks, the doubts and questions he had been harboring within the rigid orthodoxy of the Communist Party became unbearable. It was then that he boldly published his protest in the form of a book: *Czechoslovakia: Socialism as a Problem*.[39]

When my critics pointed to my association with Petkoff, I would tell them that the image of Petkoff in an embrace with the American ambassador should be enough evidence that Petkoff wanted "in" to the Venezuelan political system. Still, people with less experience than I wondered what in the world I was thinking.

Some of my Venezuelan friends had tried to explain my actions by pointing to my own history of watching the decay of the Communist idea in Europe. After serving in Italy for two years in the US Navy, I had watched the Communist Party of Italy become disrupted by Khrushchev's revelations of Stalin's criminal and cruel legacy in the USSR. The US policy of the 1960s, which forbade US relations with the Italian Communist Party (PCI), had been effective in keeping the PCI irrelevant in the current Italian political environment. But there was a catch. Combined with the "no relations" policy, the US, with its elaborate financial support of the Christian Democrats, had built the Catholic, anti-Communist Christian Democrats into an unassailable force, which had in turn led to a resurgence in opposition to the US role. So, while US political and financial support propped up the Christian Democrats as a political actor in Italian politics, the Communists, as the largest opposition party, were reestablished as a formidable factor in Italian politics. I did not want the same thing to happen in Venezuelan politics.

Though my arguments in support of my embrace of and the rehabilitation of Petkoff seemed to fall on deaf ears, I would then emphasize my belief that the US's strong opposition to Petkoff would likely make him a bigger personage than he actually was.

Ultimately, Petkoff's unrelenting opposition to Communism and later his persistence in opposition to the dictatorship of Chavez, would make him one of the loudest defenders of a free Venezuela. Petkoff's voice became the loudest and most effective against Chavez socialism during Chavez's accumulation of power. Petkoff never got a chance to challenge Chavez's power or authority in the democratic process that he had come to admire. Nor did he have the power to keep Chavez from destroying the Venezuela that I came to know and love during the eight years I lived there.

In 1978, shortly after I presented my credentials as ambassador to President Carlos Andrés Pérez, I proceeded to seek a meeting with the minister of interior, Octavio Lepage, who, like Pérez, was an old friend. My intent was to discuss the case of William Niehous, an American citizen who had been kidnapped and was being held hostage. Bill was the former CEO of Owens-Illinois, an American company in Venezuela that made glass. Bill had been kidnapped from his home in Caracas on February 27, 1976. By the time I met with Lepage, Bill already had been in captivity for over two and a half years. There were no new reports of his situation, but I was convinced he was alive. In my talk with the minister of interior, I said I was operating on the assumption that Niehous was alive and would be discovered by the Venezuelan police or armed forces during my time as ambassador. I asked Lepage to give me his word that Niehous would be transferred to my custody within twenty-four hours of his release. I expressed my concern that were he to have to stay in Venezuela for any length of time, he would become the center of much media attention and speculation, as well as mired in the judicial and official investigation to determine the identity of his captors. The minister, who was skeptical that Niehous was still alive, agreed readily to my request.

Less than a year after my arrival in Caracas, I was hosting a conference on human rights with the Diego Cisneros Foundation, which had been started by the father of Gustavo Cisneros. The conference was to support democracy and democratic values, free-market trade, and innovation. Gustavo Cisneros had become a willing and creative partner in our public diplomacy efforts in Caracas. We had as our guests to the conference: Pat Darian, the assistant secretary of state for human rights and humanitarian affairs; and our close friends, Thomas Wicker, a columnist for the *New York Times*, and his spouse, Pam Hill, who was a VP of ABC News and an ABC producer. Arthur Schlesinger, too, was part of the group. A noted historian and former adviser in the JFK White House, Schlesinger was also a friend.

While at dinner at the residence to celebrate the close of a human rights conference, as if on cue, I received a call from the embassy duty officer informing me that the Venezuelan military had found Bill Niehous wandering free from his captors near Ciudad Bolivar, in southeastern Venezuela. It was June 30, 1979. I immediately called Lepage, who confirmed that the Venezuelan security forces had Bill Niehous in protective custody at a small town on the Orinoco River. I told the Air Force attaché about the report that Niehous was free. He agreed to fly the King Air that was under his command to pick up Niehous in Ciudad Bolivar. In my stead, the deputy chief of mission (DCM), Bart Moon, would also travel to Ciudad Bolivar. Their trip was successful, and Bill Niehous was brought safely back to Caracas that evening. He decided not to spend the night at the embassy residence, which I had offered. Instead, he chose to spend the night at the house of the current incumbent of the leadership of his former company, Owens-Illinois. It turns out that Owens-Illinois executives seemed unsurprised when they learned that Niehous had "escaped" his captivity. They had a plane standing by in Jamaica to come immediately to Caracas to pick him up and fly him back to headquarters in Toledo, Ohio, where his wife had been living during his three plus years in captivity.

The Venezuelan government agreed to my request that he be allowed to leave the country within twenty-four hours, but they wanted to have him undergo a full physical checkup first. The minister of interior wanted to be certain that Niehous was in good condition, given what he had been through. I picked up Niehous the following morning and drove him to the hospital for his physical exam. He turned out to have no serious problems.

I then drove him to the airport, which is about one hour from Caracas. During the car ride, he related some of his experiences. I first asked how he had managed to survive his captivity for over three years. He calmly said he maintained a regimen of physical exercise, and then he said that his faith helped him a great deal. He was a Roman Catholic. The most stunning aspect of his survival was his method of "maintaining his sanity." He told me that he had been a very intense baseball player and had always been able to summon up the baseball games he had played as a young man. "I had been able to recall all of my plays of all my games, so I went through them, over and over," he said. This reminded me of similar mental constructs that have enabled people to survive terrible situations. Many of Vietnam's former prisoners of war described playing chess by numbers with themselves or with their prison companions. Soviet dissident Vladimir Bukovsky, in his book *To Build a Castle*, describes how he created a castle brick by brick in which each room was elaborately furnished in his mind. He would receive visitors in different rooms of the castle all in his imagination.

I have long questioned the story in the Venezuelan press which described a shoot-out among the Niehous captors and the Venezuelan police. It did not tie together for me the story of his being freed by policemen in search of cattle rustlers—a story that included the killing of two of Bill's captors by the police as they tried to escape. I chose not to make a fuss because the US government has a strong policy against paying ransom of any type. My own impression had been informed by the fact that Owens-Illinois executives seemed ready that weekend for his release (because they had an aircraft standing when he was released). I decided not to raise my suspicions so as not to involve

Bill and his wife, Donna, in an extended hassle with the media and with the US and Venezuelan governments after the fact.

The one footnote to this event that stays with me is that Venezuelan authorities continue to claim that the terrorist who led the group of kidnapers was Nicolás Maduro, the current president—or rather dictator—of Venezuela and the former right hand of dictator Hugo Chávez.

My most important partnership in Venezuela was my friendship with Patty and Gustavo Cisneros, who shared my concern that the citizens of Latin America sensed that their culture, their language, and their thinking were somehow not appreciated by North Americans. Gustavo and Patty organized regular conferences and other meetings that involved bringing prominent Americans to Caracas to discuss democracy, human rights, freedom of the press, and artistic freedom in democratic societies. A week after my arrival as ambassador, the Cisneros Foundation had held a full-fledged conference on the values of democratic governance. They invited prominent Americans to Venezuela and Latin America to expose them to this kind of discourse, an experience none of them had had previously. Gustavo, who had been educated in the US and was a well-known and wealthy Venezuelan entrepreneur, and his wife, Patty, turned out to be the perfect partners to build a shared community between the US and those Latin American nations that had a common interest in democratic values.

Patty Phelps de Cisneros had a particularly strong, well-informed passion for the visual arts. It bothered her that when

Iman, Wendy, Bill, Patty Cisneros,
Gustavo Cisneros, model, Oscar de la Renta.

looking at the arts of Latin America, Americans seemed to stop or
be blocked by the powerful images of the great Mexican muralists
Diego Rivera and David Alfaro Siqueiros, and by Frida Kahlo, a
unique woman painter who falls under no common category.
The Rivera murals were filled with large, muscular, seminude
laborers that suggested an almost primitive culture, which was far
from reality. More to the point, neither the muralists nor Frida
Kahlo were representative of the rich exploration of abstract, geo-
metric, and kinetic art that characterized the artists of Venezuela,
Brazil, Argentina, and Uruguay during the first half of the twentieth century. These "modern" artists were often seen as being
derivative of European and American artists, when in fact the
artists were profoundly influenced directly by the same seminal
artistic influences that stirred the creativity of the Europeans and
North Americans. The Russian suprematists and Italian futurists

contributed directly to the artists of Argentina, Venezuela, and Brazil, as well.

Patty's profound insights into this limited vision of North American museum collectors, and the limited vision of the leadership of the North American art community more broadly, led the couple to a large-scale, long-term commitment of philanthropy to enhance the understanding of Latin American art in the United States and Europe. It also strengthened the strategic presence of great Latin American works of art in US institutions, which has brought about a fundamental shift in the way that North Americans now think about the visual arts in Latin America.

With Patty's recognition of American thinking about Latin America to guide it, the Cisneros Foundation set out over the next two decades, through the strategic positioning of their philanthropy, to educate Americans on the stunning visual-arts

Patty and Gustavo Cisneros.

communities in South America. She accomplished her task through the creative use of philanthropy in museums, by working directly with museum directors and key curators, including Glenn Lowry, the director of the Museum of Modern Art in New York, and curator John Elderfield.

The dramatic increase in the appreciation in North America for Hispanic culture has become a central part of our nation's culture. When this expanded awareness of the visual arts is joined with the greater appreciation of Latin creativity in other aspects of culture, such as popular music—I am thinking of the smashing success of the musical *Hamilton* by the Puerto Rican–American composer Lin-Manuel Miranda; the enormous attraction of the literature of such Nobel laureates as Gabriel García Márquez, Octavio Paz, and Mario Vargas Llosa; the sensation of José Antonio Abreu's El Sistema and the teaching of music as the core to education in Venezuela; and the brilliant El Sistema student Gustavo Dudamel, who will become director of the New York Philharmonic—the power of Latin culture to impact us all is extraordinary.

The visual impact of the Cisneros Foundation has been transformative. To quote the Museum of Modern Art director Glenn Lowry:

> Over the course of five decades, [Patty Phelps de Cisneros] assembled a collection of Latin American art that has, it is no exaggeration to say, fundamentally helped to change our understanding of the art of the region, and not just in this country but around the world, including Latin America. With its favoring of the rational and the conceptual over the exotic and the fantastical, the

collection of Cisneros has remained remarkably coherent, especially given the broad range of geographies, artistic practices, and eras represented; and it is this heterogeneity within a cohesive whole that allows for so many possible conversations across time.[40]

Gustavo and Patty Phelps de Cisneros became two of my closest friends in the world. Gustavo is a visionary, not only in industry but also in politics. As Glenn Lowry has said, Gustavo is able to see around corners and anticipate rather than react.

About a year after assuming my job as ambassador to Venezuela, I had already gotten to know Gustavo well. One morning, out of the blue, I had received a call from David Rockefeller. David wanted to ask me about my opinion of Gustavo, whom David was considering asking to be a member of the Chase Bank's international board. David reported to me that he had found mixed reactions from the American business community about Gustavo. I told Mr. Rockefeller, whom I had not met before, that my impression of Gustavo was that he wanted to model himself after what the Rockefeller family had succeeded in doing for New York and the United States: he wanted to promote civility and the arts in social and intellectual intercourse in Venezuela.

It's fair to say that over the course of my diplomatic career, and my career in the arts that followed, there is no family I feel closer to than the family of Gustavo and Patty Phelps de Cisneros and their three children. I am particularly close to their daughter, Adriana, who is somewhere between a goddaughter and a protégé to me. They occupy a special place in my consciousness.

We were all fascinated by the art generated by the Yanomami and other Indigenous tribes in Venezuela, such as the Makiritare

Bill and John Updike with Yanomani indigenous tribe.

tribe. One of the most memorable trips the Luers family and the Cisneros family took was to Amazonas to show John Updike the unique and rich culture of the Yanomami. (It was that visit that provoked John to write his outrageous and flippant *New Yorker* piece "Venezuela for Visitors.")

Patty was very interested in the many types of art of the Yanomami, and over the years the Cisneros family would amass a collection of art created by the Yanomami, which would travel across Europe. The exhibition became extremely popular with Europeans who had long been fascinated by the vitality and energy of the New World. In fact, the experience of getting to know the Indigenous peoples of Venezuela greatly enriched and refreshed Patty's belief in the importance of expanding North American and European appreciation of the rich and glorious challenges resting in the cultures of the nations of Latin America.

In the early 1990s, shortly after I arrived at the Metropolitan Museum of Art in New York as its president, the museum made a major contribution to the transformation of American and European blind spots regarding the culture of Latin America. At that time, it mounted its most ambitious exhibition on the arts of Mexico with a show called "Mexico: Splendors of Thirty Centuries." Many of the Met's top curators contributed to making "Splendors" a game-changing and formidable tribute to the arts of the United States' southern neighbor, and the show raised the appreciation of US citizens for the culture of Mexico.

In October 1990, Octavio Paz received the Nobel Prize for Literature. To celebrate, we invited Octavio to give a museum lecture following the Nobel Prize announcement, which enabled him to make the case that Mexican culture has been coherent and compelling throughout the centuries. Paz, who was the intellectual force behind the "Splendors" exhibition, drew on Xochiquetzal, the Aztec goddess of flowers, vegetation, fertility, and love, to tell the story of Mexico and her long traditions of art.

Another formidable couple that shaped my knowledge and appreciation of Venezuelan culture was Carlos Rangel and his remarkable wife, Sofia Rangel. Sofia was the director of Venezuela's leading modern museum. She wrote a weekly column on the arts in Venezuela for a leading newspaper, *El Universal,* and, with her husband, hosted a daily television interview program on culture and politics. She and her husband interviewed virtually every American artist and intellectual who visited us in Caracas. That list included John Updike, John Cheever, Peter Matthiessen, Frank Stella, Richard Diebenkorn, Edward Albee, Arthur Miller, Bill and Rose Styron, and Larry Rivers. Our goal was to bring writers and intellectuals from the United States to

(clockwise) Octavio Paz
and Bill at the Met.

Carlos Rangel and Bill with
model of *Museo de Arte
Contemporanio*, Caracas.

Bill Styron and Peter
Matthiessen in Venezuela.

Richard Diebenkorn,
Phyllis Diebenkorn at
King Ranch, Venezuela.

(top to bottom) Bill, John Kenneth Galbraith, and President
Betancourt.

Vice President Bush greeting Marines at the Embassy.

Wendy and Barbara Bush at residence.

Bill, Wendy, and Jeane Kirkpatrick.

Bill, Joan Mondale, President Carlos Andrés Pérez at Presidential
Palace.

Venezuela for what was often their first visit ever to Latin America, so that they could learn directly about the realities of that part of the world. In almost every case, the Americans' first encounter proved surprising and uplifting. Latin Americans, and Venezuelans in particular, while seeking to mimic the successes of their high-achieving peers in the US, tended to be highly critical of themselves. Such self-criticism has been a burden for Latin American writers and for Latin American democracy.

––––––––––

The decision of the British government to send a fleet of nearly fifty warships to defend the Falkland Islands (Islas Malvinas) against an Argentine effort to take control of the Falklands in April of 1982 turned upside down most of the assumptions about US relations with Latin America and Europe. It also saw America fumble in her diplomatic efforts to prevent a war.

The first US mistake was to seek to play the role of mediator between Argentina, a member of the Rio Treaty (which bonds it to the US), and the United Kingdom, a NATO country. The US was stuck between a rock and a hard place. The UK claimed that Argentina had committed aggression against them and invoked Article 5 of the NATO Treaty, which provides that in the case of an attack against a NATO member, every other NATO member shall assist their fellow ally, if it is deemed necessary. Yet, when the UK decided to act against Argentina, their doing so threatened to overturn one of the longest traditions in US foreign policy, the Monroe Doctrine, the purpose of which was to place the US against European colonial powers exercising military power in the Western Hemisphere. At the outset, Secretary of State

Alexander Haig signaled a neutral posture. Secretary Haig's intention to mediate the conflict was no doubt motivated by the sterling example of Secretary Kissinger's shuttle diplomacy in the Middle East after the Yom Kippur War.

The world was surprised when the Thatcher government dispatched one half of the British fleet to travel eight thousand miles to recover territory that most people outside the British allies had never heard of. The European community of nations surprised themselves by approving a decision to sanction all Argentine imports. This embargo surprised, angered, and stiffened the Argentines, who had always been closer to Europe than the Americas.

Meanwhile, Secretary Haig began his shuttle effort with the government of Venezuela, and I joined him in his talk with the Venezuelan foreign minister. Haig was surprised by the already clear Venezuelan support for the Argentine response to the British dispatching warships to the island. This shouldn't have come as a surprise, as Venezuela itself had a long-standing dispute with the UK over the territory of the Essequibo. Haig had miscalculated the degree to which Venezuela's attitude was shaped less by its bad relationship with the conservative president of Argentina, Leopoldo Galtieri, than by its long-standing dispute with the British government.

The EEC countries fully expected a speedy resolution before a miliary conflict could take place or before the sanctions had an impact. After the May 2 sinking of the Argentine ship *Belgrano,* it became clear that the decision to sanction Argentina might have been unwise, as the sanctions reenforced the punishment of Argentina but not a peaceful settlement.

The US surprised the British and the Europeans by trying to

act as a mediator for three weeks, thereby failing to join NATO allies. Immediately opposed to Argentine aggression, the Europeans were surprised that we were torn by our dual commitments. But when the US decided, on April 30, to shift to full support for the UK military buildup, that decision surprised and angered many Latin Americans. This change put the sincerity of our mediation effort in doubt. Latin Americans never expected us to support Argentina. The US mediators lead by Secretary Haig were surprised by the apparent confusion in Argentine government, which then made it difficult to play the mediator role in Buenos Aires. Meanwhile, the US public was surprised that the Reagan administration had waited so long to support the British, who were genuinely perceived to be in the right.

Meanwhile Secretary Haig, who was following by instinct a tradition to support the UK, ran up against the influence of President Reagan's ambassador to the UN, Jeane Kirkpatrick, who was very close to the Argentine government and wanted the US to support Argentina. The Argentinian army surprised many Latin Americans by surrendering without a major fight after having persuaded many governments and militaries that the war on the Falkland Islands would be bloody. The Argentine foreign minister Nicanor Costa Méndez, in a dramatic speech on the Falklands at the Organization of American States (OAS), had "committed the honor of his country to his Argentinian brothers"[41] that "the Argentinian flag will not be lowered while there flows a single drop of blood through the veins of the last soldier that is defending the Malvinas."[42]

The Latin American nations surprised each other by taking positions on the conflict that reflected the national interest of each nation rather than a regional commitment to Latin

American solidarity. Feeling powerless to stop the conflict and having no desire to enter it, Latin nations, with the sole exception of Peru, avoided involvement in the mediation efforts. Venezuela's democratic government—a longtime severe critic of Argentine military governments—surprised the Argentines by becoming their strongest supporter. Colombia surprised and angered Venezuela by becoming Argentina's strongest critic—and so on!

Not the least of the many surprises was for the British people, who have had to pay for this expensive little war (nearly $2 billion), to sustain a force of three to four thousand troops on the Falklands indefinitely to protect 1,800 islanders, and have had to pay for the economic recovery of the islands ($200 million). All this has more closely wedded them politically to those distant islands and has taken them further away from a political settlement to a problem that will not go away without Argentine agreement.

Had diplomacy persisted and worked, that silly war in the South Atlantic could have been avoided.

Venezuela, which was so blessed with natural resources and a two-party system, and without the tradition of a caudillo, a military authoritarian leader, seemed destined to prove that the negative self-image of Latin Americans was not justified. Then came the Bolivarian socialist revolution of Hugo Chávez, which destroyed all that had been built during the three decades of Venezuelan democracy. Looking back, it is difficult to understand how such a populist revolution could have arisen in

Venezuela. Ultimately, I believe that the corrupting influence of the cash flow of this petroleum-rich country was a major factor in bringing down Venezuela's democracy. So too was the rapid population growth (the population virtually doubled in size from my first arrival in 1969 to my departure in 1982), which did not permit Venezuela's government to continue to build a middle class through government employment. Concomitantly, there was a severe lack of investment, which could have built a private sector and created employment and built productivity outside of government. Some have argued that the Venezuelan and American private sector should have driven Venezuela on investments that would have resulted in 10 percent annual growth of the economy drawing on the China example. It is hard for me to imagine how such forced investment would have been acceptable politically.

Yet another factor that brought on the socialist populist revolution was the failure of the two leading political parties, Acción Democrática and COPEI, to invest in educating technocrats who could then run the government and make wise decisions about how the government spends its money. Venezuela also failed to develop efficient agriculture and food production. This increased the need to import food from abroad. One of the better books on the rapid deterioration of the Venezuelan political and economic system under Hugo Chávez and his successor Nicolás Maduro, *Things Are Never So Bad That They Can't Get Worse: Inside the Collapse of Venezuela,* was written by William Newman. A sorry tale of socialist mythology and its attraction of charismatic leaders—even though Chávez was nothing compared to Castro on the measure of charisma. Interestingly, Castro personally considered Chávez to be almost an equal to him in "manipulating the masses," as Fidel told me years later, during a long talk in Havana.

Today, Venezuela is a shell of her former dynamic self. The dictator Hugo Chávez, who ruled Venezuela from 1999–2013, and his chosen successor, Nicolás Maduro, who has ruled since the death of Chávez, have laid waste to this extraordinary and rich country, and sent into exile over seven million of its citizens. I mourn the gross misrule that has brought poverty and hunger and death to that beautiful country. It is a tragedy for the Western Hemisphere.

CHAPTER 10

Looking for a Place in the Reagan Administration

In 1982, I was transferred from the embassy in Caracas back to Foggy Bottom in Washington, DC, and then to Princeton, New Jersey, where I had been named a director's visitor at the Institute for Advanced Study (IAS).

The Institute for Advanced Study is a magical place; it also has a short history. Founded in 1930, its mission was and is to be a place to facilitate "fundamental inquiry into the unknown." It is a place for scientists and scholars and specialists to read and study and think and write. It was an incubator for the computer and for the atomic bomb; J. Robert Oppenheimer had been a fellow at the institute, as had Einstein, who was not there when I was there. Though located in Princeton, it is independent from Princeton University and has its own campus.

On accepting the invitation to be his visitor, director Harry Woolf and I agreed that I should not have a specific research task during the year, but I should think about what I might write about someday. I wrote a long paper about the Falklands War, which I had recently experienced as ambassador to Venezuela. I agreed with the director that I would not try anything more ambitious, but my thoughts for this book began to take shape at the institute.

Harry and Pat Woolf in Caracas, offering Bill the
Director's Visitorship at the Institute for Advanced Study.

In the summer of 1982, I was invited to teach a graduate
seminar at the Woodrow Wilson School at Princeton University,
while I still had no ongoing assignment. The seminar I taught
was on the progress of the Kissinger Commission in Central
America. My star student in that senior seminar was Michael
Froman, who was recently named president of the Council on
Foreign Relations. Kissinger had asked me to write my opinion
on the commission from the standpoint of a liberal Democrat.
My colleague, Elliott Abrams, was asked to write the conservative opinion on US interests in Central America. We eventually
published both versions with the American Enterprise Institute.

I also spent my early months at IAS writing a paper on
the Falklands War. Over the years, I had worked alongside the
Brits on issues affecting the hemisphere, and we used to meet
with them on the Falklands. The American view was, Why don't
you work this out and find a way to make a deal with the

Argentineans? The fact was that the people living in the Falkland Islands were British farmers who were ignored by London. They were a colonial outpost that the Brits cared little about, except it was theirs and they didn't want to give it up because of the sea rights and because of the possibilities that there could be oil out there. They came close to a solution a couple of times. But the US was torn in its policy: on the one hand, our position against imperialism and in favor of the Monroe Doctrine would argue that the British should not have more territory in the Western Hemisphere, and yet, we were inclined to oppose anything for the Galtieri government of Argentina, which was a military junta that had disappeared thousands of Argentines. When the war began, my instinct was that we should help make the Argentine effort fail diplomatically and avoid the use of force. I didn't think the US government should get involved militarily, but if the Brits were able to do it and wanted to do it, it was something that would help establish the UN principle against taking territory by force. The advantage of what happened is that it was so humiliating for the Galtieri government that it was the end of military rule. I still believe that the greatest benefit of that stupid war was the fact that Argentina got rid of the military junta.

Apart from my writing, I spent a good deal of time with George Kennan; we lunched together frequently. I also attended the Thursday lunch sessions when the scientists who were fellows that year at the institute made their presentations.

The "campus" of the institute was composed of many small Breuer Bauhaus houses that were identical: they had three

George Kennan at IAS, 1982.

bedrooms, one bathroom, a dining room/living room, and a very small terrace. Wendy and I moved from the large residence of the ambassador of Venezuela to this small cottage with two children, a nanny, and two dogs. We lived there and rode our bicycles around the campus, rather than being driven from location to location with a backup police car. Our lives and lifestyles changed dramatically, and we got to know many of the fellows at the institute. I found the biggest challenge was that there was nobody to take care of my outbox; I had to write all my own letters whether it was responding to correspondence or asking for an appointment—activities that, before, the embassy staff would manage efficiently. Our year in Princeton was a happy one for

Wendy and me, and we made enduring friendships, particularly with Peter Benchley, the author of *Jaws*, and his wife Wendy. Our life in Princeton was unusually rich from an intellectual point of view because of the professors we knew at the university and the remarkable fellows at the institute. I was also asked to take on several tasks for the State Department during my time at Princeton. For example, I was asked to do a paper on US policy toward Guatemala, which had been troubled ever since the US overthrew the government of Jacobo Árbenz in 1954.

In the spring of 1982, I was informed I had been selected to be ambassador to Spain. Wendy was thrilled, as was I, since we both knew the prime minister, Felipe González, who had frequently visited Venezuela and was a close friend of Gustavo Cisneros. Spain is a post rarely given to a career diplomat and I felt honored that apparently secretary of state George Shultz had approved or promoted this assignment. But within a month of first learning the possibility of going to Spain, I was informed that I'd be going to Peru, not Spain. The current ambassador to Peru was Frank Ortiz, who had, I presumed, bumped me out of the Spanish assignment. It turned out that I was right: Ortiz was already preparing to go to Spain. I heard from others that he had been supported in his quest by some of the senior female friends of the White House. Ortiz was a conservative diplomat who was close to the Reagan administration. Having left the institute, we moved into the house of Wendy and Peter Benchley. And we reenrolled our children in Princeton Day School.

Still later, I was told by the director general of the State Department, "We want to send you to Nigeria." And I said no. I knew nothing about Nigeria and had never served in Africa. It would have been a waste of talent and language skills. This

Peter and Wendy Benchley, Princeton.

guessing game went on for some time, when finally Larry Eagleburger, the deputy secretary of state, called and said, "Bill, there's a Class 3 embassy that we could offer you, but you're too senior for this . . . Would you go to Czechoslovakia?"

Without a moment's hesitation, I said I would. And that surprised the hell out of him.

"That's interesting," he said. "I hadn't expected it but I—"

"Look, Larry. I want to go to Moscow as ambassador, and Czech—and Prague is on the way to Moscow."

And Larry quickly responded with his characteristic wit, "Luers, for you, Prague is on the way to Sofia!" (The capital of Bulgaria.)

———————

Prague was a Class 3 embassy, which meant that Czechoslovakia was a small mission. It also happened to be at the bottom of the heap of Soviet satellite countries of interest to the United States. At that time, our approach to central European Soviet satellites was determined by the degree to which they were developing some independence from Moscow. Tito's Yugoslavia was the number one dissident in central Eastern Europe. Romania, after Yugoslavia, was number two. At that time, our approach to Central Europe, which we called Eastern Europe then, was that they would get extra benefits from us for the degree to which they were developing some independence from Moscow. Romania was number one; Nicolae Ceaușescu had kept his distance from the Soviets on many issues important to the US. And he had not joined in the 1968 invasion of Czechoslovakia. He had retained a certain level of independence. Poland has always had its own support from the United States, and it had Solidarność, known in the West as Solidarity, an independent trade union, which by then was already established. Also, by then, Hungary's Goulash Communism had begun to ease up, even though János Kádár was still in power. Hungary was changing; it was reforming internally already. Bulgaria was thought to be basically a quasi-Russian country in terms of the language, which is so close to Russian, and it had not shown much interest in breaking that historic relationship. East Germany (GDR) was always sort of the toady of the Soviets, but East Germany was important because of West Germany. We had no reason to take much interest in Czechoslovakia. No assistant secretary had visited Prague since the Soviet invasion in 1968. The highest level their ambassador could see in the State Department was a deputy assistant secretary or, on very important occasions, maybe an assistant secretary, so . . . we had them downplayed. For me, because of our history with it, because of the invasion of 1968—and just because I liked the history of the place—I said yes to Czechoslovakia. And I never looked back.

———————

Before things got rolling with Czechoslovakia formally, we were invited by Gustavo and Patty Phelps de Cisneros to spend two days at a quail shoot with President and Mrs. Carter in Albany, Georgia, near the Carters' home in Plains. After dinner the second night, the president and I talked for a long time about his strategy in 1978 to encourage Somoza to leave voluntarily as president of Nicaragua so as to avoid the Sandinista takeover of Nicaragua, which seemed inevitable. At the time, the US government and Venezuela had identified an admiral who was serving as Nicaragua's ambassador to an Asian state who was willing to come back to succeed Somoza as President of Nicaragua. We first had to persuade Somoza to leave voluntarily and cede his presidency. We called the process *Somozismo sin Somoza*.

I explained to the president that he had been very close in 1979 to succeeding in his plan. It depended on Ambassador William Bowdler successfully making it work and hinged on whether

Somoza could be persuaded to leave, neither of which happened. I told President Carter it was too bad the plan had not been successful. If it had, the US could have avoided the long-running Central American wars that followed the Sandinista takeover in Nicaragua. The president turned candid and said, "Bill, my plate was very full during that fall of 1979. I had to negotiate the Camp David Accords in the fall of that year. At the same time, we were swamped negotiating the establishment of diplomatic relations with China. Moreover, the wild card was the return of the Ayatollah Khomeini to Tehran."

Carter pointed out that the Camp David Accords were reached in September 1978. Only months later, the Shah of Iran was forced out of Tehran in January of 1979. And the United States signed an agreement with China in 1979 that led to the reestablishment of diplomatic relationships between the two hostile nations. President Carter said these were highly political issues that required his presence and involvement. He then asked rhetorically how the president's involvement could have been called off or delayed in such demanding moments. We exchanged views on whether a president could pass or transfer the responsibility for such important decisions to his vice president or others in his cabinet. President Carter's association with establishing diplomatic relations with China and the Camp David Accords were paramount to his presidency. It is hard to imagine how he could have ceded the responsibility for those actions to another person.

Carter's heavy focus and unique negotiating abilities gave him a special role in completing these two important steps for US foreign policy. He and I discussed the problems faced by a president when dealing with world issues of such momentous importance. He assumed that I was expressing frustration at his inability to focus enough on the Nicaragua problem. I was pleased that he, unlike his predecessors, had not ordered the removal by covert operations of Somoza or his assassination, as his predecessors had done as revealed in 1975 by the Church committee report. The plan to ask Somoza to depart was similar to the US pressure on Jean-Claude Duvalier (Baby Doc) to leave Haiti and Ferdinand Marcos to leave the Philippines. I knew Jimmy Carter did not advocate the assassination of either president; to do so was neither his style nor his instinct.

The next president I was to serve, I was less familiar with.

That summer of 1983, needing President Reagan to put forward my name as ambassador to Czechoslovakia, it was time to do a little politicking of my own.

I had been slow to comprehend the significance and dangers implicit in the anti-Communist rhetoric of President Reagan. Having been President Carter's ambassador to Venezuela, I was perceived to be in agreement with the Democratic view of US foreign policy. The only Reaganite I knew well was Jeane Kirkpatrick, who had been appointed his ambassador to the UN and was very much a part of the ideological hostility to the USSR that shaped the Reagan foreign policy agenda. She was a superhawk on Communism and fully supported President Reagan's extreme opposition to détente with Moscow. I realized that if I wanted another career appointment, I had better become more acquainted with the real Ronald Reagan and his administration. The opportunity came in the summer of 1983.

Vice President Bush and Bill discussing ambassadorship.

Bill and Senator Tim Wirth, a friend who
encouraged Bill to lead the UNA-USA.

The occasion was my first meeting with Michael Deaver, the White House chief of staff. His title did not come close to capturing his close relationship with the Reagans. Perhaps most importantly, he was a close confidant of Nancy Reagan.

Kay Graham had invited Deaver to that notorious gathering place of Democrats and liberals on Martha's Vineyard to get closer to Nancy and President Reagan. This was in the early days of Reagan's presidency when partisan rancor had begun to grow intense. Dems and Republicans would not party together except when Kay Graham, the formidable force who was publisher and owner of the *Washington Post*, would summon them to an occasion. Over her decades in Washington, Kay had tried to get close to all of the presidents no matter the party (President Nixon, particularly after the Watergate revelations, was a large exception). Her house in Washington was one of the very few places in DC where senior Republicans and Democrats would agree to meet and talk politics. During most of the Cold War years, politics in Washington worked because of the social network kept vibrant by the famously powerful hostesses in Washington. Since her death, the informal politics made possible by those informal dinner parties and lunches have been impossible to sustain. Kay was uniquely committed to her role as informal mediator between the Democrats and Republicans, who I had hoped would have become our presidents. Yet, I was well aware that career diplomats—FSOs—never favor publicly or campaign for a political party or candidate. In fact, we all must perform our tasks loyally for whomever becomes our president. By then, I had served under Republican and Democratic presidents.

Rose Styron, whose home was just down the way, knew I was playing tennis with Deaver the next day at Kay's house, so that he and I could meet, and he could get to know me. Rose also knew I was hoping to go to Prague and was always ready to enter a conspiracy with me for a good cause; the day before our tennis date, Rose introduced me to Mike Deaver directly, as we were both at the Styrons' place, out on their front lawn.

In talking with Deaver, our conversation inevitably circled around to US relations with the USSR—and to my belief that sustained communications at all levels, but particularly the highest levels, were essential. This was the conversation I was angling for. In preparation, I had ordered my own thoughts on what had motivated every president from FDR to Carter to keep the current Soviet leader as the central focus of US national security. There on the Styrons' lawn, I turned and said to Mike, "Every president I have followed and worked under eventually came to the view that improved US national security required open lines of communications at the top."

Mike turned defensive and blurted out loudly, "No, not my president. He will never be drawn in by a Soviet leader. He is too clear about the nature of the Soviet system."

Thus warned, I took my time to explain my view that communications with the current Soviet leader were *the* key to improved relations between our two countries. I realized I needed to proceed carefully, for these were my opinions alone—and could affect my nomination for the ambassadorship in Prague. But history was on my side.

Taking a deep, steadying breath, I started my "speech" to Deaver: "Mike, this is what I know and have observed. First, FDR established diplomatic relations with Stalin's Soviet Union because, even in the 1930s, he already had conceived of the need for an alliance with the Soviet Union against the rising threats from Nazi Germany and Imperial Japan. Truman was focused on winning the Second World War, and in his tense alliance with Stalin, he too saw the possibility in and need for Soviet strength in bringing the war to an end, not only in Europe, but against the Japanese in the Pacific. Eisenhower realized direct talks with the Soviet leader would be required to mitigate and manage the new threat of nuclear arms. Ike even invited Khrushchev to visit the US in a bold move. Ultimately his outreach failed because of our U-2 that was downed by Soviet missiles. But Ike and Khrushchev made immense strides while they were talking at Camp David. Next, we go to JFK. Kennedy also saw direct talks with the Soviets as necessary to manage the nuclear arms race. Additionally, he saw direct communication as a way to deal with the shaken but somewhat chastened USSR after the Cuban Missile Crisis. LBJ, who had seen the writing on the wall as far as Vietnam went— and was not even running for president—was so desperate to talk to the Soviets about nuclear weapons that he was willing to meet with Soviet Premier Alexei Kosygin in Glassboro, New Jersey, rather than wait for talks with Brezhnev, who was the *real* Soviet leader. LBJ saw this meeting as an opportunity to talk directly with the Soviets—any member of the Soviet leadership. He was willing to speak with the Soviet leader *who was available.* In August of the next year, on the day before the US and the Soviets were to announce the culmination of the Johnson administration's bridge-building campaign—the opening of arms limitations talks with the Soviets—LBJ announced to his staff that it might be the greatest accomplishment of his presidency. Clark Clifford said Johnson was "just about as excited about it as anybody I ever saw." And even the next day—yes, the next day— when the Soviet Warsaw Pact forces invaded Czechoslovakia, LBJ took the call from Anatoly Dobrynin, Soviet Ambassador to the United States. The other NATO countries were outraged and seeking ways to register disapproval. Johnson got on the phone. Later, Nixon and Kissinger designed US foreign policy around ways to better limit Soviet power by engaging the USSR as an equal to the United States. Carter had to endure the extreme disappointment of the Soviet invasion of Afghanistan interfering with *his* nuclear agenda.

"Mike, what is common to every single one of these American presidents is that each of them toward the end of his term thought of the Soviet leadership as the main target of their foreign policy." My speech over, I tensed to see how Deaver had received it. I hadn't planned on giving him such a long history lesson, but that's what it turned out to be.

To my surprise, Mike did a double take. When he spoke, his words surprised me.

"You may be right about President Reagan," he said, finally.

Then he went on to tell me the story of a specific event that suggested a possible scenario pointing toward a strong concern Reagan had in his mind about relations with Soviet leader Brezhnev. Deaver said that when President Reagan was shot in the first spring of his presidency, Mike went with him to the hospital and stayed close during his several unconscious hours. When he regained consciousness, he asked Mike to bring him a pad of paper and pen. Mike, as he had done many times before, got him the pen and long yellow pad. After a few days, when he was recovering, the president handed back to Mike the pad on which he had drafted in longhand a letter to Brezhnev. It was a warm letter with only a few hints of President Reagan's hostile view of the Soviet Union.

The draft letter is available to anyone at President Reagan's library. It begins warmly with, "My Dear Mr. President" and moves into recalling their first meeting with President Nixon at San Clemente a decade ago, reminding Brezhnev that he had been the governor of California. He then wrote, "When we met, I asked if you were aware that the hopes and aspirations of millions and millions of people throughout the world were dependent on the decisions that would be reached at your meetings." Then he added a touching personal note, "You took my hand in both yours and assured me that you were aware of that." Reagan concluded his heartfelt letter to Brezhnev with an appeal: "Mr. President, should we not be concerned with the elimination of obstacles which prevent our people—those we represent—from achieving their most cherished goals? And isn't it possible that some of those obstacles are born of government objectives which have little to do with the real needs and desires of our people?"

I took that story to demonstrate that that relationship between the US and the USSR was clearly central to President Reagan's thinking as president, as he faced death or a long recovery. This also seemed to confirm for Mike my thesis about the subliminal attitudes of American presidents toward the Soviet Union.

That discussion with Mike Deaver never left me. Not his immediate aggressive answer about Reagan's staunch disdain for the Soviets nor his thoughtful reflection—and change of mind—about the president's possible willingness or openness to refocus US foreign policy on active communication with the Soviets. At a time of virtually no communications, such a change of mind on Deaver's part opened a door I was determined to walk through.

Only months later, President Reagan nominated me for the position of ambassador of Czechoslovakia. After two stressful

months of preparations for my new post, including some intensive language training at Berlitz to try to retread my Russian
into Czech, which proved difficult since the Czech language is
much softer and melodic, with more inflections, than Russian.
(There was not enough time to send me to the Foreign Service
Institute language program, which I knew well, having learned
the fundamentals of Russian there.) I also had to prepare for
my confirmation hearings before the Senate Foreign Relations
Committee, whose chairman was Senator Claiborne Pell, who
had served as a diplomat in the Consulate General in Bratislava,
the capital of Slovakia. My friend Senator Adlai Stevenson III
from Illinois came to introduce me to the Senate committee. The
confirmation went smoothly, but virtually no senator had
interesting questions about Czechoslovakia, except to ask what

Swearing in for Prague, 1983. Connor, Ramsay, Amy,
William, David, Mark, Chief of Protocol Tim Towell,
Wendy, Bill, and Larry Eagleburger.

could be done with that repressive Communist regime. They generally wondered whether that Communist government in Prague could be brought into the Helsinki process that would lead toward an agreement by which Prague would sign a bilateral agreement with the US to have regular bilateral official discussions on political relations (which both sides wanted); commercial and economic relations (which Prague wanted); and the "third basket" of the Helsinki Accords—human rights (which Washington wanted).

The Senate confirmed my nomination later that fall, and I received my formal appointment on November 14, 1983. Less than a month later, Wendy, our two daughters, and I boarded the plane for Prague.

CHAPTER 11

US Ambassador: Czechoslovakia, Part I

It is almost impossible to understand the Czechoslovakia of 1983 without first understanding what happened to the country and her people in 1968.

On January 5, 1968, the Stalinist leader of Czechoslovakia's Communist Party (KSČ), Antonín Novotný, was toppled by the more moderate and lesser-known Alexander Dubček, who was then named first secretary of the Communist Party. Though Czechoslovakia had a president, Ludvík Svoboda, it was the first secretary who ruled the country. Almost immediately, the Communist Dubček began instituting a series of reforms, both economic and political; increasing the freedom of speech; and liberalizing civil rights and personal freedoms.

The effect of this "action plan" on the citizens of Czechoslovakia was electric. Thanks to an underground movement that had prepared for just such a moment, new political groups arose quickly, opposition groups formed, the Communist youth movement collapsed. Soon, there began to be demands for real democracy. These events and the time in which they occurred, in the spring of 1968, is called the Prague Spring.

The West watched with bated breath, as it seemed that Czechoslovakia was transforming before their eyes. But also watching were the USSR and the members of the Warsaw

Pact—the alliance between the Soviet Union and its satellite countries: Albania, Bulgaria, East Germany, Hungary, Poland, and Romania. Worried about the effects on their own citizens, and shocked at the breadth and direction of the reforms—and the full-throated embrace of these reforms by the peoples of Czechoslovakia—on August 20, 1968, twenty-seven divisions of the armed forces of four members of the Warsaw Pact backed by two thousand tanks of the Soviet Union, invaded Czechoslovakia. The total number of troops who invaded the country would eventually top five hundred thousand.[49] With this invasion, the Prague Spring was over.

Paradoxically, though Dubček was eventually removed from power, and the new government under Soviet-chosen Gustáv Husák proceeded to put the country through a program of "normalization," the people of Czechoslovakia—and particularly the writers and cultural leaders—did not give up their dreams for a more free and more democratic Czechoslovakia: they simply retired and went underground, bruised but not broken.

One group of these individuals coalesced into a group that emerged as a result of the Helsinki Accords that were signed in early 1975 to protest the arrest of the psychedelic rock band Plastic People of the Universe for "organized disturbance of the peace" but really for being everything the government despised: creative, outrageous, uncaring of whom they displeased, and determined to chart their own path. Not coincidentally, the Plastic People of the Universe had caught the attention of the playwright Václav Havel, who in the months after their arrest gathered together a band of intellectuals, writers, and fans and wrote a document demanding greater freedoms for the people of Czechoslovakia. The document was "addressed to the

Czechoslovak government[;] it protested against the violations by the state against the basic human rights guaranteed by the UN and the Helsinki Conference, to both of which Czechoslovakia had subscribed."[50] This group and their demands were called Charter 77. For their efforts, members of Charter 77 were brutalized, beaten, and jailed. Yet they would hang on. With Havel as one of its founding members, Charter 77 would plant the seeds of the Velvet Revolution that would unshackle Czechoslovakia from the bondage of Communism, twelve years later, in 1989.[51]

It was in this interim period that Wendy and I arrived in Prague. It was 1983, six years before the Velvet Revolution occurred.

I arrived with my wife, Wendy, and two daughters, Ramsay and Connor, to live in Prague on December 17 of 1983. We were greeted by the charge d'affaires, William Farrand, who would immediately become my deputy chief of mission. We were also met by the Foreign Ministry's chief of protocol, who greeted us with characteristic Central European graciousness. I was scheduled to present my credentials to President Gustáv Husák in a few days as ambassador plenipotentiary (meaning I had full powers to represent the US government with the government of Czechoslovakia) of the president of the United States of America.

I made a protocol visit to the foreign minister, Bohuslav Chňoupek, prior to my meeting with President Husák. Chňoupek would prove to be an excellent ally in helping achieve one of our objectives in Prague. Having received no

DCM Bill Farrand greeting Bill at Prague Airport.

specific instructions from the president or from the secretary of state about my mission in Prague, I had formulated my own. I had two main objectives as ambassador: First, I needed to persuade the Czechoslovak government to sign an agreement with the US under the Helsinki Accords. This had been suggested by the senators in my confirmation hearings. No official in the State Department who followed Europe thought that such an agreement would be possible with Czechoslovakia, considered to be the most conservative and obedient of the Soviet satellites. However, I took on the task as my traditional diplomatic objective. My second objective was to mount a campaign for an exchange/visitation program to help open up the long-isolated Communist government of Husák to the outside world.

Wanting to meet most of the leadership in the government and the party, early in my time in Prague, I asked Chňoupek the best way to do so. He suggested that I could informally meet most

of the major leaders in the government and party if I would join
him in his weekend shoots for pheasants, wild boar, and hare.
I told him I had never hunted game and knew nothing about
shotguns. He said he would teach me, since no prior American
ambassador in his lifetime had agreed to partake of this way of
life, which was so rooted in the culture of Central Europe. (I
recalled to myself that when Dubček went to Moscow after the
Soviet invasion of Czechoslovakia and was told he would have to
step down, he reportedly said to Brezhnev, "But I do not understand; we have shot boar together.") Chňoupek said that all I
needed to do was buy two double-barreled Brno shotguns and
agree to join him in the regular pheasant and wild boar shoots
he organized for other diplomats and for some senior government officials. He said that, officially, I would not be allowed
to meet with any of the ministers in Husák's cabinet in their
offices because US relations with his government were so frigid
and because their ambassador to Washington, DC was frozen out
of all visits with US senior officials. But I would have the opportunity to develop close relations with some senior officials if we
shot and drank together on his shoots.

I learned during my tour that Chňoupek was correct about
the access I could get through attending his shoots, which I did
regularly. And I carefully drank less than my Czech and Slovak
partners. During one memorable shoot, I sat with the head of
the Ministry of the Interior who oversaw the secret police. And
he, being completely in his cups, bragged about how much they
knew about my activities in Prague. He was highly motivated to
explain in detail the "efficient reach of the STB" (the Ministry of
State Security—the Czech version of the KGB).

Two hours after meeting with Chňoupek, I presented my

credentials to President Husák in the Czech language, after which I had the full authority to function in Prague as the American ambassador, even if they succeeded in freezing me out of all of senior official contacts, which they had traditionally nurtured around all representatives of the US government.

Husák devoted much of our session to a discussion of the deployment of the Pershing missiles in West Germany. He announced at the outset of our conversation, "Welcome Mr. Ambassador. You unfortunately take up your mission at the worse moment in the history of US relations with my country."

I replied that that was quite a statement given the bad times I could recall in our relations. Nevertheless, the overriding political/security issue in Europe in the fall of 1983 was the deployment of Pershing missiles (intermediate-range ballistic missiles) with nuclear warheads in Western Europe. This was being done to bring up the NATO force to be comparable to the Soviet deployment of their SS-20 medium range missile, similar to the Pershing, in the eastern Soviet Union. The proposed deployment of the Pershing missiles by the US and NATO coincided with some heightened rhetoric from the Reagan administration, including the announcement of US plans to build a military missile defense system, which came to be known as Star Wars. The Soviet military and intelligence agencies believed that such a weapons system was a real possibility. The Soviets began a campaign reflecting their argument that the US was planning a first nuclear strike strategy against the USSR. In the middle of this period, the Soviet alert system picked up a false signal that the US had launched a missile against the USSR. A smart, young Soviet military officer chose not to alert his top commanders, judging that the alert was mistaken. In this environment, both sides thought that nuclear war had been averted again. But the controversy over the Pershing missile deployment mounted in Germany brought over one million Germans to the streets to protest the American action. The controversial US decision was denounced by many political opposition parties in Europe as a provocative act by the Reagan administration. Moscow and other Warsaw Pact capitals (including Prague) were screaming that the Pershing deployment would provoke a third world war. The Reagan administration, which I would soon speak for in Prague, was determined to deploy the Pershing missiles, in part to get Moscow to pay attention to the significant, unbalanced growth of middle-range nuclear weapons in Central Europe, which was a security threat to NATO. Two years later, the new Soviet leader Gorbachev and President Reagan would sign the Intermediate-Range Nuclear Forces Treaty (INF Treaty), which eliminated the medium-range ballistic missiles in Europe. This treaty was one of the long-range objectives of the Pershing deployment.

President Husák then warned me that he and his people feared that we were on the verge of war because of the US decision to station Pershing missiles in West Germany. I explained why the US had decided to deploy the Pershings and gave him my opinion that the other NATO members fully supported the deployment to better balance the buildup and presence of Soviet middle-range ballistic missiles in the eastern USSR. I assured him that I would do what I could to improve relations in these troubled times and hoped I could work with him on improving the ties between our two nations. I outlined my view of the value of building on the bilateral cultural relations that had been so strong for so many years in the twentieth century. He had little to say on the matter of cultural ties. I excused myself and thanked him for receiving me. And I said I was honored to have been asked by President Reagan to represent him in Prague, in a country that I had traveled in and admired greatly for its beauty and its lasting contribution to the arts in Europe.

Wendy and I had decided that our first and second big objectives could be organized along similar lines, with distinct events and targeted audiences. We designed an active two-to-three-year program of diplomacy, intending to flood Prague with visits by prominent American writers, artists, and intellectuals, as well as publishers, editors, and political leaders to convey to the outside world that Václav Havel (and his Charter 77 movement) was an active intellectual force for change, and that the Czechoslovak government was an important partner to our commitment to the Helsinki Accords.

Havel had just been released from five years in prison in early 1983—less than a year before I arrived in Prague. Those five years had witnessed the growth of Charter 77 as a vehicle for promoting awareness and adherence to the 1975 Helsinki Final Act resulting in the Helsinki Accords. Havel and his dissident colleagues signed on to Charter 77, which became the guiding document to encourage the active participation of Czechoslovakia in the Helsinki process, the objective of which was to open up Europe and the US to a new effort to reduce tensions by expanding formal and informal relations between the East and West.

The Charter 77 group was not as well known to the outside world in 1983 as the more flamboyant and politically active

Václav Havel.

Solidarność, or "Solidarity," movement in Poland. Havel was not a charismatic political labor leader like Lech Wałęsa, who enjoyed vast support inside Poland. Nor was Czechoslovakia a Catholic nation with the special support of Pope John Paul II, a former Polish cardinal who had been pope since 1978. Moreover, unlike the Slovaks, who were a Catholic nation, the Czechs had clung to their Protestant roots (which went back to Jan Hus and Tomáš Masaryk) as an expression of their resistance. The irony was that many Czechs found in the Catholic Church a refuge from the emptiness and repression of their Communist government. By the 1980s, priests were being ordained in Czechoslovakia without the full authority or presence of a cardinal. Wałęsa and Havel had already begun their clandestine meetings in various locations along the common Czech-Polish border. Havel chose not to portray himself as a political opposition leader. Instead, Havel preferred his role as a member of Czechoslovakia's substantial arts community and as an essayist on the freedoms of speech.

The second and most important objective of our mission in Prague was to mount an exchange/visitation program to help open up Czechoslovakia. In the absence of any formal US-Czechoslovakian cultural exchange programs, Wendy and I and a very bright, engaged professional embassy staff executed our ambitious plan of encouraging dozens of high-profile American visitors to visit Prague. We wanted the Husák government to take notice that an American ambassador, through personal contacts, was making an effort to attract to Prague some of America's most prominent media leaders and public and cultural figures. We had concluded that the dissidents and Havel would welcome an effort to encourage the Communist Czechoslovak government toward a more open approach to the Helsinki process, which was a major objective of Charter 77, as long as the US pursued policies that supported human rights and freedoms within their country. We calculated that a regular flow of well-known Americans to Prague would get the attention of the Czechs and Slovaks and the other Communist governments of Central Europe, who paradoxically seemed to be in competition with the other governments of the Warsaw Pact to win favor from the US. The US policy of differentiating among the Soviet satellites was precisely designed to provoke such a reaction.

We knew, for example, that the Romanian leader Ceaușescu was worried about indications that the US was considering trade arrangements with Poland that had not been offered to Romania. Ceaușescu worried that Poland would try to replace Romania as the US's favorite member of the Warsaw Pact, because of the Polish pope and Polish American influence in Washington, DC. Ceaușescu had earned his reputation as the US's favorite through a series of steps differentiating his policies and actions from those of the Soviet Union. For example, Romanian forces did *not* join the Warsaw Pact forces when they invaded Czechoslovakia to crush the Prague Spring in 1968.

Our overriding objective was to bring to Prague, as our guests, dozens of friends who were prominent Americans to help keep the light (i.e., the publicity) shining on Havel as the leader of a vibrant culture in Prague. If the world admired Havel as the leader of a rich cultural legacy in Prague, the Communist government was less likely to throw Havel back in jail than if he were portrayed by the US government as the leading Czech political dissident. Havel himself preferred his image as a person of the arts rather than the person leading political opposition against the Communist Party.

Charter 77 was formed after the Helsinki Accords were reached in 1975. They established the framework by which all European states (East and West) would relate to each other and the US. Charter 77 would issue occasional statements of human rights and freedom of expression. The Communist regime's arrest and persecution of Prague's favorite rock band, the Plastic People of the Universe, forced Havel and his group to become more political by setting up the Charter 77 movement.

In Havel's own words, the Czechoslovak antitotalitarian

opposition was chiefly the members of Charter 77. The Chartists "were people with a broad range of positions, from Trotskyites to reform communists, various types of socialists, people who declared themselves liberals, Christian Democrats or conservatives, as well as many people who refused to be put into any kind of predefined pigeonhole."[52] Charter 77 would name a new spokesperson every year. Havel was not the designated leader but represented its active presence and the philosophical spirit of its work.

Our first big cultural event was held at the Ambassador's Residence, which had been built in 1929 by the Petschek family and was a grand copy of the Petit Trianon in Versailles. The building had been offered to the US as the residence of the American ambassador in Prague following World War II, at a time when the Czechoslovak

Petschek Palace, the residence of the
American Ambassador in Prague.

government was more favorably disposed to the United States. The vernissage we held was for the first showing of the contemporary American art we were hanging in the residence. The paintings came from the Art in Embassies program. We had borrowed pieces from painters and galleries and private collectors. The Art in Embassies program had been the centerpiece of our cultural program in Caracas. Originally founded in 1963 as an office within the State Department, it was used to promote cultural diplomacy. From MoMA and other museums across the United States, we asked for catalogues of their recent exhibitions. When hundreds of catalogues started arriving, we laid them out on tables all around all the rooms in the residence and encouraged our Czech and Slovak visitors attending the vernissage to take catalogues home with them.

We had spent the past two months compiling a list of addresses and contact information for all the writers, artists, academics, university students, and all the members of Charter 77, we could locate. Fortunately, we had already met with Michael Żantovský, who was one of Havel's closest advisers. Michael had assured us that Havel would come to our first evening and bring along many of the artists and writers we would get to know over the next two years. I had asked the embassy staff how best to get invitations delivered to the growing list of invitees. They recommended mailing them. I questioned whether the Communist government's postal service would even deliver invitations from the American Embassy. In fact, we checked by phone, and no one had received an invitation from our first mail drop. So, we had copies of the invitation delivered by embassy staff. The invitees preferred to have a document inviting them, since the police were checking outside the residence to determine who

was invited. The police were not concerned about the security
of the residence or the ambassador. They were mainly concerned
about checking to see which citizens were being contacted by the
American ambassador and why. We learned over the years that
virtually everyone who visited the residence, or me or Wendy in
another part of town, would be stopped after the meeting and
interrogated about the matters that were discussed and the questions we had asked. Wendy once asked a prominent dissident
whether he was ever worried about coming to the residence. He
said, "No. And besides, Wendy, you have whiskey."

On the night of the vernissage, we realized we were on the
right track by leading with culture. We had managed to hand-
deliver 250 invitations to the event. By 6:00 p.m., at least two
hundred people were lined up at the front door to come to the
reception. Our guests of honor from the US that night were
the painter Cleve Gray and his wife, the writer Francine du
Plessix Gray. At a little after 6:00 p.m., I walked down the long
winding stairs from the living quarters upstairs to the first floor,
which was crowded with Czechs and Slovaks. They were writers
and painters and critics and translators and museum directors
and students and professors and a very few low-level officials
from the Foreign Ministry and Ministry of Culture. Most of
the guests were engaging in conversation with the embassy's creative, Czech-speaking American staff, who were surprised to be
seeing and talking with so many citizens in that huge American
space in the center of Prague. I saw in the library my friend and
house guest Francine talking in a circle of the guests to a short
man whom I recognized from pictures as Havel. I welcomed
him and his wife, Olga, to America's house, then watched as he
interacted with the groups of other guests, one of whom was

President Barack Obama and William Luers at American University at the celebration of the Iran Nuclear Deal, 2015.

Castro Dinner 2000, Palacio de la Justicia, Havana, Cuba. *Left to right:* Mercedes Garcia Marquez, Roberto Fernandez (Casa de las Americas), Patricia Phelps de Cisneros, Wendy Luers, Carlos Marti (UNEAC), Gabriel "Gabo" Garcia Marquez, Helmo Hernandez, Abel Prieto (Minister of Culture), Arthur Miller, Ismael Gonzalez, Inge Morath, Mort Janklow, Fidel Castro, William Luers, Rose Styron, Bill Styron, Linda Janklow.

Family, Black Point Beach, Martha's Vineyard, 2013. *Top row:* Ramsay Turnbull, Will Luers, Sergio Missana, Leonard Sklar, Amy Luers, Bill Luers, Wendy Luers, David Luers, Mark Luers, Ken Ishiguro, Connor Turnbull. *Bottom Row:* Luis Missana, Maya Missana, Arden Luers, Mika Ishiguro, Cedar Sklar-Luers, Seiji Ishiguro, Carl Luers, Erin Luers, Riley Luers, Sofia Missana.

Bill's retirement dinner, Metropolitan Museum, January 1999. Will Luers, Katie Whitney Luers, Connor Turnbull, Leonard Sklar, Amy Luers, Ramsay Turnbull, Bill Luers, Wendy Luers, David Luers, Sergio Missana, Sheelin Wilson, Mark Luers.

Bill's eightieth birthday. *Standing:* Wendy Benchley, Jodie Eastman, John Eastman, Wren Wirth, Fred Baldwin, Nancy Rubin, Geoffrey Hoguet, Wendy Watriss, Rose Styron, Annalu Ponti, Gustavo Cisneros, Tim Wirth, Aileen Adams, Geoff Cowan, Frank McCourt, Ellen McCourt. *Seated:* Patty Cisneros, Bill Luers holding Eva Griffin, Wendy Luers, Tomas Orinoco Griffin, Adriana Cisneros.

Quail shoot, Albany, Georgia, with former President Jimmy Carter and Wendy Luers.

Portrait of William Luers by Zverev,
Moscow 1964.

Richard Diebenkorn, *Ocean Park #94,* 1976,
oil and charcoal on canvas.

Polly Kraft, Václav Havel, and Wendy
Luers, Hrádeček, Czechoslovakia,
August 1989.

William Luers tying the tie for
president-to-be, Václav Havel,
Prague, December 27, 1989.

Oprah Winfrey and William Luers, Chicago, 2003.

Bill Gates, William Luers, Hank McKinnell, CEO and Chairman of Pfizer. UNA-USA Dinner, New York.

William Luers, Cardinal František Tomášek, Senator Bob Dole, Prague, 1986.

Ramsay Turnbull, William Luers, Wendy Luers, Nancy Reagan, President Ronald Reagan, The White House.

William Luers, Laura Bush, President George W. Bush, and Wendy, The White House.

Jill Biden, Wendy Luers, William Luers, Hillary Clinton, Praemium Imperiale announcement, The White House, 2023.

Wendy Luers, Martin Scorsese, William Luers, Tokyo, 2016.

David McCullough, William Luers, Geoff Cowan, Metropolitan Museum, 1995.

Václav Havel, William Luers, former President Kwaśniewski of Poland, Rolling Stones concert, Beacon Theater, New York, 2006.

Standing: Mia Farrow, Wendy Luers, Martina Forman, Stephen Sondheim, William Luers, Miloš Forman. *Seated:* Jack Rosenthal, Ronan Farrow, David Furnish, Elton John, Holly Russell, Luers' house, Connecticut, early 2000s.

Frank McCourt, William Luers, Nick Griffin, book party for *Ping Pong Diplomacy* by Nicholas Griffin, Luers' house, Connecticut, 2014.

Tom Wicker, Bill Luers, Bill Styron, at Lach and Jennifer Phillips' house, Washington DC, 1981.

William and Wendy Luers, Lee and Walter Annenberg, Martha's Vineyard, 1997.

Richard Diebenkorn, *Recollections of a Visit to Leningrad*, 1965, oil on canvas.

Michael Žantovský. Žantovský was becoming indispensable to Havel and one of his closest advisers. He would later be Havel's biographer.

During the evening, an aura seemed to glow around him. (Years later, when I welcomed Princess Diana to the Metropolitan Museum in New York, I saw an aura around her, which was of a beautiful, majestic woman. Havel had an aura of a very different type.) I sensed that everyone around him was affected by this man. Auras are in the eyes of the beholder, but they often suggest the presence of a leader. The two American presidents who had an aura for me were JFK and Barack Obama. Like the two of them, Havel was always the center of attention when he entered a crowded room, and somehow there was invariably humor when he was with a group. It was clear to me that Havel's appeal to the Charter 77 signers and members was in his humor and his theatrical gestures. As I have said frequently, the Velvet Revolution that would follow six and a half years later, with Havel at the helm, was most certainly launched by a philosopher who inspired his fellow revolutionaries with big ideas and who united them with laughter—a natural characteristic of the Czech nation. The quick wit of former secretary of state Madeleine Albright is probably more attributable to her Czech-ness than anything else. Her bold ease with humor became more pronounced as her relationship with Havel became closer.

Years later, in 2019, Wendy and I were in Prague for the thirtieth anniversary celebration of the Velvet Revolution, when I spoke to 140,000 people in Wenceslas Square. One night, we were invited to an event at the Magic Lantern Theater, where Havel's small group had plotted the revolution thirty years earlier. Those planners who were still alive stood on the stage and

Francine du Plessix Gray, Havel, and Bill.

Wendy after the party.

Bill speaking to 140,000 people in Wenceslas Square, 2019.

reviewed for a few invited friends the days and nights when they met to manage the revolutionary events. They laughed the entire time—laughing at the review of Soviet reactions to the event's spontaneous performance of the Velvet Revolution, which turned out to be an onstage comedy. It must be said that the Communist government of Czechoslovakia had not been nearly so cruel and violently repressive as the Ceauşescu government in Romania. Ceauşescu was an authentic Communist dictator, despised and feared by the Romanian people, as evidenced by the fact that he and his wife were killed by the people. This was in sharp contrast to the Velvet Revolution, which allowed for a peaceful transition in Prague. My personal experience with Ceauşescu resulted in my writing a note to the secretary of state after the Romanian leader's last state visit to the United States, which said that no other American president should again be asked to dirty his hands by greeting Ceauşescu in the White House. Ceauşescu was an example of a Communist leader who did not always follow Moscow's demands on East-West relations.

Based on the reach we achieved in our first evening introducing our collection of American contemporary paintings to a relatively large group of dissidents and artists, we planned to implement a long-term (two-year) strategy of visits of prominent friends to Prague, including visits with several major objectives.

We set out to promote the message through the Western media and create general buzz among the "chattering classes" that there was an active cultural and dissident life in Czechoslovakia and that Havel was the vital mover and shaker in that movement. We also set out to emphasize that Prague was a center of artistic and creative activity and that governments and the media in the US and Europe should pay attention. To that end, we chose to invite many writers and artists from the United States to visit and encouraged them to let the media know about the life of artists in Prague. We also invited a number of media giants to visit Prague and meet with Havel and his close group. As an example, we organized visits from Kay Graham, the publisher of the *Washington Post,* who came with her editor in chief, Meg Greenfield.

We would normally have our guests first meet with the officials of the Czechoslovak government and the state-run media, and then with the local official media, and finally with the Charter 77 spokesperson. Then we would try to arrange for meetings and interviews with Havel and one or two of his closest advisers, such as Jiří Dienstbier, his "shadow" foreign minister who would become the actual foreign minister in Havel's government. We encouraged the publication of articles on the Havel phenomenon, articles about writers, and articles about Havel, Prague's playwright who was also its leading dissident.

In addition to Kay Graham, we had visits from Henry Grunwald, the editor in chief of *TIME* magazine, along with the *TIME* bureau chief stationed in Vienna. We were also visited by Robert Bernstein, the CEO of Random House. Bob later founded and became the chairman of Human Rights Watch. We also had in Tom Wicker—one of the lead columnists of the *New York Times.*

The second category of visitors were the potential supporters of Havel's work. For example, George Soros visited Prague and stayed with us for two days, during which I introduced him to Czechoslovakia's deputy foreign minister, central banker, and minister of finance, none of whom would have come to the residence without the opportunity to meet Soros. After one of the dinners with official guests, one of the brighter members of the staff, Bill Kiehl, took Soros to meet Havel. From that time, Soros provided support to the Charter 77 Foundation that had been working out of Stockholm to support Havel's group in Prague.

The third category of visitors were prominent American political and intellectual leaders; John Kenneth Galbraith was well known in Prague for his views on the convergence between socialism and capitalism that had given much hope for the Communist economists. The dinner for Ken was attended by senior officials and financial leaders. We even managed to get an agreement to bring this leading American economist to speak at the Institute of Economics in the Academy of Sciences, the first time that had happened since the 1968 crushing of the Prague Spring. The turnout of Czech economists was exceptionally large and included individuals the embassy had not seen since the Prague Spring. Each of them brought their tattered, personal copies of Galbraith's books for him to sign. It felt almost like a church gathering.

George Kennan was also a big hit. He had served in the embassy in the 1940s and had been well known as the diplomat historian who had designed, in his "long telegram from Moscow," the containment policy for the US after World War II. All of the many guests we invited for a luncheon with Kennan knew that he had begun to distance himself from the militarization of the US containment policy during the Vietnam War and had become a strong advocate of negotiating with the Soviets.

The creative writers were the most welcomed by Havel and his colleagues because the visiting authors fostered a sense in the Czech and Slovak intellectual communities that they were now a part of the larger Western literary community. Moreover, it built a similar sense among the vast reading population of Czechoslovakia who were familiar with American writers, either in English or their own language.

Kurt Vonnegut and the Pulitzer Prize–winning poet Galway Kinnell visited Prague in the fall of 1984. I had asked Galway, a friend, to visit Prague to bring a letter by hand from Washington, DC, from President Reagan to Jaroslav Seifert, who had just won the Nobel Prize for Literature. I had written the letter and asked that President Reagan sign it and the White House return it to me as soon as possible. It was all handled very efficiently by the desk officer for Czechoslovakia in the Bureau of European Affairs. The desk officer is the universal and invaluable eyes and ears in Washington for American ambassadors in faraway countries.

I then asked Seifert if he would come to a meeting at the embassy, so that I could present him with the letter. He wanted to meet at his home. Seifert spoke little English, so I asked his family to produce a good interpreter for the meeting. The interpreter they sent was a gorgeous young Czech woman. The meeting was

Galway Kinnell congratulations on the
Nobel Prize to Jaroslav Seifert, 1984.

Kurt Vonnegut signing
books Čapek bookstore.

(below) Karel Srp and
John Updike planting
a tree at Jazz Section,
Prague.

flawed (or enhanced) by the fact that neither Galway nor Seifert, who were of an age, had written much about lust, and talked frequently of their female friends in their poetry, could take their eyes off the interpreter.

At the same time that Galway arrived in Prague, so did one of our most popular American writers. Kurt Vonnegut, whose books and contemporary avant-garde writing was greatly admired by young writers and readers, spent four days with us in March 1984. Kurt was very active. He signed books for dozens of Czechs at the Čapek Bookstore that sold books by American writers in both Czech and English. He also started a new tradition of planting a tree near the Jazz Section headquarters in the suburbs. The Czech secret police (StB) then started their own tradition of digging up the just-planted tree the following morning. Kurt also went with us to the dissident theater in Brno called Theater on the String to watch a play adapted from one of

Updike and Petr Oslzlý, Goose on a String Theatre.

his more admired books, *God Bless You, Mr. Rosewater*. The production was done by Havel's good friend Petr Oslzlý who agreed to become, for a short time, Havel's minister of culture. Following the production in Brno, I watched as Kurt was surrounded by a small group of local citizens. I walked into the group just at the moment when one of the Czechs was telling Kurt that a letter that Kurt had signed months earlier to officials had gotten him released from prison, and the man was told by police that it also saved his life.

Just after the Vonnegut visit, we were visited by our close friends, the writer Bill Styron and his poet wife Rose Styron. Thanks to the Styrons, we had come to know many of the writers who visited us in Prague. The Styrons were at the center of a world of intellectuals that doesn't exist in the US today. They were the post–World War II generation, largely white, largely male, who had been in the war and were telling the stories of

William Styron signing the wall at the Čapek Bookstore in Prague.

their lives in the military and the impact of the war on American society. The Styrons had visited us regularly in Venezuela with other writers such as Peter Matthiessen. In Prague, they met with Havel and most of the other Czech and Slovak writers we knew. Bill signed copies of *Sophie's Choice* that had been translated into Czech and Slovak at both the Čapek Bookstore and the American Embassy library. Rose Styron met separately with young writers and poets. We also met with Jaroslav Seifert, the Czech poet and Nobel laureate.

As part of my ongoing strategy to get to know the Communist government of Czechoslovakia, I developed a plan to informally "run into" Prime Minister Lubomír Štrougal, who was thought to be the most "liberal" or open member of the post-1968 government. Štrougal was the senior Czech in the government the Soviets set up after their invasion in 1968. Most of the power was put in the hands of the Slovaks, who the Soviets and Russians had always felt closer to. The Prague Spring was led by the Czechs, not only because of Havel but because the vast majority of the dissidents and reformist leaders in the Dubček government were Czechs—even though Dubček was a Slovak.

I managed to literally bump into Štrougal at the large Brno Trade Fair in the fall of 1984. I surprised him and apologized in Russian. (I knew he spoke excellent Russian and was close to many members of the Soviet Politburo.) We had a brief but courteous exchange, during which I asked to call on him. He was positive about the idea and gave me a number to call for a meeting the next week. I called, as he had suggested, and I had my first meeting with him the following Thursday evening. After dark. He arranged to have a car pick me up and drive me to his office rather than have my car seen parked there. During my first meeting, I expressed my delight with my mission and with Prague, and described my strategy of inviting prominent Americans to Prague and my hope that the US could eventually sign a bilateral agreement with the Czechoslovak government under the Helsinki Accords. He listened carefully and politely, demonstrated interest in a bilateral agreement, and complained a bit about the poor state of US-Czechoslovak relations. I told him of my talks with his foreign minister about improving relations. When it came time for me to leave, I asked the PM whether I could come see him again, particularly in case important matters were to arise out of US relations with his nation. Štrougal was surprisingly positive about the possibility of another meeting. He said, "You have the number to call if you want to meet again." I left in his car, which took me back to my driver.

Within a few months of my first meeting with Prime Minister Štrougal, Mikhail Gorbachev replaced Konstantin Chernenko as first secretary the Communist Party and became president of the USSR. Knowing that Štrougal was close to the Soviet Politburo, I called the phone number he had given me. I wanted him to explain to me the Gorbachev phenomenon. I was granted a meeting for the next week. When I arrived in Štrougal's office, I explained the reason for my particular interest. I said that my daily routine involved getting home by 6:00 p.m. every night to work out on my stationary bike while listening to Moscow TV, which was broadcast directly and live every afternoon. I told him that about a week ago I had watched Gorbachev speaking to a meeting of the local leadership of the Communist Party. I said that I had been watching Politburo leaders for years speak on TV to such groups and I was stunned by Gorbachev's informality: He did not speak from notes; he was leaning on his podium; and he called on party members to speak informally to the group and answer his probing questions about life in Leningrad. More than curious, I asked Štrougal, "Who is this new guy? He seems to be a completely new type of Soviet leader."

The prime minister was slightly amused by my questions and astonishment, and replied with modesty and great control. "Gorbachev is definitely different from Chernenko and Brezhnev," he said. "He is much younger and came to the leadership in a different way." Štrougal then went on to say that he knew a bit about Gorbachev because he had two close friends in the Politburo who told him the identical story. President Gorbachev was summoned to Yuri Andropov's bedroom, where he was lying sick. Andropov told Gorbachev that he, Andropov, would not live long and that Chernenko would die soon. Andropov then told Gorbachev that he would replace Andropov as leader, after Andropov had left the scene. Andropov alerted Gorbachev that there was likely to be less than a year from the time of Chernenko's death to the time that Andropov would die.

Andropov then turned serious and charged Gorbachev to prepare to reform the Soviet system. He warned that the only leader with any experience in reforming the system was Khrushchev. He urged Gorbachev to find Khrushchev's reform team. He said that the Soviet Union could not keep up with the United States in technology and was way behind in many sectors. The USSR must find a way to get access to the American know-how to get things done. William Taubman, in his biography of Gorbachev, suggests a more complex transition of power from Chernenko to Gorbachev, and includes a discussion of the long relationship that Andropov maintained with Gorbachev.

Indeed, at one point, as chairman of the Harriman Institute at Columbia University, I introduced Gorbachev to a crowd at a large dinner party and told the story I had heard from Štrougal in Prague. At the end of my introduction, I asked Gorbachev whether the story was accurate. He smiled at me and said, "It is certainly true that Andropov was one of my great patrons."

Another close adviser on Soviet reforms was the prominent sociologist Tatyana Zaslavskaya, whom I had known through a close friend, Boris Grushin. Grushin was the founder of the first polling institute in the USSR. It was called Vox Populi. Grushin, along with Zaslavskaya, had been part of Khrushchev's reform group, many of whom had been exiled after Khrushchev was dumped by the Politburo in 1964. They spent their exile in Prague, working with some of the Communist front organizations that had headquarters in Prague. This group of reformers were in Prague during the buildup to the Prague Spring—the reform effort in Czechoslovakia that sought to build Communism with a human face, and which provoked Brezhnev and the Soviet leaders in 1968 to order the Warsaw Pact invasion of Czechoslovakia. Boris Grushin reported that the Soviet reformers who were in Prague in the mid-1960s often referred to themselves as the Club of Prague.

Grushin, a philosopher and writer, returned to Prague to live with his family after the dust had settled from the Soviet invasion. He spent two years doing the research for his book, published in Czech, *In Pivo Veritas* ("In Beer Is Truth"), which is the result of his research into nearly one thousand beer halls in Prague, each of which has its own favorite saying on the wall about beer.

Edward Albee and Wendy.

In the spring of 1986, we finally arranged for Edward Albee to visit Prague. Edward and I had been friends since our time together in the Soviet Union in the early 1960s. I knew that Edward was directing three one-act plays by Sam Shepard at the English-language repertory theater in Vienna. He agreed to drive with his acting troupe to Prague from Vienna to perform those three plays for the official theater organization in the Old Town of Prague, at their small theater. The deal we made with this very conservative official section of the Prague theater world was that the embassy would invite fifty people from the American side and the theater organization would invite fifty from their official theater groups. In fact, we invited many Czechs from the avant-garde theater world instead of Americans. We chose not to invite Havel to that event since that would probably be an overreach on the "hospitality" of our Czech hosts. Instead, we arranged for Havel to meet with Albee and the actors in the courtyard of the theater, prior to the performance. At the time the performance was to begin, we were invited into the theater. The director of the theater was to introduce me, then I was to present Edward, who would then provide the context for the Shepard plays. The opening did not go as planned. Instead, the director stood before the audience and announced that there had been a mishap: Mr. Albee had been locked outside in the courtyard. So, the large officious key lady was asked to unlock the large door to the hall and let Edward into the theater. Edward walked in with dozens of additional young theater people. After that embarrassing episode, which demonstrated the closed environment in which the theater operated in Prague in those years, the three plays gave that Czech theater audience a good sense of what the avant-garde was like in the US.

After the performance, we had invited all the guests from the official theater organization to come to the residence for a late, buffet dinner. We invited Havel to come to supper, as well. I was relieved that none of the officials walked out of the dinner. It turned out that none of them even complained to me. We sat at a long table. At one end were Edward, Havel, and Wendy. At the other end of the table, with me and the embassy cultural officer, were Czech theater officials.

About halfway toward completing our agenda of visits to Prague, we began to question whether the elaborate plans were worth the strain on the staff of the embassy and on Wendy and me. Years afterward, in 2014, Michael Žantovský published his prize-winning biography *Havel: A Life*, and we got a partial answer on page 250:

It is true that prison taught him (Havel) some elements of self-preservation and discretion that he had previously lacked. But if anything he exhibited more energy and discipline than before, most of it spent on the dissident cause and a large part directly outside the country. Keenly aware of how much the protests had contributed to his largely indifferent if not kind treatment in prison and eventually to his release, and how close the Charter came to extinction during his absence, he realized that there was not much future to the fight unless he made it global. He had some help from several quarters.

Thanks to the remarkable diplomacy of William Luers, who had been American Ambassador to Prague from 1983–1986, his wife Wendy, and a few of his fellow diplomats, Charter 77 and the whole Czechoslovak intellectual opposition had never been cut off from the world of ideas and politics from across the ocean. One of the things that made life in "normalized" Czechoslovakia more bearable if not trouble-free was going to the Ambassador's grand Residence in Prague and meeting with Kurt Vonnegut, Bill and Rose Styron, Edward Albee, John Updike, and Philip Roth and others. This called for an elaborate choreography since the government bureaucrats that the Ambassador had to entertain would not be caught in the same room with the washouts and self-appointed. They would not even be caught with them in the garden. On his arrival at the 1985 US Independence Day Celebration in Prague, a brilliant sunny day, the deputy Czechoslovak Foreign Minister Jaromir Johanes, representing the communist government, took about a minute before he recognized Havel among the guests milling about the lawn. Johanes said "he is here," spun around and walked out with all the other officials from the Foreign Ministry.[53]

The issue of whether to invite dissidents to national day celebrations of the NATO states—like our celebration of the Fourth of July—that had embassies in Prague had become highly contentious among NATO ambassadors there. We met monthly in one of those embassies that had a safe room. At virtually every one of our meetings, one of the ambassadors would raise the question of whether to invite Havel or members of Charter 77 and risk irritating the Czech government.

We had invited Havel to my first Fourth of July as ambassador. According to Žantovský, the only other ambassador who did something similar was the French ambassador, who invited to Czech government officials at noon and the dissidents at 4:00 p.m. In effect, he celebrated Bastille Day twice, separately. This made Havel and the other dissidents feel like second-class citizens. The discussions on this issue among Prague's ambassadors occasionally became heated, since some ambassadors claimed that the American Embassy's approach to Havel and company was interfering with the work of the other NATO embassies. None of my colleagues was ever able to show me how the US practice of inviting Havel was interfering with goals of our NATO allies. I contended that the US actions were fully consistent with the Helsinki Accords, to which we were all signatories. Given the unusually close historic connection between the US and Czechoslovakia (whose constitution was signed in Philadelphia, and whose first president, Thomas Masaryk, was a close friend of the US), and since there were many Americans whose families are Czech or Slovak, I wanted to make a special effort to be conscious of the human rights aspect of my work in Prague.

Eventually, I became convinced that the government was complaining to my NATO colleagues about our practices, which left me particularly disturbed.

Then, when I returned to Washington in August of 1984, shortly after my first celebration of July 4, I was invited to a meeting in the office of the assistant secretary for Europe. The assistant secretary had agreed to receive a visit from the Czechoslovak ambassador in Washington, who had requested to come in to complain about Ambassador Luers's conduct in Prague. I joined the meeting willingly and heard the Czechoslovak ambassador complain that I had arrived in Prague as the American ambassador accredited by the government in Prague and not by a group of private citizens who opposed the government. The assistant secretary fully supported my inviting of Havel and others from Charter 77 to the American national day. He then invited me to respond directly to the ambassador. I said very seriously, "Please do not ask us to choose between these two groups." That ambassador, who I had known well in Prague before he was assigned to Washington, departed the meeting having carried out his formal instructions and having been rebuffed, as was often the case in relations between our two states during the Cold War and after the Soviet intervention in the Prague Spring.

In the fall of 1985, I received a welcome call from an old friend, J. Richardson Dilworth: the board of the Metropolitan Museum of Art in New York City had voted to offer me the job of president of the museum. I was thrilled and honored, and a bit surprised by the opportunity.

But before I left for New York, there was much left to do in Prague. The other dimension of our strategy of dealing with the Czech government diplomatically and traditionally had borne fruit: we had gotten approval from the US and the government in Prague to sign an agreement that provided for two years of scientific and cultural cooperation. Foreign Minister Chňoupek wanted this agreement to make certain that a full assistant secretary of state would visit Prague, but also to demonstrate that he had been able to take his country out of the pariah category the US had placed them in for twenty years. The grand signing was set for April 16, 1986. Assistant Secretary for Europe Rozanne Ridgway would arrive in Prague for an overnight before the signing. Roz was to arrive midday, by commercial air, on April 15.

As usual in dealing with relations between Prague and Washington, stuff happens to complicate even the best planned events. I woke up on the morning of April 15 to the news that President Reagan had ordered an attack on Libya, which had taken place that morning in retaliation for an attack by Libya on a bar in Berlin in which two Americans had been killed. Now, Czechoslovakia had close friendly relations with Libya. The issue was how to manage what was going to be an even more hostile than usual Communist government in Prague. The deputy foreign minister, who was to join me in welcoming Roz, asked me whether Roz might have been involved in the decision to bomb Libya. I assured him that she could not have been in on that decision

Bill signing the CSCE Agreement.

and why. When Roz arrived, she handled all the questions along that line professionally and reassuringly. When we met the foreign minister that afternoon, he looked as though his world was collapsing. But he was measured. He asked what I thought the Soviet reaction would be to the bombing. I tried to reassure him that the Soviets would complain a lot but would not likely take any severe action. Before dinner with the foreign minister that night, I went home to change and listened to Voice of America, with the clear message from Moscow that they were cutting back all cultural and educational exchange programs with the US. When we got back to the Foreign Ministry for dinner, Chňoupek looked at me quizzically, as if to ask *What more have you heard?* I told him nothing specific from Moscow. I recommended we go forward with the dinner and the signing of the agreement after dinner, as originally planned.

(both photos) Ambassador Luers commemorating the
American liberation of Southern Bohemia, WWII.

There was at least one other behavior of the American Embassy that offended the government in Prague. For years, the ambassador would lead a caravan tour by embassy staff, including the military attachés in full uniform, to remind citizens in the country about the role the Americans played in liberating fourteen towns in southern Bohemia and about the American pilots who were shot down over eastern Czech lands and Slovakia. This tribute is called the Convoy. The military attachés, who spent a great deal of time planning these annual visits, found these trips inspiring and fun—they made possible real contacts with local citizens on an important issue for both nations. We all felt the trips were important, as we knew that the Communist government of Czechoslovakia was determined to run information and educational programs that were designed to help people forget about their history—and particularly America's role in it. Our tours in the spring and fall were designed to revive memories of the US role in the victory over Nazi Germany. A particular favorite stop for me was me Říčany, a town just north of Plzeň, which was the closest town to Prague reached by Patton's tanks. There was always a large turnout there, and we had come to know many of the community's members who were regulars at those annual visitations. This pattern had grown and been formalized over a number of years. Each year, the staff would prepare a speech for the ambassador that explained the specific characteristic of the liberation of each town. The speech would be translated into Czech, and the American ambassador would prerecord each speech (twenty-four or twenty-five a year) in Czech for Radio Free Europe. The words of the American ambassador's speech in Czech would then be broadcast, starting two weeks before the visit, specifying the time and location of the event.

The embassy team would arrive in five or six cars, with the ambassador's car flying the American flag on the front right fender (as permitted by international protocol). The ambassador's speech would normally be overridden by loudspeakers playing national patriotic music, strategically positioned around the square we had selected to hold the event. Local officials were encouraged by officials in Prague to be creative in disrupting the American events.

The authorities in Strakonice, on my final tour before leaving Prague, may have gotten overly enthusiastic about how best to send a message that the American Embassy cease these annoying events to promote the memory of America's effort, during World War II, to liberate their country. In Strakonice, we had traditionally managed to gather one of our largest crowds. In May 1986, after my speech in St. Wenceslas Square to a crowd of around a thousand, a group of older men moved toward me, pushing an old woman in a wheelchair. She had in her hand a plate holding a piece of bread. I recognized the offering—Slavs welcome visitors with bread and salt. The Russians have a verb that is literally "to bread and salt a person" (*xleb y solovats*), which means to welcome them. This woman offered me the bread, which I accepted and took a bite of. I bowed and thanked her for the welcome. Wendy and I left the church square and went directly back to our car. Waiting for us was our official driver, a Czech man called "Shorty," who unquestionably was an official in the Czech secret police (StB). Shorty was to drive us to Munich, about fifty miles across the German border. Going back to the car, I began to feel a pain in my gut, which I thought was provoked by eating the bread and salt.

By the time we were in the car and heading toward the

German border and Munich, the pain had become severe, unlike anything I had ever experienced. Wendy, my innovative and activist wife, found a way to call our Consul General in Munich. The duty officer in Munich found a German hospital not far from where we were. Shorty drove us to the hospital, which had been alerted by the consulate. Three doctors, all dressed in comforting white, greeted Wendy and me at the hospital's emergency entrance. They immediately took me to a room where they administered a general antidote and proceeded to take steps to reduce the pain. Within a matter of minutes, I was feeling better. The doctors agreed that if I had ingested poison it would not be traceable in my blood by then. The only way to confirm that I had eaten poisoned bread would be to examine the piece of bread. Wendy and I looked at each other: *"The bread!"*

We realized we had left it in the car with our driver, Shorty. Wendy went to the car, and, not surprisingly, he had already tossed away the bread. We would not be able to recover it. So we had a quandary. The German doctors said they thought I had ingested poison and treated me accordingly. But they could not prove it.

Driving back to Munich, Wendy and I discussed whether we should make a fuss with the government in Prague or even tell the Department of State about our suspicions. The next day, in Munich, I met with the American doctor in the consulate. We both concluded that it would not make sense to charge the government of Czechoslovakia with foul play, and agreed that without some proof, I should not make an issue of my suspicions to the US. Meanwhile, the doctor took some blood tests and examined me thoroughly to determine whether he might find traces of poison. He agreed with the German doctors that traces of arsenic and most other serious poisons leave the system rather quickly. In the end, I decided not to report the unhappy moment to anyone.

Back in Prague the following week, we were still trying to wrap up my tour as ambassador and my career as an FSO, and prepare for my responsibilities in my new job at the Met.

We left Prague on April 24 for a new life in New York. By that time, I had lived half of my mature life outside of the US. New York had become a particularly appealing city for me since I had attended Columbia University for graduate school in Russian studies, after my tour with the US Navy.

As a matter of record, I did not completely leave Prague. Wendy and I continued to keep in touch with our many Czech and Slovak friends. We kept in very close touch with Havel and his many colleagues from Charter 77, many of whom came to stay with us in New York.

The doorman at the apartment building on Fifth Avenue owned by the Met, where we would live while I was president of the museum, knew that if a visitor speaking Czech or with red hair came calling (all six of our children are redheads), they would be welcome guests of the Luers.

CHAPTER 12

The Metropolitan Museum of Art, Part I

I was informed by J. Richardson Dilworth, in the fall of 1985, while still serving as the American Ambassador to Czechoslovakia, that the Board of Directors of the Metropolitan Museum of Art of New York had voted to offer me the job of president of the museum. It was a step I was ready to take, even after my exciting tenure as ambassador in Czechoslovakia.

Dick Dilworth and I had come to know each other while I was the director's visitor at the Institute for Advanced Study, in Princeton, NJ. I had been invited to the institute by Harry Woolf, a prominent historian of science at Princeton who also was the director of the institute at the time. George Kennan, whom I had long admired and served with, was at the institute working as a resident scholar. At the time, he was working on the manuscript that would become *The Fateful Alliance: France, Russia, and the Coming of the First World War*. Harry, knowing of my regard for Kennan and our similar interests, had invited me to the institute, also to write. Kennan and I had offices next to each other.

It was while I was in Princeton that I met Dick Dilworth, as he served as chairman of the board of the institute. He and his wife became close friends with me and Wendy during the nine months I was there (1982–1983). As it happened, Wendy

Wendy and Bill in the American Wing.

had been close friends for years with the Dilworths' daughter, Melissa. Bunny Dilworth, Dick's wife, was deeply involved in the arts and was very interested to learn of my own involvement in, and efforts through the years to promote, the arts and culture while serving as ambassador to Venezuela and earlier in the Soviet Union. Bunny would later urge Dick (who was also on the board of the Met), to propose me for a senior position at the Met. Dick and Bunny would go on to be frequent guests of ours in Prague.

In 1983, several months before I was confirmed by the Senate to be ambassador to Czechoslovakia, Dick Dilworth was promoted from vice chairman of the board of directors of the Metropolitan Museum of Art to chairman of the board. He replaced the venerable Douglas Dillon, former secretary of the treasury and ambassador to France. Then, in December of 1983, a few weeks before I was to depart for my new post in Prague, Dick asked me whether I would consider becoming president of the Met—a position he thought might open up in the next couple of years. I said I would be greatly honored to be considered for the position. Out of principle, I never said no to theoretical offers of employment. But Dick's offer came as a complete surprise.

When I learned, three years later, that I had been selected as the next president of the Met, I immediately began to plan how to prepare for that challenging new post in a city I did not know well. First, I had to learn the museum's context and language. I had made a number of friends in American museums over the years, and I began to invite them to come stay with us in Prague. In particular, I had gotten to know Bill Rubin, the director of the Museum of Modern Art (MoMA) in New York. I had also gotten to know many museum directors in Central Europe and the Soviet Union, and Wendy and I were good friends of the director of the National Gallery in Prague, with whom we had worked in concert on multiple occasions to highlight the work of Czechoslovakian and American artists. Another good friend was the painter Richard Diebenkorn, who was already due to visit us in Prague. We invited John Richardson, the Picasso scholar, to visit us again. Richardson had taken us to see the precious collection of Picasso masterpieces in the Prague National Gallery. We called on and received the prominent gallery owner, André

Emmerich, who had visited us in Caracas as a lender of one of the paintings to be displayed in our residence in Caracas. Finally, we had a stream of painters and collectors who had already visited us in Prague, including the painter Cleve Gray and his wife, Francine du Plessix Gray; collectors Sid and Anne Bass; and Patty Phelps de Cisneros. Sid and Patty, as it turned out, were on the board of MoMA in NYC. Following the announcement of my appointment, I also invited Philippe de Montebello to visit us in Prague. Philippe, with whom I would be working side by side for many years, was the director of the Met.

My second big task for my new job was to prepare myself to read balance sheets. A close friend from Martha's Vineyard, Sheldon Hackney, was the president of the University of Pennsylvania. I asked Sheldon whether he could put together a crash course for me on budgeting and understanding balance sheets.

At the Met, I was to be the chief administrative officer of the museum, with the title of president, while Philippe would continue to be the director of the Met. Philippe's primary responsibility would not change: he was responsible for the art. My primary responsibility was to manage budgets and finance. Government officials, particularly ambassadors, are not known for their savvy on budgets; I wanted to be different. Sheldon set up a crash course for me in June and July of 1986 at the Wharton School. The experience was profoundly worthwhile. Within months of my assuming the responsibilities of president, I learned that one of the biggest dysfunctionalities in the Met's management was the secretive way the budget was built. Money is power, and the allocation of money defines who has the power. It was no different at the Met. The first person I replaced was the CFO, who was a Princetonian and well known by the

Princeton graduates on the board. He had served at Citibank as a personnel manager, but had no experience managing budgets or money and was one of the most secretive men I encountered in my years at the Met.

When I arrived, the responsibility for creating the secretive budgets had been shared between that CFO and Philippe's longtime assistant. After the CFO departed, Philippe asked his assistant also to leave. In a remarkable short period of time, they were both gone. Philippe's decision to fire his longtime assistant gave me the opportunity to find both a new CFO *and* a budget officer who would build the annual budget for the Met more transparently. Philippe and I agreed on a new, more open way to build the budget, and we moved forward with alacrity and transparency. The new CFO and budget officer designed a new budget process that created a program of meetings with every department head to discuss that department's needs and expectations for the coming year. One big goal had been met. We were able to accomplish this early in my tenure.

I knew from everyone I had spoken with at the Met, including Dick Dilworth, that the biggest and certainly most important challenges would be how I dealt with Philippe and the curatorial staff who had been opposed to the Met's experiment with divided leadership, which had started in 1978. I was only the second full-time president of the Met.

Eight years before my appointment, the Met's Board of Directors had been guided by the chairman of the board and President Douglas Dillon. Douglas held that as a volunteer part-time president he was unable to keep in touch with the daily operations of the museum and balance the decisions taken by the museum staff. Douglas believed that the job of president was too large to be held by a part-time member of the board of directors. Douglas's stature was so large that the board of directors chose to follow his recommendations and sought to identify a candidate to fill the new job of president and CEO. The CEO of the Met subsequently selected William Macomber to be the new president and CEO to run the museum. It was probably that initial decision— to make the new president the CEO—that set off the fury among the curatorial staff, which suggested a downgrading of the traditional role of the director. Indeed, when I became president, I was told by the board that I would share with Philippe the leadership of the museum, leaving the CEO issue ambiguous and requiring the president and director to work together closely to resolve the big issues that might arise. The Dillon decision to divide the leadership was not arrived at easily; nor was it a decision that was accepted with enthusiasm. I already had some intimation of the heat that still circulated around this issue. Some of that heat had been present when Philippe and I had breakfast during my trip to New York for the interview with the board.

Dick Dilworth had invited me to breakfast with Philippe. Dick introduced us and then left us alone. I decided to go directly to the point. I said to Philippe, "If I were to be selected as president of the museum, what would be the one thing you would want to tell me that worries you about that?" He was taken aback by the directness of my question. I presume he expected us to dance around the issue for a while, until we got to know each other better. He thought about my question for a short while, then said, "What I would worry about is that you would appear on the *Today* show, or some other TV show, to talk about a special exhibition at the Met."

My question and his answer opened a good discussion

about how he defined his job as director and what he thought the president's role should be. It became clearer than it already was that Philippe and the Met's museum community considered the director to be the intellectual leader of the museum and the spokesperson for all art, education, and aesthetics. Knowing this, I entered the job understanding the guideposts on my role and the limits of my responsibilities. Over my thirteen years at the Met, there were differences between my office and Philippe's over methods and certain policies. But the museum thrived, and our collaboration worked well, mainly because Philippe and I wanted to make it work, as did the senior staff and the board.

Another big uncertainty in taking on the job of president of the Met was whether I could raise money. My guru on this matter was Dick Dilworth. He told me, "All you have to do is ask the right person at the right time." On timing for new donors, he gave me an intriguing generalization about New Yorkers. He said, "When ambitious men come to New York, they first want to 'get on,' that is, make a great deal of money. Then, they want to 'get honest,' that is, clean up their act, if necessary. Then they want to 'get honor.'

"You want to ask them for money between phases two and three; honesty and honor," Dilworth advised.

With this as a philosophical base, I had a long talk with Larry Tisch, who had become my second guru on the Met board. He was kind, welcoming, and a wise and generous philanthropist. After he repeated several times that the biggest hurdle for most beginners in fundraising is to get to the point of asking for the money and describing the project to be funded, I looked directly at him and asked whether he and his brother (they made their large commitments together) would give $10 million to fund a large (twenty thousand square feet) gallery that would be used for our special exhibitions at the Met.

"The Met needs the money for the new Tisch Gallery," I said. "That gallery would become the prominent location for our special exhibitions." (Special exhibitions drive attendance at the Museum.) Larry said yes, they would indeed donate the $10 million. He also said that they would pay off their pledge over ten years. This struck me as a long time, but Larry had committed his foundation on the spot and followed through with a signed promise agreement.

It was a promising, generous first step. But I now needed to raise an additional $40 million—the amount needed to build the new wing of the museum, which would house the new Tisch Gallery.

So, having raised $10 million from the Tisch brothers, I set out to raise money for the new courtyard, which would be created in tandem with and as a part of the new wing. As part of this effort, I began to speak with a new donor about the Met's needs vis-à-vis the new wing. Our talks were positive and continued for several months, but he kept putting me off. Finally, I told him that I felt he did not truly want to commit to funding the new space at the museum. He agreed and said that if I could find another donor who would agree to contribute the amount of money I was seeking, he would gratefully step aside. That night, I was attending a large reception in the city. While we were there, I noticed that Henry Kravis was there as well. I had been on shooting trips with Henry, and once even took him on a tour of St. Petersburg. I began talking to him about the new wing of the Met. When he began to show real interest, I asked him whether he would make a $10 million gift to the museum for the new wing. He immediately said he would like to do it, and we agreed to meet at his office the following Wednesday with his lawyer to draw up the agreement. We met that next week and signed the agreement for what is now the Henry R. Kravis Wing of the Met.

All along, I was keeping Larry Tisch informed on my progress in raising funds for the new wing. He had become engaged with my efforts and noted that he played bridge on Saturdays with Bernie Cantor, whom the Met knew well. Cantor was in the process of donating a number of Rodin sculptures that were being cast as part of a collaboration with the Rodin collection in Paris to produce copies of Rodin's complete oeuvre. Larry Tisch said he would ask Bernie Cantor whether he would join him in providing a $10 million contribution to the museum, again for the new wing. Bernie agreed, and we now had $30 million that, together with the money we had received from smaller donors and from the city, was enough to start to build the new wing.

Underlying all of this good news in my first year at the Met was my understanding that the talents needed for the job were not too different from those required by my profession of diplomacy. I was becoming more confident that I could make this venture work.

Continuing my role as one of the guardians of the Met's finances, I became a tennis partner and friend of David Dinkins, the mayor of New York City. He invited Wendy and me to take two diplomatic trips overseas as official members of his delegation. The mayor was important to the Met because he was able to earmark gifts for capital projects within the city's budget for the Met, in addition to the substantial annual support the city gives to the Met. The Met building is essentially owned by the city, even though the works of art are owned by the corporation, a not-for-profit entity run by the board of trustees. I also developed a close working relationship with the Cultural Institutions Group, which is composed of the leaders of the city's cultural institutions that are supported by New York City's government. The Met, which is by far the largest recipient of city funds, has a permanent membership within and partnership with this group. The Met must also work closely with the City Council, the mayor's office, and the mayor's commissioner for cultural affairs, who became a close friend. The outside work of the Met president is an essential element of the senior Met leadership. Wendy and I lived in a splendid Met apartment at 993 Fifth Avenue across the street where we entertained constantly for the Met.

When I arrived at the Met, the museum was open to the public on Tuesday evenings, which was a night that clearly was not drawing large crowds. Moreover, our visitors were mainly elderly. This was a concern, as our long-term objectives were to increase weekly attendance and reach a lower average age of regular visitors for whom visiting the Met was a habit. I began questioning Dick Morsches, our long-term chief of operations, why the museum was open Tuesday evenings. Would it not be better to be open on Friday and Saturday evenings, when most New Yorkers look for relaxing evening activities, go out on dates, and meet up with friends? Dick said that opening on Friday and Saturday nights would mean that we would have to pay the guards overtime because of the contract we have with the union. The math suggested that the payment of double time to the guards for

Bill, Bishop Tutu, and Wendy.

Curator of Japanese Galleries Barbara Ford, Wendy,
Crown Prince, Crown Princess of Japan, interpreter, Bill.

their overtime would eat up any revenue gain from an increase in visitors. Dick and I continued to talk about the guards and he became characteristically creative by rotating the guards around their preferred days of the week for work, and freeing up non-overtime hours.

With that issue resolved, we took the idea of opening on Friday and Saturday to the senior staff, most of whom were enthusiastic about the idea. Emily Rafferty, who managed the membership of museum visitors and was always ready for any good idea; the press office; the finance office; and the membership and admissions offices all chipped in with additional ideas to make Friday and Saturday evenings at the Met more special. Some of these ideas included adding music in the Great Hall, making drinks available for purchase, and advertising "Saturday Night at the Met" as the least expensive date in New York City. The changes were marvelously successful; over the next two years, every major museum in New York was opening on Friday and

Jules Feiffer, Wendy Gimbel, Rose Styron, Henry Grunwald,
Beverly Sills, Steve Rattner, Walter Cronkite, Bill, Louis Grunwald,
Wendy, Maureen White, Michael Kramer, Lynn Forester.

Saturday evenings, as well. Making the visual arts available on weekend nights to culturally minded New Yorkers and visitors from around the world—as Broadway was and as the too-numerous-to-count concert venues were—was one of the most popular decisions made during my tenure.

Another innovation we created specifically targeted our international visitors. By the mid-1980s, the majority of visitors to the Met were not from the US. During one of my periods volunteering at the round visitors' desk at the entry to the Great Hall, I watched as the docents or volunteers answered questions on what was on display and where certain objects could be found. "No, we do not have the Mona Lisa on display" was a frequent rejoinder.

It was then that I realized how many of our visitors had little or no fluency in English. I discussed this clear shortcoming with Emily Rafferty and with Dick Morshes. We agreed to ask our docents, many of whom were fluent native speakers of non-English languages, to sit at a table in the Great Hall to answer complex questions about the museum and current exhibitions to visitors who were not Americans. We eventually began publishing brochures and maps in languages other than English and conducting tours of the Met in languages other than English. Our polyglot volunteers contributed generously and abundantly to internationalizing the Met and opening it to the world. Good things were beginning to happen, and I was pleased with the changes we were making. But much larger goals beckoned during my first year.

In the fall of 1986, my first year on the job, Wendy and I were invited to dinner at the apartment of Mort and Linda Janklow, two New Yorkers at the core of New York's leaders of the arts in the city. Mort was the head and founder of the most prestigious literary agency in the city, and Linda was the chairman of the Lincoln Center Theater and was from one of the most important families (she had been a Warner) in the film industry. She had lived most of her life in Hollywood.

We came to know the Janklows shortly after we arrived in NYC. The dinner that evening turned out to be just the four of us. The Janklows had an agenda, as we discovered during the postprandial discussion when Mort said that he and Linda had decided that I was the perfect person at the Met to ask Walter and Lee Annenberg for their priceless collection of impressionist and postimpressionist paintings for the Met and New York. Mort had thought through a strategy to get the Met to win this extraordinary collection, which was sought by many of the major museums in the US.

In detail, they explained to us the Annenbergs' frustration and even anger with the Met's management over many years, particularly during the years in which Thomas Hoving had been the director of the museum. Hoving had persuaded the Annenbergs that the Met should undertake to sponsor a series of films about its collection. Ambassador Annenberg bought into the idea, including Hoving's proposal that the Met build a new, large wing, funded by the Annenbergs, on the backside of the Met's main building. This new wing would house the production facilities for the new film venture, which would be funded by and named after Walter Annenberg.

When word got out that the Met was planning to go into the film industry and build a new building in Central Park, the media flew into a rage . . . against Walter Annenberg. The Met lost control of the publicity *and* the media coverage, which began to take on an anti-Semitic tone.

The hostility in NYC toward this new film venture ultimately killed the project and, according to the Janklows, almost
killed any chance the Met would have of receiving the much
sought-after Annenberg collection of masterpieces. Mort and
Linda speculated on which other museums had a shot at the
collection. The Philadelphia Museum of Art probably had the
first call on the Annenberg collection because Philadelphia was
their home and the base of Walter's media empire. The Annenbergs knew the director, Anne d'Harnoncort, well, but the Philadelphia museum was not large and was not a major world class
museum like the Met.

Another contender was certainly the Los Angeles County
Museum of Art, since the Annenbergs' favorite house was Sunnylands in Rancho Mirage, not far from LA. Their paintings
hung permanently in Sunnylands, where they were seen regularly by the top leaders of the Republican Party establishment—
Richard Nixon, Ronald Reagan, and Gerald Ford, all of whom
called California home.

The Janklows agreed the most serious competitor of the Met
was the National Gallery of Art in Washington, DC, because
Walter Annenberg was a patriotic American who was particularly proud of his service as the ambassador to the Court of
St. James's. An important element that could swing the choice
to the National Gallery of Art was the charm and savvy of the
National Gallery of Art's director, Carter Brown, who was strategic, polished, and extremely well connected politically. The
Janklows indicated they would be surprised if Carter did not
already have a deal with Walter: the two of them already had a
close relationship.

I asked Mort and Linda what advantage the Met had in this quest. They replied in rapid fire that *I* was the logical person to ask Walter because Wendy and I knew both Walter and Lee personally, because I carried none of the baggage of the Met from the era of Tom Hoving, and because Lee was a member of the board of trustees and would most likely favor the collection going to the Met, because it was in New York and it was the premier museum of its scale in the world.

"If you can cut out all the noise, Walter and Lee will see that all the arguments favor their collection going to the Met," said Mort. He and Linda also put a large emphasis on the role I could play as a former ambassador in enhancing the Met's chances.

As the night went on, it became clear to Wendy and me that the Janklows' only agenda was to help the Met succeed in greatly upgrading its collection and its position among the world's museums. They had prepared their case with great care and with an impressive grasp of the issues, in the ways many New Yorkers do, for their city.

I was impressed by their presentation and knew that it was a strategy I needed to discuss with Philippe. I was already quite alert to his sensitivity on the divided leadership, and I needed to use caution in my approach. After doing some research, I first had a conversation with Ashton Hawkins, who had been general counsel during the Hoving years and was the most knowledgeable staff person on the dynamics among the board of trustees. Ashton confirmed most of the Janklows' report and also confirmed the likely competition the Met would face in attracting the Annenberg collection. He doubted that any approach would carry the day with Walter, who remained quite angry that the

Met and New York City had so mismanaged the public relations side of the film venture wing planned for the Met. I also discussed it with Emily Rafferty who also had worked at the Met under Hoving during that controversial episode.

When we finally met with Philippe, the general consensus was that the Janklow analysis was correct: Walter had been soured on the Met by the melee caused by his $20 million offer to fund a center for communications on art, which would eventually give graduate degrees and would be run by Tom Hoving. Philippe and others concluded that it would be extremely unlikely that Walter would think positively about a Met approach about leaving his collection to the museum.

In the end, the Met leadership decided that I could do no harm by asking Walter whether he might consider leaving his collection to the Met. I told the leadership that I needed to inform myself about the event that had so soured the Annenbergs. Over the next few months, through careful reading of the files and minutes of board meetings, I learned that Walter disliked and distrusted André Meyer, after whom the current impressionist galleries had been named. I also learned that Douglas Dillon, then chairman and president of the Met, had recommended to the board, without any prior agreement with Meyer, that the new nineteenth-century European paintings and sculpture galleries, located in the new Rockefeller Wing on the south end of the Met, would also be named the André Meyer Galleries. I learned, too, that there had been no contract between André Meyer and the Met committing us to naming those galleries after him. This was important should there ever be a chance that we could name those galleries after the Annenbergs.

Having received the "mandate" from senior leadership that

approaching Walter would do no harm, I scheduled a private meeting with him during the Met's spring board meeting, which is traditionally held in the Cloisters in Fort Tryon Park in Upper Manhattan.

As planned, Walter and I met together at the Cloisters during the 1987 board meeting of the museum. There is no more lovely setting at any museum. It was a clear sunny day; the weather, the timing, and the setting seemed to bless my mission. Or rather, my mission seemed to be blessed until I asked Walter to sit with me in a small chapel adjoining the board's meeting space. At that point, Walter warned me, "Bill, if you are going to ask me for a large amount of money, let's not have the conversation in a Catholic chapel." This, obviously, cast a different light on my mission, which had seemed "blessed" only moments earlier. I smiled and moved us to the ramparts, a sunny terrace only steps away, to two stone benches where we sat facing each other. He waited for a pitch from me for a big gift, as he must have done thousands of times during his life as a megaphilanthropist.

I asked Walter whether he and Lee had decided what they planned to do with their magnificent collection of paintings yet. He was clearly surprised by that question. And I was pleased that he did not say, "Sorry, Bill, we have already promised the collection to the National Gallery of Art."

I do not think he had yet had this discussion with any other museum. When he gathered his footing, he said that he and Lee had not decided, but they certainly were not going to sell the collection. "You must understand," he stressed to me, "we think of these works of art as our children. We have discussed turning Sunnylands into a destination site commemorating our life together and our art collection. We have thought to use the

location as a site for the study of the collection and as a location
for international gatherings of statesmen, to continue the way
Lee and I have used our home. We might also leave the collection
to a museum for the expanded study of the art and so that more
of the world's population can experience this collection."

We spoke for another half an hour about the fate of his "children," and he ended by thanking me for the interesting conversation. I said I hoped we could return to the subject. He then
told me that I could be in touch with his trusted lawyer William
Heinrich, at a law firm in Philadelphia.

After my talk with Walter, I called Philippe to report what
Walter had said, noting that he had not denied my request. I
explained Walter's comments about the plans that he and Lee
had been discussing for the future of their "children" and that
one of the possibilities was to leave it with a museum. I told him
we had left the issue by agreeing to remain in touch and that he
had told me about his lawyer William Heinrich in Philadelphia.

I made a particular point of stressing the importance of Lee
Annenberg to the process. I was not at all certain that the muse-
um's professionals and some of the trustees had a high regard for
Lee as a force in Walter's decision making. I told Philippe that
I had first gotten to know Lee in 1982, when she was President
Reagan's chief of protocol and I was ambassador to Venezuela.
The president of Venezuela was making a state visit to Washington, and Lee and I had connected and bonded over this collaboration. Over the years, I had had many dealings with her and
found her very intelligent, savvy, and with good judgment. I told
Philippe that I was convinced that Walter honored these qualities
in Lee. I also told him that my wife, Wendy, was working closely
with Lee to establish a private sector NGO, the Foundation for

Art and Preservation in Embassies (FAPE), of which Lee became chairperson and Wendy became president. FAPE was established when George Shultz was secretary of state. Wendy confirmed to me on an almost daily basis the savvy and good judgment shown by Lee at every roadblock that came up in the process of establishing the new complex institution.

I told Philippe that I was optimistic that Walter and Lee would end up deciding to leave their collection with the Met. Philippe said he did not share my optimism. Indeed, he retained this pessimism almost through the entire time of our negotiations. Perhaps this was because the issues he had to resolve were the most complicated. What did the gift consist of? Would it be only the paintings? Or would it include the Steuben glass art objects, the many photographs, and the Wyeth portrait of Walter? Would such personal memorabilia need to be included

Lee Kimche McGrath, Lee Annenberg, George Shultz,
and Wendy at inaugural dinner for FAPE, 1986.

in the presumed Annenberg Galleries? Could Walter's works of art be allowed to go outside the Met on loan? Could they be loaned to exhibitions at the Met, as long as they did not leave the museum? Questions and complications abounded.

Despite his skepticism, Philippe remained creative and committed to the venture throughout the negotiations. One encouraging indicator that there was reason for optimism is that Philippe and I, plus our wives, were invited to spend a weekend in Sunnylands in February, less than a year after I made the first approach to Walter.

A vital adviser to Philippe and Walter throughout the process was Gary Tinterow, who was a world-renowned expert on impressionist and postimpressionist art. Gary, who is now the director of the Museum of Fine Arts, Houston, was a valuable and perhaps indispensable player in this Met project.

One of the creative preparations that Philippe and Gary undertook was to build a large scale model of the new Beaux Arts galleries that we were proposing to replace the current Modernist André Meyer Galleries. Philippe and Gary worked with the Met architect Kevin Roche to create a large model. The model sat upon a twenty-foot table on which Gary had placed small photographs of the Annenberg paintings in the new "Annenberg Galleries" and added to the adjacent galleries the small photos of the Met collection to make the point of the strength of the Annenberg collection when added to the strength of the Met's current collection. When the model with the "hung" photocopies of the various paintings was ready to be shown to the Annenbergs, I accompanied the two of them, along with architect Kevin Roche and Gary Tinterow, to the unveiling of the model in the elegant boardroom of the Met. Philippe had had a conflict that morning and arrived after the unveiling. From the moment Kevin lifted the cover off of the model, we could see that the Annenbergs were smitten with what they saw.

Once Philippe joined, there was much rejoicing, as plans about the time frame for the construction of the new gallery spaces, for which Walter pledged $500,000, were discussed.

Meanwhile, I had been concerned about making certain that the André Meyer family was aware that we were planning to rebuild the gallery space and rename the André Meyer Galleries. I wanted to assure the family that we would name some of the galleries in that new space after André Meyer, and that some of them would be named after Walter and Lee Annenberg as recognition for their giving their collection to the Met. I asked Michelle David Weill to arrange a meeting for me and Phillipe Meyer (André's son) in Paris. I flew to Paris for one night to meet him. During that time, I explained to him the situation and showed him the minutes of the board meeting in which Douglas Dillon, as board chairman, had recommended that the new galleries, which were completed in 1984, be named after André Meyer because of his close association with the Met (and not as a result of a contractual or legal commitment). Philippe had no objections to the change of naming, and later I got similar response from Meyer's daughter. Her two sons, however, were more reluctant to accept the new arrangement, but they did not take any action to stop it. Since their mother had accepted the arrangement, they chose not to make a public fuss over the name change. We also sought and got the full approval of the Met board for the name changes.

On March 12, 1991, after over four years of discussions between Walter Annenberg and his lawyer and the Met leadership, Walter and Lee Annenberg announced that they had decided to bequeath their fifty-three impressionist and postimpressionist works of art to the Metropolitan Museum of Art. Referring to the future, Walter said, "I believe in strength going to strength. We have got to think of this when we are no longer here and the ultimate repository has to be very carefully thought out. My wife and I share the view that the paintings belong to the public. I had the opportunity to sell them to a Japanese syndicate and the banker who phoned about that mentioned a very sizeable figure. When I responded, 'You're asking me to sell members of my family. I would never do that,' he was surprised."[54] The Met was ultimately chosen because the Annenbergs considered it the only whole museum in the United States and only one of two great whole museums in the world. The other, they pointed out at the time, was the Louvre.

There were strings attached to the bequest: The paintings should hang together; there would be no lending (except to exhibitions in the Met); and there must be no deaccessioning. In a letter to the *Wall Street Journal*, Philippe de Montebello responded to criticism by a *WSJ* journalist that the Annenberg Collection would be segregated from the Met's impressionist and postimpressionist pictures. Philippe noted that, "on the contrary, the new galleries, which would house the Nineteenth Century European Painting and Sculpture Galleries, will resolve the need to define the Annenberg pictures as a collection and the desire to integrate them into them in the Museum's existing collection. This resolution enriches both collections and creates a whole that surpasses the sum of its parts."[55]

The Annenberg bequest was a sterling example of what can happen when the Met leadership works together. The director and

Kevin Roche the architect of the Met, unidentified participant,
Bill, Diane Coffey, Ed Koch, Philippe de Montebello,
Punch Sulzberger, looking at a new wing of the Met.

his curators worked directly with Walter and Lee on the conditions of the bequest and the design of the new gallery space, plus
the best way to have the Annenberg Collection hung together as
one collection—which was possible thanks to the creative imagination of the architect Kevin Roche and his team, and the genius
of Gary Tinterow.

The transformational nature of this acquisition demonstrated
the ability of the divided leadership to succeed when working
toward common goals. It also built my own confidence that
Philippe and I could make this work.

CHAPTER 13

Reagan and Gorbachev

In May 1988, when I already had been at the Met for two years, Wendy and I prepared to visit Moscow to open a collaborative exhibition between the Pushkin Museum and the Met. The timing of our trip coincided with a trip being taken by President Ronald Reagan, who was to meet with Soviet leader Mikhail Gorbachev. Long before this trip, in preparation for my meeting with Michael Deaver, out of which came my more intimate knowledge of Ronald Reagan, I undertook to learn more about the attitude of President Reagan and his relationship with the Soviet leadership. I, of course, had heard and read a great deal from Soviet and American diplomatic colleagues about the freeze in US-Soviet relations under the Reagan administration. I had also heard much from my Soviet and American diplomatic colleagues about Reagan's condemnation of the Soviet Union as an "evil empire." This epithet worked perfectly to evoke maximum disapproval among the American Christian population, but it profoundly put off the Soviet leadership. Soviet Ambassador Dobrynin asked Secretary of State Alexander Haig, "How is [President Reagan] going to do business with us?"

In his first press conference after his inauguration, President Reagan had said, "The only morality the Soviet Union recognizes is what will further their cause. Meaning they reserve unto themselves the right to commit any crime, to lie, to cheat."[56] He later

*To William Luers
With best wishes,* Ronald Reagan

Ronald Reagan and Bill, 1983.

followed this up by saying "The only morality they recognize, therefore, is what will advance the cause of socialism."[57]

In February 1980, a series of events caused then first secretary Andropov to tell a visiting West German journalist of the real threat of a nuclear war. As this gloomy picture further darkened, moderates in Moscow and in Washington began to look for ways to break the downward spiral in the standoff. It was then that Suzanne Massie, a superb scholar of Russian history and the Russian Orthodox Church, came into the picture with President Reagan and his main advisers. After having lunch with

Massie, Reagan had been persuaded that she should go to Moscow to urge the Soviet leadership to agree to renew the cultural exchange agreements that had been dormant since Reagan came to the presidency in 1981. Suzanne had convinced Reagan and his advisors that the agreement to renew the cultural exchanges would be sufficient to reignite the discussions between the US and the USSR, since neither side wanted to seem anxious.

Jack Matlock, the president's special national security assistant for Soviet affairs, and later his ambassador to Moscow, recognized the key role Suzanne could play in moving forward the discussion on renewing the US-USSR cultural exchanges agreement. Following Suzanne's meeting in the White House, Matlock was authorized to call her and ask her "to discuss with her contacts in the [Soviet] Ministry of Culture how best to go about getting negotiations started."[58] Both governments realized that neither side wanted to appear to be soliciting the other or to appear weak or anxious to ease the tensions between the nations. Suzanne's telling of her successful meetings with Andropov's advisers in Moscow is quite amusing. In her book *Trust but Verify: Reagan, Russia, and Me*, she writes, "I didn't give up, persistently insisting that it was essential to have some kind of discussion with the US. 'Talk about anything,' I urged, 'talk for two years, but talk.'"[59] (Talk should be the motto of all diplomats—it certainly was in this case, when US–Soviet relations almost went off the rails in the absence of talk.)

I had come to know Suzanne during this period. She is a passionate scholar of Russian culture and a forceful advocate for improved US relations with Russia. I got to know President Reagan only after I went to be the president of the Metropolitan Museum of Art, years after I had been Reagan's ambassador to

Group photo with Ronald Reagan, Bill, and Nancy Reagan.

Prague during the collapse of the Soviet hold over Central Europe. While at the Met, Wendy and I spent two long weekends with the Reagans and Walter and Lee Annenberg at Sunnylands, the Annenberg's home in Rancho Mirage, California. From our first meeting, Reagan talked a great deal about Gorbachev. And in our very first conversation, I disagreed with his firm conviction that Gorbachev was a Christian and a capitalist. I argued that it was highly unlikely that Gorbachev could be a Christian as first secretary of the Soviet Communist Party. Since my talks with Reagan, I read enough about his conversations with other people to understand that he had ceased on certain anecdotes to point to his assumption that Gorbachev may have had some interest in the Russian Orthodox church. However, Gorbachev clearly had no knowledge of capitalism, because he gave no leadership to the transition of the USSR from a Communist state to one aspiring to be organized on the principles of free enterprise. Gorbachev never even acknowledged the success of Deng Xaoping in astutely leading the Chinese Communist Party on its transition to a system based on capitalist practices.

I learned, much later, that British Prime Minister Margaret Thatcher had had that very discussion before with President Reagan. Reagan was never able to persuade her that Gorbachev was a closet capitalist, either. At a dinner party that Wendy and I were invited to by a member of the Met board, I was sitting next to Margaret Thatcher. I told her at dinner of President Reagan's assurance to me that Gorbachev was a capitalist and a Christian. The prime minister threw her head back and virtually shouted out, "Oh Ronnie always got that wrong." She explained how she and President Reagan had had disagreements over that very issue. Mrs. Thatcher and I were in agreement: Gorbachev was neither a Christian nor a capitalist. If any more proof is necessary, we can refer to the words of Anatoly Dobrynin, the wise Soviet ambassador to Washington (1962–1986). Dobrynin wrote in his book on this period, *In Confidence*, that Gorbachev "believed strongly in socialism and resisted drastic changes in our economic structure."[60] Nevertheless, Gorbachev's "secret capitalist tendencies" had nonetheless become an important factor in Reagan's attitude toward Gorbachev. In my sessions with Reagan at the Annenbergs' home, he was compulsively interested in discussing the Gorbachev he thought he knew.

Like many who were attracted to President Reagan, I found him an appealing, warm, and charming leader who was easy to talk to but whose thinking was difficult to track. In his book, Ambassador Dobrynin tries to sum up his take on President

Bill with Gorbachev.

Reagan, who was, he claims, "the most unusual American president in the postwar history of our relations. My compatriots perceived him as a peculiar yet vague political leader."[61]

In the last week of May 1988, President Reagan and Mrs. Reagan made a long-planned visit to Moscow to meet with the general secretary of the Soviet Union, Mikhail Gorbachev, in what was being called the Moscow Summit. The two leaders were scheduled to discuss strategic weapons and missile defense, Angola, Cambodia, the Iran-Iraq War, and the Soviet pullout from Afghanistan, among other issues.

It was during this trip, when asked by the press about his 1983 "Evil Empire" speech, that Reagan said, "I was talking about another time, another era." Reagan also spent time walking in Red Square and around the Kremlin, speaking with students at Moscow University, and declaring the Cold War to be over.

I had been assured by Reagan's advisers that the president had read Suzanne Massie's masterwork on Russia, *Land of the Firebird: The Beauty of Old Russia.* Nancy Reagan, too, had prepared herself for the trip by consulting James Billington, the librarian of Congress and a celebrated American scholar on the Russian Orthodox Church. (Billington's masterpiece was *The Icon and the Axe,* a scholarly treatise on the role of the Orthodox Church and military power in Russian history.) Jim joined the president on Air Force One to Moscow and helped shape the president's meetings with Orthodox leaders—a complicated world, since the Russian church then, as always, had internal differences over relations with the Soviet leadership, with the KGB, and with the entire Communist system as run by the Communist Party.

Wendy and I chose to go to Moscow at the same time, taking advantage of the strong relationship that the Met maintained with many of the Soviet museums. Philippe de Montebello and I agreed that I would go to Moscow to open a joint exhibition that had been in the works for months between the Met and the Pushkin Museum, which for decades had loaned many paintings to the Met. The director of the Pushkin was the legendary Irina Antonova, whom I had come to know well over many years, as she had served in that same position since my tour in Moscow (1962–65). The Met exhibition of Impressionist paintings was scheduled to open during the visit of President Reagan to underscore the depth of America's cultural interaction with Soviet Russia, which had been encouraged by Washington and Moscow.

But opening the Met show at the Pushkin was not my only mission during that trip. I had two additional missions to carry out. One was to meet with the Russian nuclear physicist and human rights activist Andrei Sakharov. This meeting had been requested by Wade Green of the Rockefeller Family Fund. My second mission was much more prosaic: I was to deliver toner and some equipment for the copy and printer machine used by Lev Kopelev and his Soviet human rights organization.

The equipment we were transporting was provided by Human Rights Watch, which had packed it in a large, very heavy suitcase. Since I still had a diplomatic passport, we assumed that I would be able to get the suitcase through customs without difficulty. The night we arrived in Moscow, we took all the luggage to our hotel room, including the heavy bag. We then took the heavy bag with the equipment in it and arranged for a taxi to take us to an apartment complex on the far perimeter of Moscow. We only had the address of Kopelev's apartment, not his organization's office. It took about an hour to get there by taxi, and it was not easy to find, but our driver was very smart. When we got out of the cab, the driver was insistent on taking the bag out of his trunk: he must have wondered what I had in it, as it was so heavy. We then went up to the fifth floor, to Lev's apartment. When we arrived at the door, we knocked; he opened the door and put his finger over his lips so as to say *Don't say a word*. So we didn't talk the whole time, which was unfortunate because I had known Lev from my time in Moscow in the mid-1960s. He was part of the literary group that met with Steinbeck and Albee, Updike and Cheever. Lev had been an authority on German literature and was married to the scholar of American literature Raisa Orlova. After the American writers left Moscow in the mid-1960s, when I was living there, Lev and Raisa became regulars at the movies we showed at our apartment for the next two years. We showed American films to Soviet dissidents and the literary community that spoke English; showing American films became an extra way to entertain Russian writers and other intellectuals in Moscow. But that night, when we arrived in Lev's apartment, because I couldn't remind him of our friendship of a decade earlier, we did not get to have a reunion. He quietly installed the equipment and gave us back the empty bag, which we took back to the taxi. The driver grabbed the bag from my hands and put it in his trunk, clearly realizing we had dropped off something with substantial weight. On the drive back, he did not ask me what we were doing at that apartment or what we left there. I presumed he was a representative of the police, otherwise he would not have taken us to the apartment in the first place. During the trip back to Moscow, we talked about the new situation with Gorbachev and Reagan meeting in Moscow and the easing of relationship between the US and the Soviet Union. I was trying to distract the driver from thinking too much about what we had done. I asked him whether he listened to the Voice of America, not certain whether it was still being jammed. The driver immediately asked me why it's a good thing to have some unemployment. He said he was listening to the Voice of America and heard of the value of unemployment to the US economy. In the Soviet Union and Russia, the government was proud to say that everyone was employed. I tried to explain to the driver in Russian the best I could the economics of having a flexible workforce that can move from one job to the next, without losing the opportunity to work. We finally arrived. The driver let us off outside the hotel without driving to the main entrance, clearly disturbed that he did not know what we had just done and what we had just left at the apartment.

That evening we met with our friends in the media, including Peter Jennings, who was working for ABC News. He asked me for unique stories. I told him that I was always convinced that the Soviets had invented wind machines to keep the Soviet flag flapping in the wind even when there was no wind. I suggested he ask the Soviets to explain to him why the flag was always flying in the wind. He did not find that an interesting story and did not pursue it. Tom Brokaw, who was the NBC correspondent covering the Moscow Summit, was not interested in my story either.

I had been asked by Wade Green, who was working with a member of the Rockefeller family, and by Jerry Wiesner, the president of MIT, to explain to Andrei Sakharov, if I could see him in Moscow, what the word "foundation" would mean in Russian. They were hoping to get Sakharov to endorse and cochair, with Jerry Wiesner, a new foundation for the saving of humanity, which would be organized as a US-Soviet initiative. They were concerned that Sakharov had not understood, from their correspondence with him, the goals of this new foundation.

I was to explain to Sakharov that his stature as a humanitarian and human rights leader would help to ignite global support for the foundation's many values. This International Foundation for the Survival and Development of Humanity had grand ambitions. It was supported by large segments of the American private sector and the US government, and it seemed to have the full support of the Gorbachev leadership, which was already doomed to disappear. It represented a fleeting moment in which some elements in Moscow and Washington seemed to come together to take on a leadership role in bringing together nations that had been so divided during the Cold War.

As an example of the type of work the foundation sought to do, funds would be used to launch a satellite that would provide all nations of the world with up-to-date information on medicines that were available for specific diseases.

I was asked to help Sakharov understand that the foundation was designed to raise money from individuals and governments, so as to be able to execute their programs' goals. The second thing Sakharov needed to understand was the way this entity would be used to achieve the goals. When I met Sakharov and his outspoken, strong-willed wife, Yelena Bonner, in his by-now famous kitchen in their Moscow apartment, I realized that Sakharov indeed had not understood the meaning of a "foundation," or even the word itself. My explanations in Russian did not help, since the entire idea of raising private or public funds for philanthropic purposes was alien to Soviet thinking. Then, when I told him the objectives of the foundation were to provide all doctors and hospitals that could get access to the satellite important and current information on medicines available for specific diseases, he was clearly befuddled. He replied loudly and firmly, "My people do not even have access to one aspirin, never mind information on sophisticated new medicines for new diseases that are still being identified." Sakharov said he would prefer a program that made medicines more available to all Soviet citizens. "Information on new medicines is not helpful if you cannot get access to those new medicines," he said.

I explained Sakharov's reactions about the new foundation over the phone and later in New York to Jerry Wiesner and Wade

Green and told them I thought it best not to ask him to take on the role of cochair of the foundation or of raising money for it or for supporting its objectives. They thought I must have misunderstood; surely Sakharov could not fail to appreciate the potential help that such a foundation could provide the world.

Six months later, on the afternoon of November 17, 1988—the day of the official launch of the foundation—I spent an hour with Sakharov trying to explain the high stakes and the level of commitment this new foundation represented to a number of important institutions and pharmaceutical companies in the

Bill escorting Andrei Sakharov at the Met.

US. One of the main goals of this new foundation was to provide countries and pharmaceutical companies around the world
with up-to-date information and new medicines and treatments
for chronic diseases worldwide. Jerry Wiesner thought it would
prove to play a major contribution to the US and USSR's roles
in managing chronic diseases together. Sakharov remained
unconvinced that the reach of modern medicine could solve
public health problems around the world and, specifically, deal
with public health in the USSR, which had such limited access
to medicines. Sakharov was convinced that only medicines and
medical treatment could manage to reduce the ravages from diseases around the world.

The launch of this new foundation took place that same evening in the American Wing of the Metropolitan Museum of Art
in New York City. Walking from my office with Sakharov to the
American wing, I proposed we walk through the recent exhibition
of the painting of Edgar Degas. Sakharov was clearly delighted
by the possibility. I had discovered he knew about Degas and his
individual paintings and was clearly drawn by Degas's proclivity
to place the central focus on the painting off center. He confided
that he had spent years looking at books of Degas's work, which
reinforced my view that art is a common language among different cultures.

David Rockefeller Jr. and Jerry Wiesner, in introducing the
event, made moving and persuasive arguments for the value
added from this new foundation. Even to imagine such a foundation was an indicator of the optimism of the moment. Then,
when they called on Andrei Sakharov to support the foundation
before the international media present at the meeting, he backed
away from an unequivocal endorsement, stressing instead his

conviction that human rights had to be at the center of international political efforts. However, he was supportive of an international effort. In his rejection of it, however, he agreed to join the board of the new foundation and later agreed to become the chair of the new Human Rights Committee of the International Foundation for the Survival and Development of Humanity, along with Father Theodore Hesbergh, the former president of the University of Notre Dame.

Instead of the famous Sakharov becoming cochair of the new international foundation, Jerry Wiesner had to be satisfied with Evgeny Velikhov as his cochair. Velikhov, a distinguished Soviet physicist who did not have the global reputation of Sakharov, was then vice president of the Soviet Academy of Sciences. I assume that Sakharov's almost single-minded focus on human rights rubbed Gorbachev the wrong way, and that Gorbachev had made clear his preference for Velikhov. Another Soviet physicist, Roald Sagdeev, was also actively involved, from the Soviet side, in the creation of the new international foundation. Sagdeev was married to Susan Eisenhower, an American member of the International Foundation for the Survival and Development of Humanity and the daughter of the former US president.

In retrospect, I have concluded that Sakharov must have had a falling out with Gorbachev over Gorbachev's reluctance to take some final steps that Gorbachev felt necessary to rid Russia of the residue of Stalinism, such as the rehabilitation of all of Stalin's victims. In any case, by the time of Sakharov's death the next year, he had not reconciled with Gorbachev. Ironically, Sakharov's first meeting with Gorbachev, on January 17, 1988, took place while the foundation was having its first meeting in Moscow, well before the announcement and "coming out" party at the Met for the foundation. Yelena Bonner told the media in Moscow that Gorbachev received Sakharov in his capacity as a member of the board of the new foundation and as a cochair of the Human Rights Committee of the International Foundation for the Survival and Development of Humanity. According to the intrepid Bonner, during their meeting, Sakharov appealed to Gorbachev for the release of about two hundred political prisoners from Soviet prisons, camps, psychiatric hospitals, and places of exile. Sakharov himself had been detained in internal exile by the KGB for seven years in Gorky.

During the period following President Reagan's trip to Moscow, I had occasioned to see the president several times in New York and at Sunnylands. In both places, I was seated next to the president and had the opportunity to renew our discussion about Gorbachev and whether he was a closet capitalist and Christian. The president stuck to his convictions and I to mine, holding to the view that there was no evidence that I could see that Gorbachev was a Christian or a capitalist. I suspected that the president, who had already left office, was showing signs of his Alzheimer's. Wendy and I noticed that Nancy Reagan would more frequently draw the president's attention through a subtle kick on the leg when the president began to repeat himself.

What I was most interested in with President Reagan asserted itself across our multiple meetings. Reagan left office obsessed with his relationship with Gorbachev, just as I predicted he would in my talk with Mike Deaver some six years earlier on Martha's Vineyard.

CHAPTER 14

To the Velvet Revolution: Czechoslovakia, Part II

On February 22, 1990, President Havel addressed a joint session of the US Congress as the philosopher-president who had recently emerged for most Americans as the intellectual and human embodiment and symbol of the collapse of Communism, the fall of the Berlin Wall, and the seeming beginning of the end of the Cold War. He started speaking to Congress in the Czech language, by saying abruptly,

> The last time they arrested me, on October 27 of last year, I did not know whether it was for two days or two years. Exactly one month later when the rock star Michael Kocáb told me I would probably be proposed as a presidential candidate, I thought it was one of his usual jokes. When they arrested me on October 27, I was living in a country ruled by the most conservative Communist government in Europe, and our society slumbered underneath the pall of a totalitarian system. Today, less than four months later, I am speaking to you as the representative of a country that has set out on a new road to democracy, a country where there is complete freedom of speech, which is getting ready for free elections, and

which wants to create a prosperous market economy and
its own foreign currency.

Then he added, "It is all very strange indeed."[63]

For those sitting in the hall of Congress at that moment, and
for the millions worldwide listening to the live TV broadcast of
Havel's speech, the moment was less "strange" than miraculous,
and as joyous as it was bizarre. How could this short, soft-spoken,
and slightly bent-over playwright from a country most Americans could not find on a map be telling the world with such
conviction that the long nightmare of the Cold War was over?

Havel then spoke of his life's work in the arts:

We playwrights, who have to cram a whole human life or
an entire historical era into a two-hour play, can scarcely
understand this rapidity ourselves. And if it gives us trouble, think of the trouble it must give the political scientists who spend their whole lives studying the realm of
the probable?[64]

The most visionary moment in the already stunning speech was
what he asked from the US. We knew in advance that Havel did
not want to ask for a huge grant of economic assistance for his
country. He did not want to appear as a self-serving solicitor. He
was committed to multilateral solutions: If the former Soviet satellites were to be helped, they should all be helped in an agreed-
upon program in which all would participate.

Havel felt it undignified and wrong to make a special plea
only for Czechoslovakia. However, he did have a request:

I often hear the question: How can the United States of America help us today? My reply is as paradoxical as the whole of my life has been. You can help us most if you help the Soviet Union on its irreversible but immensely complicated road to democracy. It is far more complicated than the road possible for its former European satellites. You yourselves know how best to support as rapidly as possible the nonviolent evolution of this enormous, multinational body politic toward democracy and autonomy for all of its peoples. Therefore, it is not fitting for me to offer you any advice. I can only say that the sooner, the more quickly, and the more peacefully the Soviet Union begins to move along the road toward genuine political pluralism, respect for the rights of nations, and to their own integrity and to a working—that is market—economy, the better it will be, not just for Czechs and Slovaks, but for the whole world. And the sooner you yourselves will be able to reduce the burden of the military budget borne by the American people. To put it metaphorically, the millions you give to the East today will soon return to you in the form of billions in savings.[65]

Congress's reaction to Havel's humility and his enlightened wishes for the USSR was exuberant: they gave him seventeen standing ovations.

Our surprise would have been far greater—and perhaps turned to shock—if we had known that his words of warning, couched in a magnanimous plea, foreshadowed the future. It was as if Havel in 1990 had foreseen the resulting horrors of the post-Soviet treatment of its former national entities and the nightmare of Putin and his invasion of Ukraine.

So, why was his warning not heeded?

Perhaps Havel and the historic circumstances surrounding his speech so beguiled all who listened that the US government simply forgot the message? Havel's warning about what the Soviet Union might become if left to its own devices and its own leaders was profound and prescient. He chose not to give the US advice on how to head off the dark future for the USSR—but he was certain that the US should soon move to avoid the problems that might come from a Soviet Union or a Russia that had not taken the democratic path.

Havel's warning must have echoed in that same hall of Congress in December 2022, when Volodymyr Zelensky, also from Central Europe, also a short charismatic orator, spoke for the embattled Ukrainian people, telling members of Congress that the money and military assistance the US was sending to Ukraine to resist and overcome the Russian invasion of its neighbor was not "charity" but an investment in the future of democracy. Havel would have been justified, had he lived long enough, to have called down from the balcony: "I warned you all, but the American government either did not hear me or, if it heard, it did not choose policies that would set Russia on the democratic path."

———

It took time to lay the fires of revolution. There is no possibility that I can capture here the years of imprisonment, the thousands of written words of protest, the secret meetings with Lech Wałęsa in the Krkonoše mountains,[66] or the thousands of moments of doubt and defeat that assailed them. What I *can* do is share the demands put forth in 1977, in a document known as Charter 77, by a small group of individuals wanting only to be free, wanting only what already had been promised by the state, when the Czechoslovak Socialist Republic had signed into law two different bills: an international pact on civil and political rights and an international pact on economic, social and cultural rights.

As Charter 77 notes in its first paragraph, these laws came into effect in Czechoslovakia on March 23, 1976, and "since that time, our citizens have had the right and our state the duty to be guided by them."

The two laws were passed in accordance with the Helsinki Final Act, which is also known as the Helsinki Accords. These accords have a long history, stemming, paradoxically, from the Soviet Union's desire to strengthen its political and military positions. Specifically, it wanted formal recognition of the political borders of several Eastern European countries that had been established following the Second World War. For many years, for obvious reasons, the West had resisted this idea. But in the early 1970s, during the period of détente, conversations began that shifted—and broadened—the terms and issues being discussed. The governments of the West began to get interested. From 1972–1975, negotiations intensified, until an agreement was signed in Helsinki, Finland, on August 1, 1975. It was signed by the US and Canada, and every European nation except Albania—thirty-five countries in total. Including Czechoslovakia.

In short, the Helsinki Final Act—or the Helsinki Accords—was divided into four "baskets." The first basket covered "political and military issues" including the issue of territorial sovereignty (boundaries). "The second basket focused on economic issues like trade and scientific cooperation. The third basket emphasized human rights, including freedom of emigration and reunification of families divided by international borders, cultural exchanges and freedom of the press. Finally, the fourth basket formalized the details for follow-up."[67]

It was the third basket which caught the attention of dissidents throughout the USSR and Eastern Europe. It was to the third basket that Václav Havel and the band of dissidents around him pinned their hopes. It was this third basket that they outlined in their declaration presented to the Czech government in January 1977. Though Charter 77 was signed by only 243 people, the strength of its words would carry it to the streets of Prague in 1989. These are some of Charter 77's statements:

> The freedoms and rights of the people guaranteed by these pacts are important factors of civilization for which, throughout history, many progressive forces have been striving and their enactment can be of great assistance to the humanistic development of our society. We therefore welcome the fact that the Czechoslovak Socialist Republic has expressed adherence to these pacts.
>
> But their publication reminds us with new urgency how many fundamental civil rights for the time being are—unhappily—valid in our country only on paper. Completely illusory, for example, is the right to freedom of expression, guaranteed by article 19 . . .
>
> Tens of thousands of citizens are not allowed to work . . . simply because they held opinions which differ from official opinions . . . They are frequently the object of

the most varied forms of discrimination and persecution on the part of the authorities . . . They are deprived of any possibility of defending themselves and are virtually becoming the victims of apartheid . . . Hundreds of thousands of other citizens are denied the right to "freedom from fear" . . . because they are forced to live in constant danger . . . Freedom of public expression is suppressed . . . Publicly defending oneself against the untrue and insulting charges of official propaganda is rendered impossible . . . Freedom of religious conviction emphatically guaranteed by article 18 . . . is systematically restricted by arbitrary power by the curtailment of the activities of the clergy.

Responsibility for the observance of civil rights in the country naturally falls, in the first place, on the political and state power. But not on it alone. Each and every one of us has a share of the responsibility for the general situation and thus, too, for the observance of the pacts which have been enacted and are binding not only for the government but for all citizens.[68]

These words were written with grave seriousness and determination. Some of that determination, stemmed, I hope and I believe, from the work Wendy and I did in the embassy to rally our American writer friends around our Czech writer friends to surround them with support, counsel, and brotherhood. Brian Goodman, the author of *The Nonconformists*, has said, "It is easy to be cynical about the US Embassy's own ideological motivations for supporting Prague's banned writers. But Ivan Klíma has insisted, 'The meetings with William Styron and his wife, Rose, and John Updike, Kurt Vonnegut, E. L. Doctorow, Galway Kinnell and others, as well as with Mr. and Mrs. Luers, represented for us above all entry into the free world, a moment of exultation that imbued us with the strength to persevere, enhanced our hope.' These events were also an important (and rare) point of social contact between prominent figures associated with the dissident underground and the citizens of the Gray Zone."[69]

As Goodman rightly points out, the breadth of the impact these writers had was great: "By the 1970s, both official and underground forms of cultural exchange had opened up new channels of literary circulation, aesthetic influence, and political communication across the Iron Curtain. Famous American writers . . . established lasting solidarities and friendships with their persecuted Czech counterparts . . . including Havel. . . . By the end of the Cold War era, decades of risky encounters between American and Czech writers had helped transform the city of Kafka into an international capital of dissent."[70]

Was it the fall of the Berlin Wall on November 9, 1989, that ignited the Velvet Revolution that began exactly eight days later, on November 17? Or was it the "election" of Mikhail Gorbachev, the reforming Soviet leader, in 1985, that laid the groundwork for these two world-changing events?

I believe, as I wrote in *Foreign Affairs* in 1990:

> There were many factors—accidental happenings and political trends—that came together to create that 'velvet revolution.' [But] the person who started it was Mikhail Gorbachev. The ideas underpinning the clean sweep of the communist dominion in Eastern Europe flowed without question from perestroika and glasnost. Yet the

way in which the events in Czechoslovakia unfolded demonstrated Gorbachev's apparent lack of vision or even ignorance of the real forces at play in this important allied nation.

The spark that lit the fire under the revolution in November surely came from the explosive events earlier in East Germany, events which Gorbachev condoned if not wholly encouraged. Human waves of East Germans flowing through Czechoslovakia and Hungary [in 1989] to freedom in the West riveted the attention of young Czechs and Slovaks, opening their minds to the potential for mass action with the possible impotence of their security police. Ultimately, however, it was a uniquely Czechoslovak reaction to the prospect of reform in Eastern Europe and to the dramatic change in Soviet foreign policy under Gorbachev that formed the character of their revolution and led to the election of Václav Havel as the Czechoslovak president on December 29. . . . Gorbachev's revolution is clearly the starting point.[71]

In hindsight, the run-up to the Velvet Revolution seems so clear. At the time, though, nothing was clear. In 1988, "the demonstrations began to get serious. On the anniversary of the Warsaw Pact invasion, up to 10,000 gathered. Another several thousand massed on October 28 to appeal for new laws to permit the right of assembly, and an even larger demonstration took place on December 10. Perhaps the most impressive demonstration of public support in 1988 for an opposition cause was the 31-point petition for religious freedom signed by over 600,000 people, including non-Catholics and non-dissidents. . . . Finally, helping to set the stage for 1989 was Helsinki Watch, a human rights organization based in New York"[72] that had been founded by Robert Bernstein, the former CEO of Random House, who published Bill Styron among others, and who was a visitor to the American Embassy in Prague while I was ambassador.

The next set of demonstrations, which occurred in early January 1989, involved the anniversary of the death of Jan Palach. Palach was a Czech man who set himself on fire in 1968 to protest the Soviet suppression of the Prague Spring and the Warsaw Pact invasion of that same year. As the anniversary of Palach's self-immolation approached, Havel sent out a plea that Palach's sacrifice not be repeated. That plea was picked up by foreign radio stations and broadcast back into Czechoslovakia. For a week before the anniversary in early January, crowds gathered in Prague's Wenceslas Square to protest—and were dispersed by the police using violent measures. On January 15, the authorities arrested Václav Havel for his involvement in "inciting" the protests. In February, he was sentenced to nine months in prison. Their tactics backfired. A petition protesting his arrest and demanding his release was circulated around the entire country. Condemnations of the arrest flowed in from governments and intellectuals, including several from the Soviet Union.

As the storm clouds gathered and darkened, the Communist government in Prague grew increasingly irrational. In the late spring, I was to chair a large and impressive first meeting under a new US-Czechoslovak agreement. The government in Prague was extremely pleased with the individuals who had accepted from the American side, particularly those from the American high-tech and digital industries. Once I learned that the Communists had thrown Havel in jail again, and after consulting with the State Department, I called on the Czechoslovak ambassador in Washington, DC, and told him that we would have to cancel the excellent conference we had set up, because of Prague's decision to put Havel in jail.

The ambassador was disappointed but not surprised, since he was the same ambassador who had protested my behavior to the Department of State two summers earlier for my invitations to Havel and others from Charter 77. A few days later, Havel was released from jail.

Following his early release from prison in May, Havel authored a document titled "A Few Words," released on June 29, which called "for the release of political prisoners and other freedoms—[and] was eventually signed by around 40,000 people."[73] Though it was the most radical demand for change yet, Havel was still conflicted about mounting more protests that would invariably lead to more violence, crackdowns, and imprisonments.

Wendy and I visited Prague in August 1989, along with our friend Lloyd Cutler, who had been General Counsel to President Carter during Carter's last two years in the White House. We organized a dinner in Prague for Havel and the Charter 77 group. Our tradition, established over the last four years, was that we would hold these dinners at a restaurant in Old Town Prague called *U Sedmi Angelu*—At the Seven Angels. The following day, we drove Lloyd Cutler and his wife, the painter Polly Kraft, to Havel's isolated country house Hradicek (meaning "small castle") for lunch. While I was asking Havel about the current political environment, I noted that the student demonstrations seemed to be getting larger and bolder. I asked him what he thought about them. He replied, with typical Havellian humor, "You ask, what do I think about the student demonstrations? I don't like them because every time the students demonstrate, the government throws me back in jail."

———————

On November 17, 1989, only three months after our lunch with Olga and Václav at Hradicek, the Velvet Revolution began. On that day, students took to the streets of Prague and refused to leave. By November 20, there were five hundred thousand people in Wenceslas Square. The protests had begun to spread throughout the countryside, as well. By then, nothing could stop them: the days of one-party rule in Czechoslovakia were over. One week later, on November 28, the entire Communist leadership resigned from the government. The Communist government had been peacefully removed from power after fifty years of oppressive rule.

I will not pretend here to provide a detailed story of that amazing series of events that Havel summarized succinctly in his talk before US Congress. For anyone who would like the best-informed, intimate review of the history of the political process of the Velvet Revolution and how it related to the changes that took place in the other Soviet satellites, the best account of those times was written by University of Oxford historian Timothy Garton Ash in his book *The Magic Lantern: The Revolution of '89 Witnessed in Warsaw, Budapest, Berlin, and Prague*. The author knew well the key players in each of those revolutions; speaks Czech, Polish, and German; and is a sitting and disciplined historian—in sum, quite the brilliant historian that series of events needed to do justice to the story.

My involvement was marginal and from afar. I called Havel

on Sunday night, November 19, to ask where he thought the developments that had started the Friday before would lead. Always cautious, Havel replied that it was too soon to tell: "Give them a few more months and the picture will become clearer." I had been asked by the *Washington Post* to write an opinion piece on the protests. I was not as cautious as Havel, but did not declare the end of the Communist world, as I had done for *Newsweek* only a few months earlier.

By mid-December, an anti-Communist government had been installed. Wendy and I decided we had to go back to Prague after Christmas. We arrived on December 26, 1989. After having alerted Havel and other friends of our plans, we asked Havel to set a date when he and friends could gather again at our traditional dinner site, At the Seven Angels. He selected December 28, so we booked the restaurant for that night.

What we didn't know was that Havel had been elected unanimously by the members of parliament to be the first president of free Czechoslovakia that day. And the date for the inauguration was set for December 29, which meant that our party for him, set for December 28, would be held the night before his inauguration. It also seemed that his new government—which would include many of his fellow dissidents and friends—would be our party guests that night. Virtually every one of the regulars who attended the At the Seven Angels dinners were already designated as a minister or equivalent in the new Havel government. Since all of them were to be there, Wendy and I had many protocol decisions to make. We had to alert the American ambassador of our plans. The new ambassador was Shirley Temple Black. But she had not really begun to get to know Havel until he was almost the new president. When she arrived in Prague, she had told people she would not follow the Luers strategy and would instead devote more time to improving relations with the Communist government. Ironically, that State Department had tried to schedule me for a meeting with one of the best-known super-conservatives in the Communist Party, in my office in the Met, on the Monday following the November 17 demonstrations that launched the Velvet Revolution. I was told that Ambassador Black had taken a personal interest in the visit of this person and wanted me to meet with him. I said such a meeting made no sense and that the government's invitation was unwise. Fortunately, after the student riots on November 17, the embassy had the good sense to cancel his trip.

Wendy and I also realized the dinner was likely to be much larger than the traditional dinners we held for just the dissidents

Unknown, Wendy, Havel, Petr Pistek, Bill, Karel Schwarzenberg. President Havel Inaugural dinner, *U Sedmi Angelu* restaurant, Prague, 1989.

(twenty to twenty-five people). Fortunately, we found a number of cohosts. First was Ricca and Carl Schmidt; Carl had been the deputy chief of mission when I was ambassador. They both had been invaluable partners. Carl spoke Czech well and was one of the top specialists on Central Europe in the Foreign Service. Carl had also been a valued friend of Havel and his wife. They agreed to share costs. A most generous contributor was Miles Glazer, whom we had met during one of the visits to Prague from Dominique de Menil. Miles had been her main adviser for the Menil Collection in Houston. Miles's widow, Slavka Glazer, became one of our closest friends in Houston and New York.

There were a number of toasts that evening. Havel said some nice words and our cohosts spoke well. In my toast to the achievements of the Czechoslovak nation, of their success in achieving

Bill toasting at Havel Inaugural dinner.

Olga Havel with Ramsay Turnbull and author Ivan Klíma.

freedom from the yoke of communism, I concluded by saying that I had heard many cogent words about how the population of this free nation feels now about their success. I said some were drawing parallels to a mystical religious experience. But my own view was that it seemed like it was the pleasurable physical experiences that sustained the Czechs through the long hard years of communism—leading to this large national orgasm.

The evening went on into the early morning, more as a raucous celebration than a solemn preparation of the historic inauguration that was to happen in only a few hours.

The following morning, we went to Vladislav Hall, the large grand hall with a high vaulted gothic ceiling in Prague Castle that had witnessed the coronations of the kings of Bohemia for centuries. It was also the site of the inauguration of the Communist presidents who had sought to abscond with the great traditions of Prague—and failed in that effort.

Wendy and I stood near the aisle as Havel entered the hall. Slightly bent over, as usual, he was moving slowly. I said to Wendy, "He does have the demeanor of the person this nation and the world needs and wants as president at this moment." Then Havel arrived at his place for the ceremony, turned to the audience, and seemed to grow two feet before our very eyes. When he took his oath and spoke briefly, he had cast away the bent and shy Havel we knew, and belted out his words as the confident president of a proud free nation. Žantovský told us that he and Havel had a nightmare that at that very of moment of Havel's oath-taking, the Communist government might sweep in and shut down this little charade—that they had decided to permit this last act, but enough was enough. Of course, the swearing-in was real and achieved its objective.

After the event in Vladislav Hall, Havel, following the traditions of the kings of Bohemia, went to the balcony of Prague Castle that faces St. Vitus Cathedral (built in 1344), the gothic cathedral that presided elegantly over Prague. St. Vitus symbolized the Czech's historic preference for the gothic, even as the Hapsburgs and Jesuits tried to impose baroque architecture, along with the Catholic religion, on the historically Protestant Czech lands as a reward for crushing the Czechs in the Thirty Years' War in the seventeenth century.

As we stood below the balcony and listened to Havel's moving speech to the crowds gathered below, Wendy thought she discerned Olga Havel wearing one of the silk blouses that Wendy had brought her from New York. I was not convinced that Václav was wearing any of the presidential-looking ties I had brought him.

During Havel's speech, I felt a tug on my jacket. I looked

around and saw the former Communist foreign minister, Chňoupek, who said, "So you got your wish." He said this with a smile on his face. He handed me a book he had written on Andy Warhol, which had been published in English. Andy Warhol's family was from eastern Slovakia near the home of Chňoupek, who asked whether I could help promote his book and give lectures on Warhol's origins in Slovakia.

After Havel spoke, he went with his entourage to hear Dvořák's *Te Deum* in St. Vitus, which was not part of the tradition retained by the atheist Communist presidents nor by Tomáš Masaryk, the former president of Czechoslovakia, who was considered the founder of the country. Wendy and I were escorted into the cathedral and positioned standing behind Havel and Olga. Havel sat facing the altar in front of which sat Cardinal František Tomášek, who had become an important player for Havel and his group. Around Tomášek were gathered a group of younger priests who had helped Charter 77.

The Dvořák *Te Deum* felt right and proper in St. Vitus on that celebratory occasion. And, of course, the musical Czechs hold their composers particularly dear and close. The Czechs have a favorite expression, "Scratch a Czech and you find a violinist."

As the *Te Deum* was concluding, the young priests around the old and infirm cardinal gathered him up and carried him to a chair next to President Havel and Olga. This was a glorious and culminating moment for everyone in that cathedral. The nation had come back together at long last. I was standing right next to the Communist minister of defense, whom Havel had retained in his cabinet for the inauguration. I saw tears welling in his eyes, something that was surely happening throughout the cathedral, and a smile on his face.

It was a final act for Václav Havel's most successful drama, in which he was playwright, director, star, and producer.

―――――

Immediately upon our return from Prague to New York in the beginning of January 1990, Wendy and I started planning for Havel's first trip to New York City as the new president. He had been invited by President George H. W. Bush for a state visit, and since the Communist ambassadors were still in Washington and New York, Havel's team had asked that Madeleine Albright would organize the Washington, DC portion of his trip and we organize the New York portion. This was obviously very complicated, as Olga and Havel were bringing about eighty people— students, journalists, and friends like Prince Karel Schwarzenberg (who was now Havel's foreign minister) and Communist Prime Minister Marián Čalfa—on the plane, and they had very little money for lodging.

An interesting aside is that Havel retained Čalfa—and the former defense minister in his cabinet, including much of the communist bureaucracy and other key members of the former communist government in order to keep the state running. He told me he believed that the military would remain loyal to the country and not to the communist party. I'm always reminded of this wisdom when recalling the decision of George H. W. Bush to shut down the military leadership in Iraq once the US had occupied Bagdad, which had been one of the major mistakes of the US invasion of Iraq in 2003. Havel had figured out that he did not want to alienate the entire Czechoslovak military establishment.

An additional complication of the Havel visit to New York was that a Czech woman, Ivana Trump, was married to the controversial businessman, Donald Trump, who at the time owned the Plaza Hotel. Havel, wanting to show the Czech presence, very much wanted to stay at the Plaza Hotel. The Trumps wanted to turn the event into a political show for Donald Trump. Wendy working closely with Havel's staff said that Havel should not be trapped by Donald Trump and worked out an alternative plan by cutting a generous deal at the UN Plaza Hotel through a Czech American, who was the general manager of that hotel. He gave Wendy an excellent deal for Havel's party for the duration of their stay in New York. Havel's staff forcibly resisted Wendy's insistence, but finally acceded. As it turned out, only days before Havel was

Michael Žantovský, Bill, and President Havel
on steps of the Met, 1990.

to arrive in New York, the New York papers' headlines read that Ivana and Donald Trump were to be divorced. This increased the respect that Havel's team had for Wendy as a wise counselor.

We organized an unusually active program for Havel for his two days in New York, including a breakfast at Gracie Mansion with Mayor David Dinkins, who invited many of the prominent New York writers and artists for breakfast to start the day, which included a call on the Catholic Cardinal, a tour of the Metropolitan Museum, a meeting at Amnesty International, and a spectacular candlelit reception on the stage of the Vivian Beaumont Theater with every imaginable New York writer, playwright, or actor who had some connection to Havel. The party was funded by the publisher of the *New York Review of Books*, through its Havel-friendly editor and founder Bob Silvers, and was facilitated by Linda Janklow, Chair of the Lincoln Center Theater.

The night before saw a huge celebration at the Cathedral of St. John the Divine, which was filmed for PBS by Oscar-winning Czech film director and close friend of Havel, Miloš Forman. Thousands gathered in the enormous cathedral, holding candles and ringing little bells reminiscent of the Czechs ringing their keys in Wenceslas Square in Prague before the Velvet Revolution. Hundreds of Czech Americans and other Americans came on buses from as far away as the Midwest and Texas. Many others stood in line outside, in the freezing cold, in hopes of catching a glance of the now famous Václav Havel. During the visit to New York, Havel could not restrain his almost childlike fascination with this city of theater and Broadway, which he had visited only once before as a dissident playwright. Havel, feeling a free man, would hop in and out of the secret service limousine. On one

Wendy, President Havel, Bill, and Michael Źantovský
on Fifth Avenue, February 22, 1990.

occasion, he left the car to walk down Fifth Avenue with Wendy
and me. We heard the secret service officers who were assigned to
protect Havel speaking into their sleeve microphones in despera-
tion: "We have no control over this president!"

All in all, it was a triumphant visit!

CHAPTER 15

The Metropolitan Museum of Art, Part II

After the success of raising money and helping attract the Annenberg collection to the Met, I had developed greater confidence in my leadership abilities at the mighty museum. I was persuaded that together with the highly talented and professional staff of the museum, we could find the right course to move the museum forward and into greater success. I was also graced with growing friendships with a number of the philanthropists who worked with and supported the museum. I came to appreciate, respect, and understand how deeply "giving" meant to the philanthropists I worked with and befriended.

One February in 1994, we were spending a weekend with the Annenbergs at Sunnylands, their home in Rancho Mirage, California. The other guests present were President and Mrs. Reagan; Bill and Melinda French Gates, and Bill's mother and father; and Kay Graham and Warren Buffett, plus Mrs. Buffett. After having lunch outside, the Reagans departed by helicopter from the grand space between the tee of the first hole of the golf course and the swimming pool, to return to Air Force One and then to Washington, DC. With the president's departure, the conversation became more informal. To my surprise, Walter Annenberg rose and made an informal talk about philanthropy. Walter rarely did such things, since he had been a stutterer in his youth and had long been insecure about making informal or impromptu comments. I was, therefore, certain that he had prepared these remarks on philanthropy in advance. The talk was clearly directed at his two wealthy guests. His point was that if Bill Gates and Warren Buffett were committed to giving their money away, they should do so while they were alive so they could determine the beneficiaries of their philanthropy and take pleasure from the gifts. Walter spoke enthusiastically about the pleasures he drew from his major gifts. That afternoon, he spoke about his bequests to education—he had given 50 million dollars to historic Black universities and half a billion dollars for improving secondary schools in the United States.

The thrill Walter derived from his gifts most certainly stimulated the growth of mega philanthropy in the United States and contributed substantially to the advancement of the education system, science, and increased attention to private philanthropy.

Though his comments were directed at Buffett and Gates, the two listened patiently, but seemed unmoved and unresponsive to Walter's advice. I was sitting next to Melinda French Gates, Bill's new wife. From her body language, I could see her watching and listening to Walter with a much greater responsiveness. The Bill and Melinda Gates Foundation would be created five years later in 2000. By 2020, it had grown to be the largest global foundation in the United States, and the second largest in the world.

Six years later after that luncheon, at an announcement held at the New York Public Library, Bill Gates and Warren Buffett announced Buffet's agreement to give $31 billion to the Bill and Melinda Gates Foundation, which had already distributed billions of dollars for public health and other programs. Warren stated that he would continue to annually pledge funds to support the foundation.

Warren Buffett remained a strong supporter of the Gates Foundation until he resigned from the foundation's board in 2021, after Bill and Melinda Gates separated. I am not suggesting that Walter Annenberg was the trigger that sparked the creation of the Bill and Melinda Gates Foundation, but I do believe he was one of the many voices that persuaded Bill and Melinda Gates to establish that extraordinary institution. The Gates Foundation announced that its 2024 budget for philanthropy would be $8.6 billion to save and improve lives. It was their largest annual budget and was dedicated toward advancing global health innovations and initiatives. It will save and improve the lives of the world's most vulnerable people.

David McCullough, Met 125th anniversary, 1995.

Over the next fifteen years, the relationship that Wendy and I had with Walter and Lee Annenberg continued to build. We were invited back to Sunnylands every year until Walter's death in October 2002. And it was at Sunnylands where I began my long rolling conversation with President Reagan about Russia and Gorbachev.

One of the most interesting conversations I had with Walter was our discussion about finding a biographer for him. I offered to arrange for him to chat with David McCullough about potential biographers. David spent his summers on Martha's Vineyard. In the summer of 1992, Walter and Lee took a large yacht to anchor in Vineyard Haven harbor. I had lined up a meeting between them to discuss biographers. I had assured Walter that I doubted that David would agree to take on the task himself.

That evening, Wendy and I dined on board the yacht with Walter and Lee. We had already announced that their collection was going to the Met. They spent much of that dinner telling us how pleased they had been about the gift. In that discussion, Walter told me that he wanted to add to the collection that was going to the Met. He then announced that he and Lee already had set aside a small sum of money. Not knowing what a small amount of money might be for Walter Annenberg, I assumed it was much larger than I could imagine. I took his suggestion to heart and that evening I called Philippe and suggested that he ask Gary Tinterow to find a particularly stellar van Gogh painting to add to the Annenberg Collection. I told him I could not estimate a price and had not asked Walter what he meant by a small amount of money, but that I had gathered that he wanted to add a significant addition to his already billion-dollar gift.

Within a year, Gary had identified one of the icons of

van Gogh's oeuvre. Called *Wheat Field with Cypresses,* it was the painting van Gogh completed after *Starry Night,* which is now hanging at the Museum of Modern Art. Like *Starry Night, Wheat Field with Cypresses* had the particular haunting natural forms of the artist. Van Gogh also found the olive tree appealing and painted many of them. In fact, the Annenbergs were so intrigued by van Gogh's attraction to olive trees that one of their preferred trees they had planted at Sunnylands was the olive tree.

From the time Philippe told Gary to find a stellar van Gogh in 1991, it took us until May 25, 1993, to acquire a brilliant icon of van Gogh oeuvres from the family of Swiss industrialist Emil G. Buhrle for $57 million. In talking of his additional gift to the Met, Ambassador Annenberg said, "It's one of the great van Goghs. And when I heard there was a possibility it was available, I talked to the Met people, because I thought it was something the museum must have."

Michael Kimmelman, the legendary art critic who wrote the story in the *New York Times* about this additional gift, wrote, "*Wheat Field with Cypresses,* a painting brilliantly colored, heavily impastoed and full of turbulent energy . . . was painted in June 1889 at St.-Remy-de-Provence during a period of extraordinary productivity for van Gogh. It was then that he also painted *Starry Night* now in the collection of the Museum of Modern Art in New York."[74]

The story of the van Gogh gift and the Annenberg Collection, however, did not end there. In 2007, a *New York Times* correspondent called the Met to report that the last owner of *Wheat Field with Cypresses* was Franz von Mendelsson, who lived in Berlin. The correspondent assumed that unless the Met had more provenance information, this was a classic case in which the Nazi government had taken the van Gogh from the presumably Jewish Mendelsson family during the Aryanization period in the 1930s. We told the correspondent we knew no more about the provenance than we had announced at the purchase. We suggested to the correspondent that she explore her presumed storyline.

The correspondent reported later that she had found a member of the Mendelsson family who stated that the family had left Berlin in the 1930s and immigrated to the US. Before leaving Berlin, they had packed up their large painting collection in large crates and asked their neighbors, who were Christian, to store them in their basement. After the war, when the family could stomach the thought of returning to Berlin, they did go back to their former neighborhood and found that their former house had been destroyed, but the neighbor's house was standing. When they inquired of the neighbors what had happened with the paintings they had stored in the basement, they learned that the paintings were still there and in good condition. The family then sold them at auction.

The acquisition of the Annenberg Collection provided evidence that the director and I collaborated on a very successful project, but there remained three core sources of tension during my tenure at the Met: how to manage the role of new technology in the museum; how to deal with the repatriation of works of art with questionable provenance; and the acquisition of works of art for the Met collection.

Cambridge Associates was a private investment firm that had

been advising the Met trustees on investing the Met endowment. In that role, the Cambridge leaders had become familiar with the debate over the split leadership model that the Met was trying to make work. So, in the winter and spring of 1989, when I recommended that the senior staff, including the heads of some curatorial departments, hold a weeklong retreat off-site without the trustees, to allow all present to speak freely about concerns, Cambridge agreed.

In retrospect, the retreat was *not* a team-building experience, since I came away feeling that I was the subject of the staff's anger. What came out was that it was my very presence that was at the center of the museum's management problems. Nevertheless, our sessions were the most interesting and exhausting meetings I had ever had in my professional life. The retreat helped me calibrate the differences between the psychological hostility toward the divided leadership and the core problems at the museum. Somehow, I had become identified with the force for change that were affecting not only everyone in the museum but every institution across the globe: technology. At the Met, I was seen as the outside presence, imposed on the museum by the trustees and given the mandate to change it. Many of the staff at the retreat had been at the Met for at least ten years—and many had been there as long as forty years. The loyalty and dedication of these long-time employees were and are a major source of the institutional strength and spirit of the Met. But the length of their tenure also made change more difficult to embrace.

Despite my confidence in my own leadership and management abilities stemming from years of occupying top positions in many organizations, I found it difficult not to take personally the persistent criticism of the president's role. Nevertheless, going into those meetings, I had understood that it was going to be a bruising experience, and that I, above all others, had to learn from the experience. My diplomatic training was helpful—indeed, it turned out to be essential—as it allowed me to play a constructive role going forward.

The first source of tension—managing the changes in technology—was universally present in museums across the country. We needed to come to a decision about the role —if any—that the internet should play in the core work of the museum. Should we use digitized images of the works of art? Should digital copies be used for education? Should use be made of the internet for promotion of museum activities? And on and on. Moreover, it was generally assumed that I would be leading the charge to *impose* the use of computers. Discussing technology, the director had issued a dictum that he would not have a computer or laptop of any type in his office. He had also stated that the internet, even an intramuseum system, would never have a museum image available on it. He—and many of the older curators—were absolutely opposed to putting any Met images online. Their position was black and white: Art would not be present on any new technology that could somehow pervert its authenticity. I argued that I had thought that that Rubicon had already been crossed when Andre Malraux had published his groundbreaking book *Museums Without Walls: The Voices of Silence*, which praised the role of photography in making art accessible to millions who could not get to museums. I said the book had certainly affected my own thinking when it was first published in the early 1950s.

The issue was so confrontational that it proved necessary to create a new team to work through the differences. I was able to find a new player, named Arthur Tisi, to serve as the Met's chief information officer. Arthur had unique communication skills and could reason with curators on the potential of the internet for linking departments together. He immediately took to Philippe's charisma and leadership. The major strategy was to get Philippe to agree to designate the amazingly competent and creative Emily Rafferty, whom we had recently promoted to vice president for development (and whom I think I promoted every year), as Arthur's partner in this onerous task. Philippe, who comprehended the degree to which technology was becoming a source of confrontation through the museums world, had great faith in Emily and agreed that she should work with Arthur. The two of them formed a team approach for all department heads throughout the museum. By the end of the first year, the director had a PC at a table by his desk and had come to appreciate the efficiency of email for dealing with other directors across the vast universe of museums in which he was perhaps the preeminent leader. Within five years, the number of PCs in Met offices moved from negligible (fewer than one hundred) to over 1,200. Also, by the end of that time, we had almost completed our fiber-optic connections. Emily took most of the heat and virtually all of the well-deserved credit from the staff for her equanimity and "cool"—so characteristic of the beloved leader who later became a respected president of the museum. The fact is that she and Arthur, along with a group of allies, turned a source of tension and polarization into an opportunity for a unique form of museum-wide cooperation among departments.

Many years later, Emily told me that taking on the internet task had been, for her and Arthur Tisi, the most difficult and challenging assignment she had undertaken at the museum.

By the end of this multiyear project, much of the resistance to images being displayed on the internet had been fully accepted as a valuable tool for education and information.

The second source of tension, the repatriation of works of art with questionable provenance, remained a nonissue among the staff (except within the legal committee of the board of trustees and among trustees who collected antiquities). It only came out during my tenure when the museum faced a strong claim from the Turkish government that 363 objects in the museum's collection had been stolen from Turkish territory. The objects were gold and silver and comprised what was referred to as the Lydian Hoard.

Our lawyers at the time assured me that the statute of limitations would apply and that the Turkish claim would not be found to be valid because the Turks had been late in their claim. This legal advice caused the legal committee of the trustees to delay further action. The debate was whether we could win in court. They believed we could. It was all about winning or losing—not about doing what was right.

But what good was that if we lost public hearts and minds?

Then, about three years later, in 1992, we were informed that the federal court had granted Turkey "the right of discovery," meaning that Turkey could request from the Met the files from that period and question Met staff about what Philippe and the curator knew.

At this time, Philippe seized the moment to design a negotiating strategy for dealing with the Turkish government which would establish a new long-term relationship for the sharing of research and the displaying of objects on long-term loans, including some on the material in dispute. When the proposal was in good shape, Philippe, Ashton Hawkins, Carlos Picon, and I got an appointment, in late 1992, with the Turkish Ministry of Culture to present our plan of long-term collaboration with Turkey. We went first to Istanbul. Our talks with the government were very sensible and, we thought, positive. However, we learned after our return to New York that the ministry had rejected our proposal for long-term collaboration. So, the Special Trustee Committee (impaneled to make decisions on this issue) finally decided to give me the responsibility to work with the lawyer and to return the objects and take full responsibility for the Met's actions. Philippe, when questioned by the media, took the high ground. He said, publicly, "Turkish authorities did provide evidence that most of the material in question may indeed have been removed clandestinely from the tombs in the Usak region, much of it only months before the museum acquired it. And second, we learned through the legal process of discovery that our own records suggested that some museum staff during the 1960s were likely aware, even as they acquired these objects, that their provenance was controversial."[75]

That is what tipped the balance. When you put these two factors together, returning the objects was the only proper thing to do.

Over the years, I learned that the trustees had had vastly different reactions to my role in this drama. Robert Pennoyer, who was chairman of the Legal Committee, for years praised me for the role I had played in pushing the Special Trustee Committee to do the right thing. Whereas, another trustee, who had been a strong supporter of me at the beginning of my tenure and who was also an antiquities collector, scolded me one evening when under the influence of extra booze and asked how I could have been so courageous in standing up to the Communists and yet such a coward when confronted by the Turks.

It was these two diametrically opposed viewpoints that created such strain in the meetings of the Special Trustee Committee. Many trustees seemed focused on winning the case through the correct interpretation of an application of the statute of limitations, instead of on what the museum would lose by sinning in this way. To me, it seemed that the important question was: How would the Met respond to Turkish accusations that senior curators of the Met knew that the objects had been stolen before they were acquired?

Ultimately, the Met did the right thing, the only thing they could do, really: they returned the materials to Turkey.

As a postscript, the collected antiquities known as the Lydian Hoard spent two years in Ankara, Turkey, but were then transferred to a small museum in rural Usak—where the collection had been first been found. I'm told by several British archeologists that the Turkish exhibition of the treasure was elegant and appropriate and well-done. In 2006, it was discovered, according to the press, that the preeminent masterpiece of the collection, a golden hippocampus, was a fake. The real one had been stolen several years earlier, while under the protection of the Usak museum.[76]

The third source of tension at the Met during my tenure was the enduring sensitivity of the question: What role did the president play in acquisition? Over and again, I ran afoul of this very fine, very prickly line.

Within weeks of my coming to the Met, I had asked two close friends from San Francisco to lunch with me at the museum. In addition, I also invited Ashton Hawkins, who was now counsel to the trustees, to join us, since I had the sense that the couple, who were top collectors of photography, would want to talk about their collection. What I learned during this lunch turned out to be well known by our star curator of photography, Maria Hambourg, who had just been hired by Philippe to establish a new emphasis on collecting photographs. At our lunch, my friends began to discuss the possibility of leaving their collection to the Met because of our close relationship. I was thrilled, but Ashton, uncharacteristically, treated them with a certain disdain. My friends were so turned off by his demeanor, that they never again mentioned that possibility. I should have taken Ashton's attitude as an early warning, because I knew him well enough to realize that he was not given to being rude. But beyond that, I should have been forewarned that some curators (particularly Bill Lieberman, the head of the Department of Twentieth Century Art) and perhaps also the director resented my efforts to help acquire works of art for the Met. I had thought that the recent cooperation between the president's realm and that of the director had worked well. Certainly we had been spectacularly successfully in the Annenberg gift. At least I had thought so. But many years later, my belief in the success of the collaborative nature of our work with the Annenberg gift proved to be inaccurate.

In 2001, two years after I had left the museum as president, I got a telephone call from Lee Annenberg asking what I was doing on the following Monday. I said I had committed to attending a dinner and giving a talk about the United Nations (I was then the president of the United Nations Association). Lee wouldn't take no for an answer: "I want you to join me for dinner at the Met, since they are having a dinner to celebrate the gift that Walter and I gave."

She was surprised I had not been invited to the dinner. And she was intent on my coming: "I want you to sit next to me."

Surprise, curiosity, and loyalty to Lee Annenberg carried the day, and Wendy and I attended the dinner and heard the presentations on how the collection came to the Met which included not a single reference to my role. I was sitting next to Lee at the dinner, just as she had requested. She eloquently included a reference to my role in her talk. Another affirmation of Lee's savvy and understanding of politics, she felt it important to mention that the president was a player during the entire process of acquiring the Annenberg collection. She clarified the role I played in starting the ball rolling with her and Walter making their bequest to the Met.

In retrospect, both Lee and I felt that the role that I played had not been fairly acknowledged. And also that it was a missed opportunity to demonstrate to the board of trustees and other large donors who were attending this special evening that the divided leadership of the Met could work well together, and that when they did, the museum thrives.

Yet, even with the success of the Annenberg acquisition at my back, I was met with cold shoulders. Shortly after the Met had made the final deal with the Annenbergs, the irrepressible Mort Janklow had introduced me to a prominent collector in New York City who had a splendid and large collection of contemporary art that contained many works by artists not yet in the Met's collections. I already knew the collector well, but I had not known about the size and incredible scope of his collection. He and I began to talk about his agreeing to give part of the collection over time to the Met, with the condition that the Met would eventually buy the rest of it. I realized that this was such a big deal that I should not continue to discuss it with the collector without full approval of the director. I explained the proposal to the director and the head of Twentieth-Century Art. They agreed to meet with the collector, whom they proceeded to treat with disdain. I was deeply embarrassed. The collection eventually went to the Museum of Modern Art.

On another occasion, early on during my tour at the Met, I was lucky enough to spend some time with Helen Frankenthaler, who had studied painting at Bennington with my first wife, Jane Fuller. The two women were star students of the artist Paul Feely, who taught there at the time. Helen suggested that she would sell to the Met her iconic painting *Mountains and Sea*, which was on long term loan to the National Gallery. *Mountains and Sea* is credited with "changing the course of abstract art . . . and is a painting of mesmerizing beauty, a marvel of modern landscape painting."[77] Helen said that she would much prefer to have the painting in the Met in New York and asked whether I thought there would be a possibility of finding a buyer among our trustees who would be willing to make an offer to her for the painting.

I approached Bill Lieberman, chief curator of Twentieth-Century Art, who said he was not interested in the painting or in getting money to buy it from Helen. His reaction seemed to be driven by personal animus against Helen. The painting is now a part of the National Gallery's permanent collection.

A final anecdote, which illustrates the hurdles and bumps I faced over my role in acquisitions, came early in my tenure, just after I arrived as president. At that time, I received a call from my close friend George Costakis, who was a legendary Greek individual who had worked in the Canadian Embassy in Moscow for many decades and amassed the most remarkable collection of avant-garde Russian art in the world. He wanted to discuss with me whether the Met would have any interest in acquiring part or all of his collection. I knew George and his collection from the time that I lived in Moscow in the mid-1960s. He did not mention the price he wanted for his collection but hinted that he would sell the entire collection to the Met for $1 million. I knew, of course, that the Met did not have that kind of money to invest in the Russian avant-garde and said so to George, who replied that he was open to negotiate a price. Bill Lieberman responded to my question rudely and abruptly, saying the Met would have no interest in acquiring a collection of such stuff at any price. I told him of my meeting with Alfred Barr, the director of MoMA, who was about to acquire a different Russian avant-garde collection for MoMA from a private dealer in Moscow. But to no end: Lieberman had no interest in the material or the period represented by the Costakis collection, which is now housed in its own section of the State Tretyakov Gallery in Moscow and in the MOMus-Museum of Modern Art-Costakis Collection in Thessaloniki, Greece.

During my years at the Met, I had been asked to join the advisory board of the Trust for Mutual Understanding (TMU) that had been founded on and remained amazingly focused on supporting cultural exchanges among arts groups in the Communist world. Initially, this meant exchanges between the United States and the USSR and Eastern Europe. TMU gave grants to American theater groups, dance groups, and artists to coproduce performances and exhibitions, either in America or in Communist Central Europe and the former Soviet Union. It continues to be one of the most innovative and successful foundations working in this important space. At one point, I suggested to a professional educator on the Met's staff that the museum might ask TMU for a grant to develop an exchange of museum professionals between the Met and museums in the USSR and Eastern European communities. By the time I left the Met, this exchange of professionals had grown to be one of the most successful exchange programs of its type for TMU—and for the Met, the Hermitage, the Kremlin Museums, and the Pushkin Museum in Russia. Eventually, the program would also extend to smaller museums in the former USSR, the Russian republics, and the capitals of Central Europe. The experience we had with the amazing TMU professionals further enforced my own beliefs in the enormous value of culture in the conduct of diplomacy with all cultures, whether friends or adversaries.

Just as institutions like TMU supported the arts and cultural exchanges in America, Communist Eastern Europe, and the former Soviet Republics, New York City and New York State had its own institutions that supported our own arts and cultural scenes. One of these institutions, the New York State Council for the Art, relied over and again on one of my favorite people as their spokesperson and all around booster.

Kitty Carlisle Hart was easily the favorite leading woman for most of New York State. She had been chairman of the New York State Council on the Arts and was, by far, the most popular promoter of the arts in Albany, at the State Assembly. I had

many occasions to join her during her hearings and other meetings in Albany, and watched her wow state senators and assembly
members. Kitty was both beautiful and witty. She was the strongest supporter of the important State Council on the Arts, which
provided funds for New York City and other arts programs across
the state . . . and the most popular. For that reason, as I was preparing to organize the speakers for a special lecture series at the
Met that we called "Arts Create A City," as part of the 125th anniversary celebration of the Metropolitan Museum of Art, I asked
Kitty whether she would agree to give the lecture on Broadway
musicals. She immediately said yes. Since the lecture series was
taking place in 1995 or 1996, when Kitty was 85 or 86 years
old, I told her that we could get someone else to do the singing
and dancing, if she felt easier about such an arrangement. Kitty,
who had already begun working with a pianist to help arrange
the lecture and the music, looked hurt and surprised and said
abruptly that she planned to do the singing and dancing herself.
She had performed in the musical *On Your Toes* and other musicals, indeed Kitty was the essence of a Broadway musical.

The night of her debut performance at the Met, after pro-
longed applause of her performance, she called on the Met audience to sing "New York, New York." I said to Wendy under my
breath that even Kitty Hart will not get this audience to sing.
I was wrong, as usual. They joined her enthusiastically. Kitty
eventually refined the show and took it on the road as a performer. Earning money as a performer during that time enabled
her to take her grandchildren on trips. The success she experienced then was probably the happiest experience she had in her
later life because it allowed her to connect more closely to her
grandchildren.

Later, when she was in her early nineties, I spent a great deal of time with Kitty, as she was dating a good friend of mine, Roy Newburger. She told me once that getting old was difficult and that she knew she would stay healthy and well as long as she was needed and wanted by other people. When she became particularly unwell in her late nineties, I called up several of her closest friends and told them to call her and say how much they needed her. It worked, she recovered.

The other experiences that solidified my belief in the power of the arts to ease standoffs was a role I agreed to take on with the Praemium Imperiale. This Japanese international arts prize is given every year to five artists in five disciplines—painting, sculpture, architecture, music, and theater/film—who, through their

Teruko Secor, Misha Baryshnikov, Lisa Rinehart, and Bill, 2017.

work, "contribute to enhancing and promoting the cultures and arts of the world."[78] The prize is considered by artists to be one of the most prestigious art awards in the world. It was created by David Rockefeller, in collaboration with Helmut Schmidt, the former chancellor of Germany; Yasuhiro Nakasone, the former prime minister of Japan; Amintore Fanfani, the former prime minister of Italy; and Jacques Chirac, the former president of France. The objective was to bring high-level political attention to the arts and to demonstrate that the arts could bridge cultural and political differences. The prize, at some level, achieved the goal of bringing high-level political attention to the arts in Europe. But in the US, the Praemium Imperiale was unable to persuade senior American leaders to contribute to the awards process. David Rockefeller Jr. replaced his father as international advisor. And David Jr. asked me to replace him. As the American international advisor to the Praemium Imperiale, I came to put

David Rockefeller Jr, Susan Rockefeller, and Patty Cisneros.

a great deal of time and energy into this prize. But I was not a senior political leader, which had been the goal of the founders. When I stepped down, we arranged for Hillary Clinton to replace me as the American representative, which brings the US closer to the original goal: to convince senior political leaders of the high value of the arts and artists in bringing nations together.

———————

Serving as the president of the Met was the most fulfilling, life-enhancing, and enlarging job in my long career in public service—as a naval officer, diplomat, as an adjunct professor, and in leadership positions in foreign affairs. Nowhere else did I have the opportunity to work with such a quality group of colleagues who put such a high value on excellence in performance and on institutional loyalty.

In my early years at the Met, we hired an outside firm to survey the staff to determine the complaints of individuals regarding personal satisfaction with their work environment. The two women who conducted the professional survey told me they were astounded by the results. Aside from certain complaints about the workplace, the entire staff found working at the Met to be one of the most rewarding things they had done. Pride in the institution and pleasure from the environment overrode almost all other complaints. A former minister of justice from Romania, who was serving as a museum guard after his defection from Communist Romania, would stop me in the galleries to explain his high pleasure in working at the museum.

The preeminent enthusiast for the Met was Philippe de Montebello, who served as the director for over forty years.

Throughout his tenure, he inspired the high standards for the staff and their work. I enjoyed a collegial relationship with Philippe, and we shared many laughs. He probably had the greatest capacity for humor—despite his aura of arrogance, or perhaps because of it—than any other colleague at the museum. Harold Holzer ran Philippe a close second. Due to the high quality of the trustees and the museum's staff of professionals, and because of the spirit of millions of New Yorkers for whom the Met is *their* museum, the Met is the greatest single to attraction in New York City, which thrives on the masses of visitors from around the world. Because of all of these things, the Metropolitan Museum of Art has remained at the center of cultural vitality of New York City, and one of the world's preeminent—and greatest—museums.

CHAPTER 16

Clinton and Castro:
Dinner at the Styrons'

In August 1994, a group of us believed that we could persuade President Clinton to open up to Castro's Cuba. The stars seemed perfectly aligned. Clinton was a fresh thinker on foreign policy. He greatly admired the writers García Márquez and Bill Styron, whom he knew personally and enjoyed being with, and who, that evening, would be sitting around the dinner table together. More importantly, Castro was hurting badly economically and politically after his Russian patrons had dropped Communism and him at the same time. We were sure that Castro would be open to an historic shift in relations with the US. So we set out to test the power of three writers to change history and US policy.

Bill and Rose Styron, working with Latin American writers García Márquez and Carlos Fuentes, decided to try to convince President Clinton in person, in effect short circuiting his national security advisers. They believed it might be possible to persuade the president that a dramatic opening to Castro would add to Clinton's stature, improve the US image in the Western Hemisphere, and improve the lives of Cubans. It seemed a no-brainer.

The ambush was set for Martha's Vineyard, where the Clintons would be in August 1994, for his annual birthday celebration. The Styron "white house," which was located on a vast lawn, had been where Democratic leaders had assembled in summers

Wendy, President Clinton, and Bill at Styron dinner.

for over forty years. It was a cottage in Camelot for the liberal, intellectual, and political community who had become part of the Styron world.

The setting was ideal for Bill Clinton. He would be in the shadow of JFK and the Kennedy clan, who traditionally had sailed the few miles from Hyannis to spend the day on the Styron lawn. Lady Bird Johnson rented a house next door for decades. Vernon Jordan, the "best friend of Bill," spent his summers nearby, as did Art Buchwald. The Clintons had already become friends of the Styrons.

This group of writers would play to Clinton's strong suits—his deep interest in literature and his voracious reading habits. He was the rare American president who took readily to writers and intellectuals. He had a photographic memory. Bill Styron told me once that while talking with the president about his novel

Art Buchwald and
Ramsay Turnbull.

Nat Turner, Clinton, out of the blue, recited the last sentence of
the book. A grateful Styron shed a tear.

The secret weapon for the evening was Nobel Prize winner
Gabriel García Márquez (or "Gabo"), whose novel *A Hundred
Years of Solitude* was a Clinton favorite. García Márquez had a
long, complex friendship with Castro. The Styrons had learned
that Gabo would be willing to fly to the Vineyard for the dinner,
presumably encouraged by Castro and Mexico's president Salinas. The Styrons had found a coconspirator in Carlos Fuentes,
Mexico's leading novelist and a close friend of Gabo.

Wendy and I were involved in the planning since we had
been close to the Styrons for decades and had come to know
Fuentes and García Márquez well. We had a house on the

Vineyard a few doors away from the Styrons, and we also lived near them in Connecticut. They had visited us when I was ambassador to Venezuela and Czechoslovakia.

The other Castro connection was that I had negotiated, in 1977, the opening of the US Interests Section in Havana in anticipation of opening full diplomatic relations later that year under the presidency of Jimmy Carter. During the several months' transition to the Carter administration from the Ford administration, I was the acting assistant secretary for Western Hemisphere affairs. President Carter had wanted to move quickly on this first step toward opening full diplomatic relations, which had become one of his priority foreign-policy achievements during his first year in office. Relations between the US and Cuba had been a part of my diplomatic career since Cuba's revolution in 1959.

President Clinton, Bill, and Alan Rappaport.

In theory, our plan could lead to a changed US-Cuba policy. That was our chimera. We, the innocent plotters, had been hoodwinked. We were freelancing as diplomats and were clueless about the backstory of relations at that moment between Castro and Clinton. I had left the State Department five years before. Because there already was motion in play behind closed doors, our plan was predestined to fail to change Clinton on Cuba. But we did not know that. And the dinner conversation proved to have positive consequences for President Clinton.

Decades later, I learned that the August dinner at the Styrons' had been concocted by Fidel Castro, Mexican president Salinas, and García Márquez to influence the outcome of tense US-Cuban negotiations that were to be held at the UN in New York City in early September of that same year, only a few weeks hence. Clinton had been trying to pressure Castro, first through Jimmy Carter and then via Mexican president Salinas, to reach an agreement on managing another large flow of Cuban immigrants to Florida. Castro had been double-teaming Clinton using both Carter and Salinas, neither of whom knew the other was involved. Clinton was desperately in need of a Castro agreement to pull back on yet another vast flow of Cuban refugees that was threatening to dump many thousands of Cubans in Florida. The president did not want to send a mixed message back to Castro through Gabo.

Clinton proved instinctively savvy about the relationship between foreign affairs and domestic politics. He had won Florida comfortably in the 1992 elections and had no intention of feeding the hostility of Cuban Americans in Florida. He would need Florida in the next elections. Nor could he afford to appear soft on Castro. He won Florida easily in 1996. Al Gore failed to win the presidency in 2000 in part because of Florida, with its charged-up Cuban American population that had always been suspicious of Bill Clinton's intentions toward Cuba.

The dinner began at the Styrons' home that August evening, as planned. The president and the others came to the Styrons' fabled porch overlooking the Vineyard Haven Harbor, with sailboats bobbing and a passing ferry visible from the porch. The Styrons' dining room with Rose's mother's white-tablecloth-laden table, with her china and roses, is adjacent to the porch. Upon greeting his hosts, President Clinton headed to the kitchen to greet Daphne, the Jamaican cook, who cooked the succulent fried chicken that was a Clinton favorite.

As usually happened at the Styrons' dinners, a smaller table was added at one end of the larger dining table to accommodate all of us. Seated that night, there were the Clintons, the Styrons, the Fuenteses, García Márquez, and former Mexican foreign minister Bernardo Sepulveda, plus multiple members of the president's Secret Service contingent milling around, alert as always.

The Cuba team focused the discussion on Cuba within moments after sitting. Gabo sat between Clinton and me. Rose Styron was on the other side of Clinton with Carlos Fuentes on her right. We had him cornered.

Gabo opened with a long recitation of the Castro litany about years of US broken promises and failed opportunities. Gabo's long arguments, when translated from the Spanish, tested the president's patience on the unexpected topic. While Clinton was attempting to savor Daphne's fried chicken—a masterpiece— Gabo went through the list of US demands on Cuba: Break with the Soviets! Get out of Angola! Treat your people better! Don't force your people to come to the US! Pay American property claims!

Gabo was egged on by Fuentes, who was by no means a Fidel "groupie." Carlos assured President Clinton that Castro had a high regard for Clinton, and so now was the time to break the failed habits of the past. Both writers suggested that, were Clinton to open broader relations with Cuba, including lifting the embargo, Castro would eventually become irrelevant in Cuba and Latin America. Without the US attempting perpetually to overthrow or kill him, Castro could no longer play the martyr. He would become history.

After ten (seemingly eternal) minutes of this fusillade in Spanish, Clinton got the picture. He had been set up. His unease was palpable. His face, usually sunny, turned dark.

Seeing his displeasure, I needed to change the pace and I asked the president calmly what he would like US relations with Cuba to look like at the end of his eight-year presidency. It was a clumsy effort at a diversion for the president, a diplomatic apple polishing.

The president glowered. His dark face was punishing. In the presence of two of the hemisphere's most respected and loquacious intellectuals, he saw me asking him to declare himself for a long-term improvement in US-Cuban relations—thereby undermining his current tense negotiations with Castro (which we knew nothing about at the time), and, at the same time, committing political suicide in Florida for 1996. He chose not to dignify my statement with a response. My diversionary ploy had turned the environment even more disagreeable.

I got the message. I whispered to Gabo in Spanish to change

the subject entirely. At once Gabo asked Clinton to talk about the recent books he had been reading, flipping his role elegantly from Castro apologist to Nobel Prize winner in literature. That question relieved the tension in a flash. Light came back into the president's face and the floodgates opened. We were treated to a compelling discussion of literature by Clinton that startled and charmed García Márquez and Fuentes. It lasted for the rest of the evening.

Time and again the arts can change moods, open doors, and help diplomatic relations. American power is conveyed sublimely to other nations through a cultural openness. When an American president grasps that truism, the point is made convincingly.

When launched by Gabo, Clinton dove into the subject of literature like an alcoholic into a martini. To Gabo's delight, Clinton said he had recently read García Márquez's biography of Simón Bolívar. Clinton observed that Gabo had presented the first balanced and critical view of that iconic and unassailable Latin American hero. He said Gabo had given Bolívar a credible humanity—flaws and all. We were stunned that he had read the Bolívar book and that he completely understood the objective of the biography. Few American presidents would know much more than the name Simón Bolívar, never mind the subtlety of the iconography of his image in history.

For the rest of the dinner, Clinton captivated his literary audience with a range of his recent excursions into books. Faulkner was a favorite; he had also been a profound influence on García Márquez. President Clinton was at ease talking about one of his favorite topics—books—directing the conversation with the enormous range of his reading and his memory. Neither Cuba nor Castro were mentioned again.

Toward the end of the discussion, Clinton began to speak of one of this favorite series of thrillers by a Mexican writer that he had read in translation. He could not recall the writer's name. He did note that in the second of the three-part series, the hero had been killed off. Clinton asked Fuentes how the author would deal with the final volume without the star character. Fuentes, who looked as if he had received an electric shock, shouted out, "Paco. You speak of Paco!" Paco Ignacio Taibo II, the author of the series, was a close friend of Fuentes. Carlos had had lunch with him a week earlier in Mexico City. And again, culture brings forth great connection.

That Clinton could not recall the name of the author was uncharacteristic for him. His memory was formidable. Several years earlier, while I was still president of the Metropolitan

President Bill Clinton and Bill in the White House.

Museum of Art, I was accompanying President Clinton as he toured a special gallery located behind the vast space that houses the Temple of Dendur, near the American Wing of the Met. The president was waiting to welcome to the US all of the special international visitors, including chiefs of state, to the opening of the UN General Assembly. I was just about to escort the president into the reception when Harold Holzer, the incredibly savvy public-affairs officer, came up to him and asked whether he would like to see a baseball card that was unique. It was in the Met's comprehensive collection of baseball cards that had been left to the museum by Jefferson Burdick. Clinton replied, "Do you mean the card of Honus Wagner?"

Harold gulped and replied, "Yes, that is the card."

Stunned, I asked the president, "How in the hell did you know that?"

Clinton, without missing a beat, said, "It was in a Tuesday *New York Times* crossword puzzle."

The evening at the Styrons' produced no breakthroughs on Cuba. We may even have reconfirmed Clinton's already negative view of making a gesture toward Castro. My bias was that it never hurts to keep planting the seed and looking for ways to change the discussion with adversaries.

Over the next many years, I learned why Clinton had not succumbed to the blandishments of two of the top Latin American writers. I learned, too, that Clinton already was incredibly savvy about the world and its impact on domestic politics. I also began to doubt my assumption that, somehow, Fidel Castro would mend his ways and take the steps necessary to revive the Cuban economy and restore commercial energy to the Cubans.

Clinton had charmed and captured Gabo and Fuentes. The positive consequence of that dinner was the enthusiasm Clinton generated in García Márquez and Fuentes, who carried the story of this literary president throughout Latin American media and among political and cultural leaders. In view of the high regard that Latin Americans have for their writers, the story of the memorable night had impact far beyond that one small table. Clinton became known as the president who reads and has a passion for Latin American literature.

CHAPTER 17

Fidel Castro:
Doctrine of a Revolutionary

By 2000, I still clung to the hope that a bold American president might someday change the dynamic of US-Cuba relations. Americans, I believed, had failed to factor in whether it would be possible to modify Fidel Castro's pathology on revolution and his presumed conviction that the US was and would remain the permanent enemy of Cuba.

Yet, it did not look as if this change would come under President Clinton, who was always super attentive to domestic politics. As such, Clinton did not want to risk losing the Cuban vote in Florida and continued to take a hard line on Castro. To this end, he signed the Helms-Burton Act in 1998, which locked in the embargo and required a future president to get congressional approval to lift it.

Clinton made the right political choice for his domestic political future. And Castro, who tried to tantalize Clinton, ultimately stiffed Clinton like he had every one of his predecessors.

The status quo remained unchanged, and the embargo remained in place. As did Castro.

Yet, against all the evidence I had—over thirty years' worth—I remained hopeful that circumstances between the two countries would change in 2001, when a new president, presumably Al Gore, would be elected.

Incredibly, Gore famously lost the election because of a few thousand chads from voters in the anti-Castro region of Florida, who presumably trusted the Republican, George W. Bush, more than the Democrat, despite Clinton's holding the line on the embargo.

Whether or not a US president who was Cuba-savvy and bold would come along to change history, there remained a more important unknown: Would Fidel Castro ever agree to make a deal with any American president to lift the embargo? I wondered if I would ever have an opportunity to check it out with Castro himself.

That opportunity came in 2000. At our annual New Year's Eve dinner, on December 31, 1999, Arthur Miller burst out in his most authoritative voice, "Bill, it is time to go to Cuba."

I remember the scene vividly. Arthur's wife, Inge, was just putting on the table her traditional roast lamb dinner. We had been listening to Arthur's familiar rants against theater critics. As usual, the main target of rebuke was the *New York Times* drama critic, Frank Rich, who, according to Arthur, had, for over a decade, almost single-handedly set producers and drama critics against Arthur's plays on Broadway.

Arthur and Inge had been weekend neighbors of ours in Litchfield County, Connecticut, for over a decade. They had traveled with Wendy and me in Venezuela and Prague several times. They were good company. Perhaps Arthur was right. Maybe we should go to Cuba. The chance to ask Castro some questions was tantalizing. Also, Arthur, I was convinced, had the ability to see Castro in ways that an earnest diplomat could not.

Within a month, I had gotten approval from the US Treasury to lead to Havana a "cultural delegation" composed of the

Millers, Bill and Rose Styron, and our friends Mort and Linda
Janklow. Mort was the leading literary agent in New York and
Linda was the chairman of Lincoln Center Theater—both were
leaders of the New York arts community. The Janklows provided
a private aircraft that took us all directly from New York to Havana—a convenience greatly welcomed in view of the difficulties
in flying to Cuba commercially in those days. Our friend Patty
Phelps de Cisneros joined us in Havana from Venezuela.

Our reception in Cuba by Castro was made possible by Castro's
pal Gabriel García Márquez, who joined us in Havana, where he
was always given a residence by Castro. Gabo's presence would
probably ensure that we would spend many hours with the

Wendy, Bill Styron, Linda Janklow, Bill, Inge Morath,
Arthur Miller, Rose Styron, and Mort Janklow, 2000.

notoriously loquacious Fidel. On March 8, 2000, our "cultural delegation" arrived in Havana on a private plane provided by the Janklows.

Castro presumably saw the Miller-Styron visit as another opportunity to portray himself as the wise, sympathetic, defiant leader who had, for decades, dazzled and puzzled well-connected foreign leaders of every stripe. The Miller-Styron visit would burnish Castro's tarnished image among intellectuals on the Left in the Americas.

Most of the Left-thinking writers and journalists in Latin America had long given up on Castro's rebellion against the US. He no longer wore the anti-Yankee badge of honor among the top Latino intellectuals, most of whom broke ties after his mistreatment, imprisonment, and public humiliation of the

WRITERS UNBLOCK

T wo of the most famous writers of the 20th century, American Arthur Miller, left, and Colombian Gabriel García Márquez visit the late Ernest Hemingway's former home in Havana on Saturday. They are part of a delegation of writers who are trying to promote contacts between U.S. and Cuban intellectuals.

Gabo, Inge, Bill, Linda, and Arthur.

prominent Cuban poet Heberto Padilla in 1971. The "Padilla affair" occurred when Fidel Castro staged a show trial in which Padilla was required to publicly confess his differences with the Cuban Revolution. The event happened after Castro laid down new tighter restrictions on Cuban artists, who would be permitted to write what they wished, as long it was not against the Cuban Revolution and as long as the work furthered, in some way, the Cuban Revolution.

This repression of Cuban writers, along with his failure to provide for the Cuban people, soured his reputation with the international Left, including the American Left. Moreover, his close ties to Moscow famously frayed the patience of Octavio Paz and Mario Vargas Llosa, the two other Latin American Nobel Prize laureates who had become openly hostile to Fidel and what he stood for.

Invited to dinner by Castro shortly after we arrived, we were greeted by Fidel in the Palace of the Revolution at 9:30 p.m. on March 9, 2000. Accompanied by a large entourage of his ministers and a few cultural figures, Castro was dressed in an elegant blue double-breasted suit (seemingly from Savile Row). He immediately disarmed us by greeting all of us by our first names. Arthur Miller's first take was "Had Castro not been a revolutionary politician, he might well have been a movie star. He had that utter total self-involvement—that need for love and agreement and the overwhelming thirst for the power that comes with total approval."[79]

Holding high a handful of notes, Castro told us he had heard much about the first day of our visit. With a wide grin, he told my wife, Wendy, a former human rights activist, that he had "lost us" for a few hours after our meeting at the university.

"Did you go shopping?" he asked. "Where did you go?"

He, of course, knew well that we had spent an hour with a leader of the Cuban human rights movement, Elizardo Sánchez. Castro was "a control freak." To be so is a necessary personality trait for all successful autocrats, particularly Communist autocrats. The Leninist-Stalinist power structure had enabled party leaders to survive for many years. Castro feigned knowing all that was happening in his realm. Over the next several days, we grew to believe that this controlling approach went beyond the natural instinct of a dictator. He seemed always to be counting and citing statistics and numbers. Arthur would comment later about Castro's obsession with numbers: "There was something almost touching in this childish demonstration of his calculating ability, and one recognized again his boyish hungering for the central distinction in a group."[80]

He may have had an obsessive-compulsive personality disorder, or any number of disorders, for that matter. But psychobabble does not dispel the reality that Fidel dominated every aspect of his state longer than any other leader in modern history—nearly sixty years. His intelligence, charisma, and ruthlessness, as well as an obsession for control, contributed to this longevity. His opposition in Cuba never came close to getting rid of him.

Perhaps the most important reason for Castro's endurance as the unchallenged leader was the Leninist system that he adopted after his "conversion" to Communism. He learned quickly and mastered the tools that Lenin had designed for the Soviet Union. The three parallel and competing institutions—the Communist Party, the government, and the secret police—all reported directly to him, each controlling the other. Castro served as overlord.

The Leninist system of control was almost foolproof. Look

at those Communist leaders who kept power and died natural deaths, leaving their rule to their heirs: Lenin, Stalin, Khrushchev, Brezhnev, Andropov, Mao, Ho Chi Minh, Kim Il Sung, Kim Jong Il, Choibalsan and Tsedenbal from Outer Mongolia—and the list goes on throughout Central Europe. The only Communist leader who was murdered by his people was Ceausescu, who behaved more like a Latin dictator. I watched Ceausescu up close: He was no Castro.

Castro was not killed by his enemies—but not for lack of trying. There were multiple efforts by Cubans in and out of Cuba. American administrations famously tried to assassinate him over decades. Castro taunted the CIA for the failures of such bizarre shenanigans as Operation Mongoose, which Kennedy launched to kill Castro after the Bay of Pigs in 1962.

The US government's focus on Fidel and his cigar was a metaphor for their narrow view of the "Cuba problem." The US pounding away at the evils of Castro every day contributed to the image of Castro as the "giant killer." Our policy and propaganda focused American attention on one man, a Goliath, rather than on the nation and its people.

Americans find it convenient to respond to one hateful and recognizable face as the symbol of the enemy. With little knowledge of other cultures, our fellow citizens and often leaders find it easier to define our enemies by the iconography of their leaders: Hitler, Mussolini, Stalin, Mao, Ho Chi Minh, Kim Il Sung, Saddam Hussein, Qaddafi, and the Ayatollah Khomeini all had faces that Americans came to fear and hate. The US obsession with Fidel's face and his ubiquitous cigar drove Americans to believe he should be eliminated, while at the same time making

Joining Castro in his Mercedes.

him the hero fighter against Yankee power for millions of people around the world. That paradox should have seemed obvious.

In one of my extended personal conversations with Castro during this visit, I was seated close to him in the back of his Mercedes. He said, "Look into my eyes and look at the color and texture of my skin. Tell the CIA that I am healthy and not about to die."

At that time, in the year 2000, he was seventy-four years old. He died of natural causes in his bed, in 2016, sixteen years later, at the age of ninety.

───────────

Before dinner in his palace, we were subjected to a well-rehearsed litany of complaints against US actions against Cuba. He railed against the US Interests Section (the quasi-embassy) in Havana, saying that it had too many spies. He knew that I had negotiated the US-Cuban agreement to open the US and Cuban Interests Sections during the first months of the Carter administration in 1977.

Apropos of nothing, Castro interjected, "Clinton is an intelligent person." It was a theme he came back to during the conversations over the two days. Nevertheless, he disagreed with Clinton's position on immigration. "Clinton's immigration policy is simply wrong" and not consistent with his understandings of the agreements that have been made over the past several years (prior to 1994), said Castro. The problem, I believe, was that Clinton had never succumbed to Fidel's siren call.

When addressing Americans, Castro almost always seemed to be speaking from the position of moral superiority that flowed from his belief in Marxism, and his hatred of capitalism and of presumed American-led corruption of Havana during the Batista regime. At one point, Castro bragged about the vast Cuban medical contributions in combating the AIDS epidemic in Africa. This comment provoked Arthur Miller to describe a play about AIDS that had been presented in his honor the night before at Cuba's impressive Instituto Superior de Arte (ISA). Arthur had been struck by the surreal creative meshing of the death of Jesus on the cross, presumably from AIDS, mixed into the mysteries of the indigenous Cuban religion, Santería. Arthur asked how big a problem AIDS was in Cuba and about the sanitariums that had been set up to handle HIV cases.

Castro's energy was bewildering and exhausting. In a later interview, Arthur explained his impression of what was going on in Castro's head: "The quasi-sexual enchantment of power?

Arthur Miller speaking to students at
Instituto Superior de Arte, Havana.

Perhaps. More likely, given his history, [it] was his commitment
to the poetic image of world revolution, the uprising of the
wretched of the earth with himself at its head. And in plain fact,
as the chief of a mere island, he had managed to elevate himself
to that transcendent state in millions of minds."[81]

At dinner, our host, in a touching yet fumbling way, tried
to engage Styron and Miller in an "intellectual" conversation.
I imagine that Gabo had taken Castro aside before dinner and
encouraged him to engage the two writers and refrain from
his endless tales of combat, war, and revolution. Castro asked,
"Are writers or scientists more likely to believe in God and life
after death?" Styron labored hard to make the case for writers. I
suggested that scientists were more likely to believe in life after
death, paradoxically. Then later, Arthur, who clearly found the
discussion mundane, observed that according to a recent survey

Ricardo Alarcón, former Foreign Minister of Cuba.

in the *New York Times*, over 75 percent of the American people believe that they will go to heaven but only 35 percent expect to see anyone they know there. Fidel quickly moved on to his next question.

The seven or eight members of the cabinet and other officials who had joined us at dinner sat unmoving. During the entire three hours at the table, my dinner partner, Ricardo Alarcón, president of the National Assembly, said not a word. He spent the entire time intensely looking at the leader. Indeed, none of the Cubans present spoke unless called on by Fidel. Not even Gabo. One can imagine the thousands of dinners those poor souls had to sit through in rapt admiration while listening to the familiar and relentless babble of their compulsively loquacious "Comandante."

When speaking, which was most of the time, Castro was animated. He left virtually no space between words or sentences.

When listening, he contorted his face and moved his head to the left and right, looking straight at the speaker then seemingly pensively looking up or beyond the table, either out of distraction or a sense of the theater. He was always listening with eyes wide open while working his long, elegant fingers around his face. He would touch his cheek in a mock pensive gesture. He heard what was being said and was quick to respond or to ask for clarification. Those exaggerated mannerisms had evolved over decades of performances at that same long dining room table. Arthur commented that he was "simply a bad ham actor."

Castro spoke of the "humble conditions" his senior officials lived in compared to their counterparts in other countries. One of his ministers had once had a nice car, but when he joined the government he had to get a Soviet Lada like every other senior official. Fidel said that he managed all the cars for the ministers. The Ladas had been left to Castro by the Russian government after the collapse of the Soviet Union. Fidel said there were about one hundred good Ladas still left in reserve of the original 175. He personally was still in charge of rationing them out to ministers. He said, "If the embargo is ever lifted, I would welcome more medicine for my people, more books, and better food. Cuba will not turn into a parade of cars."

Castro spoke proudly about how well his government worked, which enabled him to spend limited time at work. "I do not try to follow everything," he said.

I interjected that he seemed to oversee all activity in the country apropos of his remark about controlling the cars for the ministers. He said responsibilities were divided up very well and carefully, and there were many issues in government he just left to others. He said with uncharacteristic false modesty, "I am a

Communist. I work within my limited capacities and receive according to my needs." His smile revealed at least a measure of his instinct for irony and falsehood.

Of that night, Arthur would write: "Castro was now in full flight, borne aloft by a kind of manic enthusiasm for sheer performance itself. Be it some perfectly well-known scientific discovery or somebody's intelligent perception of whatever sort, he spoke of it as though personally exposing it for the first time. But charmingly, not without ironical self-deprecation and some wit, he was remorselessly on, obviously anxious to occupy as vast a space around him as he possibly could."[82]

I told Castro about the book on Stalin's errors by former Venezuelan *guerrillero* Teodoro Petkoff. Fidel said he had personally taken Teodoro and his brother Luben to a boat in the early 1960s to launch them from Cuba with arms to begin their guerilla war against the first Venezuelan democratic government of Rómulo Betancourt.

I said that I had been impressed by Petkoff's powerful book, which was called *Czechoslovakia* and had been published in Venezuela in 1969 following the 1968 Soviet invasion of Czechoslovakia. It was one of the most fierce and well-informed books on the Stalinist system I had read. Petkoff had become a passionate renegade from Communism.

Castro had never heard of the book's critique of Stalin and the Soviet system. When I got home from the trip, I found an old copy of the book, which I sent to him.

During dinner, at the height of Castro's lengthy discourse on Stalin's flawed military strategy in dealing with the Nazi invading troops, Mort, Arthur, and I took at break to go to the bathroom—which Castro never seemed to require. Arthur and Mort began to speculate that Castro could be "stark raving mad." I said that he certainly seemed angry at the Soviets and about Stalin's limitations as a military strategist.

When we returned, Castro picked back up with Soviet politics, speaking of Gorbachev with disdain. He said he may be a "nice" man but "a twelve-year-old Cuban 'pioneer' [the equivalent of a party 'boy scout'] has more political sense than Gorbachev."

Gorbachev had destroyed Soviet power, said Castro. NATO would never have bombed Yugoslavia had another leader held on to Soviet power. He maintained that Russia was a powerful country with energy, minerals, intelligent people, and military power. "It needed to be reformed but not destroyed, as Gorbachev had done."

Remaining on Gorbachev, I told Castro that China's Deng Xiaoping and Gorbachev were the exact opposites in how they dealt with their Marxist-Leninist systems. Deng understood that Marxism was hopelessly flawed as an ideology for economic growth and that he needed to resort to private property and capitalist measures in order to give the vast population of China the capacity and incentives to develop the means to expand the economy of the state and allow the Chinese to take responsibility for their own well-being. At the same time, Deng had realized that the Leninist system of control was the essential political tool, both for maintaining control over the nation and to allow the beginnings of private enterprise among the industrious Chinese. Today, Chinese leader Xi would have been unable to restore such vast authority to himself had Deng not preserved the Leninist structure of power through the Chinese Communist Party. Without Deng's capitalist commitment to an annual rate of economic growth of 8 to 10 percent, China would never have achieved its economic miracle. Therefore, at least up to today, the Chinese system has been far more successful economically and politically than the USSR had been.

In contrast, because of his policies of perestroika and glasnost, Gorbachev had unraveled the Leninist system precisely because he believed so blindly in Marxism. Like Castro, Soviet leaders believed that capitalism was corrupt and decadent: it was capitalism that caused the deep divisions in the American political system that weakened the US and would eventually lead to an American implosion. These leaders thrived on the sense of moral superiority rendered by the rubbish Communist belief that personal wealth and capital were the source of all human failures. Gorbachev and Khrushchev thought socialism could work if only the heavy hand of Lenin and Stalin were lifted. If the inefficiencies of the Soviet control could be eliminated, Communism would have a "human face" (as the Czechoslovaks had described their reforms during the Prague Spring of 1968). *That* was Gorbachev's fatal flaw as Soviet leader. That is why he left the Soviet system broken. And that is why Russians, who were not by nature entrepreneurial, were so ill-prepared to take on responsibility for their own lives. They couldn't—any more than Gorbachev could give them the opportunity to do so.

Castro seemed to be listening carefully, bobbing his head, looking me straight in the eye. He then said, "Is that your idea or someone else's?" Pointing his finger at me, he said, "You are right."

I had no idea whether he had understood what I had said. Had he been paying attention while looking straight at me? I assumed he would agree with anything negative about

Gorbachev, particularly regarding the squandering of Leninist control. But that he would agree readily with the wisdom of China's private sector option was surprising, given his failure to try to replicate the Chinese and Vietnamese successes.

By then it was after 3:00 a.m. All of us were getting tired. Arthur Miller, having heard enough, interrupted one of Fidel's monologues. Looking across the table directly into Castro's eyes, he said to our host, "Earlier this evening you said to me that you had calculated that I am eleven years, sixty days older than you are. I am now eleven years and sixty-one days older than you are."[83]

Fidel immediately, without waiting for the English translation, got the point and rose from the table saying that he apologized for keeping us too long. He was courteous in showing us out of the palace. He and his entire entourage of ministers stood smiling on the grand steps waving goodbye at 3:30 a.m.

———————

The following day, our cultural delegation was driven to a showplace farm, Las Terrazas, in the hills, about two hours outside of Havana. We were lunching on the front porch of a mock rustic house when, to our surprise, three large Mercedes limousines roared into the parking lot next to the porch. Castro emerged in his signal green mufti uniform. He was accompanied by an entourage of uniformed armed guards.

He seemed determined to clean up his act with the writers, whom he might have bored with his combat and revolutionary monologues the night before. When he joined our lunch, Wendy asked Bill Styron to describe *The Confessions of Nat Turner*. This

Castro listening to Bill Styron
with interpreter Jana on Castro's right.

was Styron's controversial novel that portrayed the enslaved person in Virginia who rebelled against his owners and tried to flee his bondage. Some African Americans had criticized Bill for writing the story in the first person. However, James Baldwin and other African American friends stood by the novel.

Styron, who was at his best that day, described the legendary nineteenth-century slave as "revolutionary." Styron then pulled Castro in further with an informed discussion of how differently the Spanish, Portuguese, and English had dealt with African slaves in the Western Hemisphere. Castro was clearly fascinated by Styron's tale. I was personally pleased; as Bill had not yet engaged the performer.

This was the only time that the issue of Afro-Cubans came up. Black senior officials were rarely encountered in the Castro establishment at a time when Afro-Cubans were nearly 40 percent of the population. They had been only a small part of the massive exodus of Cubans from the island since the revolution. As a result, Afro-Cubans had become a larger percentage of the population and were far less likely to benefit from the $3 billion annual flow of remittances from Cuban relatives abroad. The Cuban leadership had (and have) difficulty reconciling their ostensible commitment to social equality with the difficult economic conditions and low level of dignity accorded the large Afro-Cuban minority.

After the few lunch hours in Las Terrazas, Castro abruptly announced that it was time to drive back to Havana. He invited me to join him in his limo. He probably selected me because I was a male who spoke Spanish. As Arthur wrote later, Castro "seemed pathetically hungry for some kind of human contact. Brilliant as he was, spirited and resourceful as his people are, his endless rule seemed like some powerful vine wrapping its roots around the country and while defending it from the elements choking its natural growth.

Bill, Gabo, Mort, and Patty with bird in Las Terrazas.

"What, one wonders, is keeping it all alive? Is it the patriotic love of Cubans, conformist or dissident, for their country, or is it the stuck-in-cement manic hatred of US politicians, whose embargo quite simply gives Castro an insurance policy against needed change, injecting the energy of rightful defiance into the people? For it is the embargo that automatically explains each and every failure of the regime to provide for the Cuban people. It will need the pathos of a new Cervantes to measure up to this profoundly sad tale of needless suffering."[84]

My conversation in the car with Castro lasted three hours. After the two-hour ride back to the hotel, we sat for over an hour in front of the hotel before I broke loose. Sitting in the back, right next to Castro, I asked if he would answer my direct questions. Since I had been taking notes, he knew I was paying attention. In the car, I had continued to scribble away, sitting almost in his lap. His memory was impressive, albeit distorted by ego and a need for justification and appreciation.

Castro boasted that the revolution he delivered in Cuba was low cost. He estimated it cost about $150,000. "Others have spent $10 to 30 million with no success either because the situation was not ripe or the leadership was weak." His success encouraged him to promote revolutions in "every country in Latin America."

Yet the Russians remained stubborn out of caution about the US's stance against revolution and would not provide him weapons. Castro assured me that he became frustrated by the Soviets' restriction on his activity. "The Soviets were more interested in 'peaceful coexistence' with the United States than support for revolutionary change." For example, Moscow opposed Castro transferring Soviet weapons to any other insurgency in Latin

America. The Soviets did not want their weapons to be found in Cuban-sponsored revolutions while they were seeking détente with the US. Castro was forced to buy guns elsewhere, and he would ship them to fighters in the region. He also said that he did not send Cubans into Central America so as not to provoke US action and not to place himself in difficult situations vis-à-vis the Soviets.

Castro said the Soviets never showed any interest in "revolution." Khrushchev supported the Cuban Revolution to improve strategic posture against the US—not because of any support for revolution. Brezhnev's decision to become involved militarily in Africa, most particularly in the war in support of Mengistu in Ethiopia, was purely and simply to establish a better strategic position for Soviet power in the horn of Africa. Again, there was no interest in revolution in Ethiopia or anywhere else.

That afternoon, as we sat in his car, his interpreter on Castro's left and I on his right, Fidel's face was about six inches from mine for the entire time. There were machine guns on the floor and a security guard outside the door. We never ceased talking. I interrupted him frequently and he would ask me questions and wait for answers. This was not the long neurotic monologue that I had by then become accustomed to. I asked him to review his interventions to start or support revolutions in Latin America and Africa over the past forty years. He agreed.

We began with the Sandinista takeover in Nicaragua in 1979. As the former US ambassador in Venezuela, I knew that the Carter administration had decided to work with Venezuelan president Carlos Andrés Pérez (CAP) to persuade Anastasio Somoza to leave Nicaragua prior to a Sandinista victory. CAP and Carter had recruited, secretly, a shadow government that would move in once Somoza agreed to depart. CAP and Carter then had a misunderstanding. CAP became angry with Carter and began to plot to move on his own to support the Sandinista military commander Eden Pastora ("Comandante Zero") to bring the Sandinistas to power.

Castro then told me that CAP had called him on September 28, 1978, to ask that Castro transfer some weapons to the Sandinistas and to tell him that he had the money to buy the weapons. Castro said that during this call, CAP kept asking for types of rockets and missiles that the Sandinistas did not need and did not know how to use. "He never understood revolution," said Castro, referring to CAP. When he received the call, Castro was in Yemen. Castro assured CAP that he could get the weapons. I did not tell Castro that we had known of CAP's call to him because of an intercept of the call.

Castro said he bought Israeli weapons for the Sandinistas using CAP's money. Castro then had to figure out a way to get the weapons to the Sandinistas. He had been training, in Cuba, fighters from other Latin American countries including Argentina, Chile, and Bolivia. By the fall of 1978, he had already provided some of these forces to the Sandinistas. Then, in the early spring of 1979, Fidel and CAP made a deal with a senior Costa Rican man of business to fly the Israeli weapons into his ranch near the border with Nicaragua.

I told Castro that as ambassador to Venezuela, I had tracked the US efforts to replace Somoza before he was thrown out. I told him that those efforts were stopped by Carter in early 1979 because of the fall of the shah of Iran, which took the spirit out of the president. I said that I had had a meeting with CAP in March of 1979, just after he had left office as president. In that meeting,

I told CAP that I had just learned from an intelligence briefing in Panama that the Sandinistas were broken and demoralized and could not remove Somoza. CAP had replied to me that I was wrong, and that the Sandinistas, far from being demoralized, had become a real military force with modern weapons. They would soon move into Managua.

Castro confirmed, in my conversation with him in the back of his car during that hot afternoon in 2000, that it was during that period that he was able to move the weapons to the Sandinistas. He described in colorful detail his personal involvement in the final phases of the Sandinista battle to take over Managua. According to Castro, for nearly two months in the spring of 1979, he did practically nothing but work on assuring the Sandinista victory. To hear him describe his role, he was the "command central," constantly in communications from Havana with the Sandinistas as they prepared for the final attacks.

He described one episode: The Sandinistas were moving into Managua and had decided to take one of the main roads into the city, which seemed open. Castro said that the fools did not realize that it was a Somoza trick. Fidel was listening to the Nicaraguan military communications, which indicated that the Nicaraguans were trying to entice the invading forces to come in on the main road and walk into an ambush. Fidel alerted the Sandinista command. Because the Nicaraguan forces began firing too soon, the Sandinistas were able to retain enough strength to enter Managua from different directions and get Somoza out of the country. Castro was showing off with this explanation of how deeply involved he had been in the Sandinista revolution, including giving daily if not hourly commands. He may have exaggerated his role, but he became increasingly excited and energized in the telling—as if it were yesterday. Castro saw himself as a warrior and permanent guerrillero. He believed that he was more able at fighting and directing revolutions than anyone.

I told Castro that I knew from many personal discussions with CAP that he found the Sandinista Eden Pastora the most sensible leader. That is why he paid to get Castro to send arms to Pastora. Fidel laughed. He said that Pastora was popular, but he was just not a fighter or a revolutionary. At one critical phase in the war, Pastora just disappeared. All the weapons bought by CAP for Pastora, said Castro, had ended up in the hands of the real leaders, the Ortega brothers. Pastora was not involved in the fight.

Castro finished by saying that revolutionaries must be willing to carry out revolutions.

Following my questions, Castro said he had been personally involved in many wars and revolutions without showing his hand to the United States. To my great surprise, he spoke of his plans in 1982 to help Argentina's far-right military leader Galtieri fend off UK military action in Galtieri's efforts to the seize the Falklands (Malvinas) from the British. He said that even though the leftist movement in Argentina had been strongly opposed to the Galtieri military government, Castro had decided to provide some military assistance to this Argentine nationalist's move to take the Malvinas. I told him that I was astounded that he had even considered support for the Galtieri military government, which was one of the most corrupt, quasi-fascist regimes in Latin America—and one of the stupidest to boot. He said he had ultimately decided against providing support, but he had considered it. It was clear this was another indication of his priorities. The British expelled the Argentine forces from the Falklands so quickly that

Castro probably never had a chance to support the impressively incompetent Argentine military.

Venezuela, he said, was an early target for revolution. He initiated and supported the guerrilla movements against the Betancourt and Leoni governments. Those revolutionary actions in Venezuela failed miserably. However, Castro was willing to wait. He considered one his great successes to have been his close relationship with Hugo Chavez, Venezuela's populist and socialist leader who had recently (in 2000) consolidated power. He told me that Chavez was smart, articulate, charismatic, and a good leader.

One of the highest qualities Castro admired in a leader, after his fighting capacity, was his ability to lead the "masses." He said that Chavez understood how to do just that. I said that Chavez did seem to have populist support in the country, but he did not have a coherent program, or a team to carry out a program even if he had one. It all seemed populist rhetoric. Castro said that the programs and the teams would come: "Chavez is an able leader whom I must support."

We next turned to Africa, which he had entered with his revolutionary doctrine. He felt that revolution had been hindered in the Western Hemisphere by the relative success of Kennedy's aid program, the US Alliance for Progress, and forceful US operations against Cuba's role. He also felt restrained by the Soviets for his adventurism and his forced disavowal of the use of Soviet weapons in the Western Hemisphere. He pivoted to Africa because many states there appeared ripe for revolution, as the old colonial powers were departing. He also had a large population of Afro-Cubans whom he believed would be effective in Africa.

Castro relayed military support to the opposition in Algeria in their struggle against the French. He surprised me with a detailed explanation of how he had sent Cuban fighter pilots to help Hafez al-Assad in Syria during the Yom Kippur War in 1973. The Soviets had rushed some of their newest fighter aircraft to Syria, but Assad's air force had no capable pilots for the new MiGs. Fidel sent a dozen Cuban pilots to Damascus, not to train Syrian pilots but to actually fly in combat against the Israelis in the new Soviet fighter aircraft. He had also sent troops to the Congo to help to Patrice Lumumba shortly after the Cuban Revolution and before Lumumba's assassination.

Castro's major African intervention was in Angola. He spoke long and passionately about Angola, where his forces were on the ground for nearly fourteen years. He said that even though his military presence in Angola reached nearly fifty-seven thousand at one point, his general level of forces was at about thirty-five thousand. He said that the Soviets were opposed to the Cuban intervention and did not get involved themselves. We have later learned that the relatively large Cuban presence in Angola over so many years resulted in many Cuban casualties and negative reactions within Cuba over Castro's placing of the Angolan revolution over the future of the Cuban people.

The difference in approach between the Soviets and the Cubans became even clearer in their deliberations over whether to get involved in Ethiopia's war with Somalia. The Soviets had invested considerable political and military effort there, for the purely strategic objectives of being in the Horn of Africa. Fidel said that he was in Ethiopia to help rid that country of the corrupt government of Haile Selassie and support the revolution of Mengistu. He described his negotiations with Mengistu, but he said he was reluctant to commit significant forces. As it turned out, Siad Barre, the Somali leader who had been cultivated by the Soviets, decided to move into Ethiopia. When the Somalis seemed intent on seizing some critical Ethiopian territory, Fidel persuaded the Soviets to join in the effort to stop the Somali invasion, thus leading to the consolidation of Mengistu's power, assuring the victory of Ethiopia against Somalia, and giving the Soviets a larger military stronghold in the Horn of Africa.

Fidel said he knew that, at the very moment he was deciding to move forces into Ethiopia and get the Soviets in as well, there was a real possibility that the Carter administration would try to open up a larger dialogue on bilateral relations (this was in mid-1977). He had had several conversations with such visitors as Peter Tarnoff and Bob Pastor from the Carter administration, but the Ethiopia events in 1977 had put the end to those opportunities. I said to him that such things seemed to happen every time when the US political system was moving toward improved relations with Cuba. Why, I asked, in this case, was Ethiopia more important than improved relations with the US and the consequent impact on the Cuban economic situation? He said simply because "that is our doctrine."

It was an expression that he used on several occasions in our talk to explain why he undertook acts that seemed against the interests of the Cuban people.

Toward the end of our conversation, I asked Castro directly whether he had any misgivings for all those violent revolutions he had undertaken over the years on behalf of other groups in other nations. I said that thousands of Cubans and many more thousands from other states had died in revolutions promoted by Castro. I said I could not think of one of those states where the populations today were better off because of his revolutions. I asked whether he had today any misgivings or regrets. He said firmly "No."

I asked him, "Why?"

He replied, "Because of the doctrine." (*Por la doctrina.*) Those words still ring in my ears today.

I asked, "What is your 'doctrine'?"

"Wherever there is injustice on a large scale," he said, "there must be revolution. It is not important whether the revolution fails—it must be tried." Castro spoke about the deep injustice throughout Latin America in democracies where the courts and national assemblies were all part of the corruption. In explaining his "doctrine," he never once mentioned Communism or Marxism-Leninism. His "doctrine" was revolution or radical change in societies—through violence.

I took away from these conversations a clearer picture of Castro's policies toward the US. He liked to have political and psychological battles against us and was never going to surrender. At the moment we were in Cuba, he was focused on winning the "battle" of getting the young boy Elian Gonzalez released from Florida. He won that one.

Castro delighted in summarizing his wins. He said to me, on several occasions, that there was no real democracy in Latin America and yet that there was still large-scale corruption in all of those so-called democracies.

At the end of our conversation, after we had been sitting in the back of his parked car in front of the Hotel Santa Isabel for over an hour, he noted again that I had been taking notes during our conversation. He said, not in a threatening manner but in a jocular way, that he had said things to me that he had not said to anyone else, and added, "I am planning to tell my own story one of these days, and I do not want someone else to tell it for me."

While in our final moments of our talks, I heard his guards outside the car jump up and cock their guns. I became frightened. It turned out that our friend Patty Phelps de Cisneros had come out on her balcony from the hotel room right above the car with the intention of getting some air and had surprised the five armed guards around the limo. After all of the talk of violence, we ended with that.

As we left the hotel for dinner the following night, Gabo asked me whether we wanted to have dinner with Castro again. He might join us at our restaurant, he said.

I said, speaking for our group, "No, thanks."

At that last dinner, I sat next to Gabo and we spoke in Spanish most of the evening. I had become fond of Gabo over our several-year relationship, in addition to admiring his novels.

The group with Gabo, center, and his
wife Mercedes, second from the right.

And I had long been curious about the Gabo-Fidel relationship. In a compelling book on the subject, the authors Angel Esteban and Stéphanie Panichelli, summarizing the long history of that relationship, wrote: "Castro, who for years would not let the Colombian Nobel Prize winner into his inner circle, later would openly accept his conspiring overtures. Gabo, obsessed with power, political bosses, and the highest levels of diplomacy saw in the Cuban patriarch a model for Latin America. Castro found in Gabo a mouthpiece to communicate his revolutionary achievements throughout the Western Hemisphere."[85]

I sensed less affection and admiration between the two of them than an alliance and a common motive to satisfy their personal objectives. I could understand Castro's reasons for using Gabo as a coveted bridge to a world he needed and wanted to cultivate for his own reasons. But I simply could not fathom how the writer of *The Autumn of the Patriarch* could not see in Castro, his own patriarch, a man who felt he would defy death and lead his country forever.

As we reviewed our visit, Gabo asked me rather bluntly why we had gone to see human-rights leader Elizardo Sánchez shortly after we arrived. Gabo, speaking firmly, said that Sánchez was unimportant. "The only important person in Cuba is Fidel Castro."

I replied to Gabo, "That is precisely the problem."

Fidel Castro continued to dominate Cuba, even after he had turned the title of president over to his brother Raúl. This became particularly evident after Raúl had agreed to President Obama's 2016 visit to Havana, as an effort to turn the page. Obama was bold and perhaps naive in trying to put the long history of troubles in the US-Cuban relationship behind us. Within days after

Obama had left Havana, Fidel, from his sickbed, crafted for *Granma*, the official paper of the Cuban Communist Party, a lengthy critique of Obama and Obama's speech in Havana. It revealed what Fidel was really thinking and confirmed my own sense that Fidel probably never would have come to such an effort when he had been running Cuba for sixty years.

In his long editorial in *Granma* (the "Official Voice of the Central Committee of the Communist Party of Cuba"), sarcastically addressed to "Brother Obama," Fidel wrote: "Nobody should be under the illusion that this dignified and selfless country will renounce the glory, the rights, and the spiritual wealth they have gained with the development of education, science, and culture."

After praising, at length, the role of Cuba in "Liberating Angola and other African nations from the empires," he went on "to warn that we are capable of producing the food and material riches we need with the efforts and intelligence of our people. We do not need the empire to give us anything. Efforts will be legal and peaceful, as this is our commitment to peace and fraternity to all human beings who live on this planet."[86]

I never met Lenin or Mao and have no idea what they were like to be close to. I do believe that Castro was not unlike those two revolutionaries, in that he believed deeply in his revolutionary mission and that belief made him so charismatic. He had a religious fervor that can only be found in some of the early religious fanatics. Surely no member of the Soviet Politburo had any intimation of Castro's belief in the injustices of the past and his own mission to correct them. Castro was followed by Cubans since he believed so deeply in their cause as interpreted by him. He was their oracle and their leader.

CODA

After nearly one half century of trying to find a formula that would keep Castro's communism at bay and enable the US to adopt a sensible policy toward Cuba and the Cuban people, one which would give them hope and opportunity, the Obama effort to open up Cuba to the private sector was crushed by Trump, who fell back on a nearly half a century of conservative platitudes about Cuba. President Obama had finally bitten the bullet and taken an approach that would serve the interests of US policy toward the rest of the world, particularly toward the Latin American states whose governments had long found the US's open hostility toward Cuba an absurd failure to comprehend the nature of US relations with the Western Hemisphere. Sadly, Trump completely unraveled the Obama "normalization" initiative, falling back on the old ideology that Castro's Cuba was somehow a threat to the US because of its terrorist traditions and its ideology and alliances, which could spread its communism.

Analysis of the Cuba problem had become a key part of American political reality since Democrats first became conscious of the Republican voting power that Castro's Cuba gave to the American voters of Florida. This Cuba fixation helped the Republicans win the crucial state of Florida in presidential elections. This phenomenon continued to create the rot at the center of US policymaking for decades, and that rot extended to the committees of both the House and the Senate that were chaired by Cuban Americans who found it politically helpful for their campaigning to perpetuate the Cuba myth. President Biden was heavily influenced in this policy by the Cuban American senator Bob Menendez, who was the chairman of the Senate Foreign Relations Committee and an ally that President Biden considered critical for his Senate strategy.

Cuban American senators also have made sure that no career diplomat who was involved in the Obama initiative on "opening to Cuba" would ever be confirmed as an ambassador posted to any country. The crushing of career diplomats based on their support for the Cuba policy reminds one of the McCarthy era, when the China lobby destroyed the careers of multitudes of talented and bold diplomats who stood for policies that did not support the Chiang Kai-Shek government against Mao, who were actually removed from their careers.

As Wendy and I watched US policy toward Cuba stagnate further, we learned of the scale of the humanitarian crisis that was happening to the long-suffering but inventive and competent Cuban people still living on the island. A large exodus (known as the Special Period) began from Cuba, driving the young and talented, on a scale not known before, to give up on Cuba for the first time since the Soviets discontinued their huge financial subsidy.

Fidel Castro's heirs and other Communist leaders (Raúl Castro and President Miguel Díaz-Canel) were immobilized and seemed reluctant to develop a positive strategy for the economy. So, Wendy and I continued to engage with the Cubans through culture and the arts. Our relationship with Bruno Rodriguez, the Cuban foreign minister who was the permanent representative to the UN when we brought Arthur Miller and William Styron to

Cuba in 2000, has been helpful. Working with other groups, we sought to urge Biden for a more savvy and humanitarian policy toward Cuba.

Our main contacts were, as usual, through culture and the arts. From 2016 on, we brought artists to Havana under the auspices of Wendy's foundation: the Foundation for a Civil Society. These trips brought leading artists such as sculptor Joel Shapiro, photographer Carrie Mae Weems, and photographer Clifford Ross to the island. The most impactful of the American artists who visited Havana with us was our old friend and prominent abstract artist Frank Stella. Frank gave a brilliant lecture to a packed audience that was translated into Spanish. As a result of Frank's dramatic impact on the Cuban art community, the director of Havana's prestigious Museum of Fine Arts asked Frank to organize a select but limited Stella retrospective in Havana to open in early 2021. Wendy spent well over a year on the project, working with Frank directly and with his people. We had gotten approval for JetBlue be the official carrier for the exhibition—it was a nearly unprecedented policy breakthrough for the Cuban government to permit the commercial sponsorship of anything to be publicly announced and publicized. As the time for the opening approached, the Cuban government, specifically the Ministry of Culture, was considering making legal changes in Cuban laws governing the arts and artists—to proscribe their rights to expression, etc. American and Cuban artists began demonstrating against the plans of the Cuban government. I kept Frank informed about the level of criticism leveled at the planned action of the Cuban government. On the eve of when Frank's large collection of paintings were to be loaded on

ship to go to Cuba—more specifically, just moments before—
Frank pulled the plug on the exhibition out of solidarity with
the mounting opposition of American and Cuban artists to the
Cuban government's pending action against artistic freedoms.
Wendy had to act quickly to turn off the multiple actors who
had worked to make the Stella exhibition a reality, including
programs scheduled across the island. I called the director of the
Museum of Fine Arts in Havana to alert him to Frank's decision to call off the exhibition and to explain why he had done
so. I suggested that the museum director inform the minister
of culture that Frank's decision to pull his exhibition reflected
the level of international attention dedicated to criticizing the
unwise action (Decree 349) the Cuban government was about
to take against artistic freedoms. Over the next months, the legal
changes that had been threatened languished. In the end, the
government never took the dreaded action against artistic freedoms for artists. I subsequently confirmed that there is a general
consensus that Frank's decision to pull his exhibition contributed mightily to the Cuban decision to forego the dreaded limits
on artists.

Today, Wendy and I continue our efforts to expand cultural
and human ties between Americans and Cubans and to work
toward more humane and sensible US policies toward Cuba. An
uphill battle!

CHAPTER 18

UNA-USA, the Iran Project, and Other International Art Programs

O n the eve of my departure from the Met, I was asked by John Whitehead, whom I had known when he was deputy secretary of state under George Shultz, and by Arthur Ross, whom I had known as one of the more important philanthropists and internationalists in New York, to become chairman of the board of the United Nations Association of the USA. The UNA-USA was a venerable NGO built to drum up support in the US for the United Nations; it had been inspired by Eleanor Roosevelt. I did not have the wealth of either John or Arthur, but they assured me that they would help me raise money for the first couple of years.

The president of UNA-USA at the time had been Alvin Adams, who had been a fellow FSO who had last been the ambassador to Peru, Haiti, and Djibouti, in Africa. I consulted with Wendy, who had been hoping I would land a job not in the NGO world but where I could earn some cash. I had been fortunate that some at the Met trustees had helped me join a few corporate boards. I was already on the Transco board at the suggestion of my brother-in-law Ward Woods, who was at Lazard Frères at the time. Another trustee included me on the board of several international funds managed by Scudder. Henry Kravis also kindly asked me to join a new company that KKR had just acquired—IDEX Corporation from Chicago.

―――――――――

Punch Sulzberger and I had agreed to retire at the same time from the Met—he as chairman and me as president. Punch was anxious to leave as chairman of the Met board and pass that responsibility to Jamie Houghton, who was next in line for the chairmanship. Punch would then return as the full-time chairman of the board and publisher of the *New York Times*. I, on the other hand, did not have an ongoing job to return to. The Met gave Punch and me a going-away dinner. I knew that Punch had an aversion to long, self-important-sounding after-dinner talks. He much preferred humor to the alternative. I decided to do a riff on the "double Ms" of the Metropolitan Museum. I called it a "mini-memoir."

> My Mission
> Mostly Management
> Minting Money
> Mounting Marketing
> Mining Millions
> Magnifying Merchandise
> Massaging Media
> Masking Mistakes
> Mobilizing Merchants
> Mesmerizing Mayors

Mentoring Managers
Maintaining Modesty
Monetizing Muses
Multiplying Memberships
Muzzling Misogynists
Magnifying Morale
Monitoring Morsches
Maximizing Montebello
Minimizing Me

The "Maximizing Montebello" and "Minimizing Me" lines drew much applause and laughter from friends and family and fit well with Punch's preference for humor over serious summations. Punch knew well the relationship between Philippe and me.

The position of president of the UNA-USA came with two very distinct, very demanding responsibilities: management of the large organization and fundraising for the same. Because there were sixty to seventy chapters of UNA-USA across the country, each had their own management and fundraising issues to be dealt with, and because the organization was struggling financially and politically, my transition to this new world proved more difficult than I had expected. However, the psychic returns were substantial: Arthur Ross and John Whitehead had recruited the formidable Elliot Richardson to speak at my installation. Many other close friends of the United Nations came out of the woodwork to welcome me to this difficult new assignment.

I quickly realized that UNA-USA would need some high-profile programs to finance our organization, which had an annual budget of $50 to 70 million a year. One of the programs that seemed right for raising money was a new idea for the UNA-USA: to help clear landmines worldwide. We began a program we called Adopt-a-Minefield and began searching for a patron. It happened that my wife Wendy's best friend from Stanford was John Eastman. John was the brother of Linda Eastman McCartney, who had been married to Paul McCartney and had recently died. And John knew his brother-in-law well. Paul was determined to marry Heather Mills, who had lost a leg in a motorcycle accident in London and saw herself as a natural leader for those who had lost their legs in the explosion of landmines around the world.

Adopt-a-Minefield quickly became a singular program for UNA-USA, and Paul McCartney enthusiastically became its promoter, with Heather's strong support. Through this program, UNA-USA contributed nearly $50 million over ten years to clear landmines in Croatia, Afghanistan, Vietnam, and Cambodia, and became one of the largest donors to landmine clearing in the UN, though not as big as the US and other large governments. Most of the money was raised thanks to annual dinners that were held in Los Angeles, to which Paul would invite his friends to sing alongside him, such as Paul Simon and James Taylor. They were always successful and raised over a million dollars at each of these dinners. Paul proved to be a remarkably effective, kind, diligent, and creative patron for this program. But Paul wanted to use all the money he raised to go into clearing landmines . . . not into overhead and administration. That required us to considerably reduce the cost of our overhead. We eventually found other ways to raise money to cover the administrative support needed for the ambitious Adopt-a-Minefield program. We used funds to entertain prominent figures who either were already associated with the United Nations, or ones we hoped would be associated with the UN. These included: Beyoncé and Jay Z, Angelina Jolie, Mohammed Ali, John Glenn, Bill Gates, Michael Douglas, Catherine Zeta Jones.

The second big program for UNA-USA was called Global Classrooms, which was designed to help public high school students in the US and in ten other countries around the world learn about international affairs. We developed a curriculum for students to learn international affairs through Model UN simulations. The Model UN proved an invaluable tool for learning about diplomacy and world affairs. Our programs were most impressively successful in China, South Korea, Lebanon, and Spain.

Merrill Lynch gave us a grant of $7 million over five years to build out the program of Global Classrooms in cities where they had official offices; those offices would support our work in their cities. I hired Lucia Rodriguez, an Afro-Cuban American out of Columbia University, to lead the program. She proved to be an ideal leader to help institute our programs in American high schools and around the world. She worked with people of color and young Spanish-speaking students. I sought private funders in each American city to support this ambitious program. In Chicago, I found a ready sponsor in Oprah Winfrey after I described to her our objectives in the inner-city schools. She "got" the mission of the program immediately and became an enthusiastic financial supporter for our work in the Chicago public school system. She never failed to meet with me and Rodriguiz when we visited Chicago. Global Classrooms was also strongly supported by the CEO of the Chicago Public Schools, Arne Duncan, who later became the secretary of education under Barack Obama.

Adopt-a-Minefield and Global Classrooms became the core programs that helped fund the work of UNA-USA during my tenure.

Meanwhile, Wendy found herself increasingly active as the president of the Foundation for a Civil Society, which she established to help the transition of the former Communist countries of Central Europe to democratic societies. She was very active traveling through Central Europe, sometimes for many days at a time. The budget for her activities in Central Europe grew to $2 to 3 million a year. Her core work was funded primarily by USAID, plus a series of private foundations such as Soros' Open Society Foundation, Ford Foundation, Rockefeller Brothers Fund, and the Trust for Mutual Understanding.

While Wendy was promoting civil society and the arts in Central Europe, I found myself increasingly working in the same territory. I went on the board of the Trust for Mutual Understanding, which was spending over a million dollars a year in the promotion and collaboration in the arts and environment between organizations in Central Europe and the United States. The trust became the funding agency for exchanges between the Met and the art museums of art of Russia on one hand and the countries of Central Europe. These exchanges became critical for developing the capacities of the museums of Central and Eastern Europe over the 1990s and early 2000s.

One of the most interesting opportunities came with my appointment to become the American international advisor to the Praemium Imperiale, which is a program set up by David

Rockefeller and the head of Fujisankei Communications Group to provide five awards to artists from around the world in five different art disciplines. The award ceremony takes place in Tokyo each year. David's objective, as announced at the first award ceremony at Rockefeller Center in New York, was to recognize the international role played by the arts in bringing nations together. David felt so strongly about this award that he was able to convince the prime minister of Germany, Helmut Heinrich Waldemar Schmidt, and the prime minister of Italy, Amintore Fanfani, plus the former prime minister of the UK Edward Heath and the president of France, Jacques Chirac, to join him as the original international advisors. After attracting this stellar community of world leaders to the Praemium Imperiale's mission, David Rockefeller stepped aside and ceded his spot to David Rockefeller Jr., his son. Two years later, David Rockefeller Jr. asked me to replace him as international advisor to the Praemium Imperiale, a job which furthered my belief that the arts could play a vital role in communications among nations and in diplomacy.

Because I was appointed in 2002, when the euro was making waves, I asked Helmut Schmidt whether he thought the euro could work as the currency for Europe. His answer was, "Never fear. With German power and French dignity, we'll make it work."

———

As an expression of our strong commitment to the efficacy of diplomacy, Tom Pickering, Frank Wisner, and I began a back-channel dialogue with the government of Iran in 2002.

President Jacques Chirac.

Helmut Schmidt and Bill.

Bill, Wendy, former president of Germany,
Richard von Weizsäcker, 2003

Bill speaking in Tokyo at the Praemium Imperiale, 2018.

Iran Project: Wendy, Suzanne DiMaggio, Stephen Heintz,
Bill, and Frank Wisner, New York, 2019.

This dialogue was made possible by the contacts that we had
with the Iranian permanent representative to the UN Javad Zarif
and Suzanne DiMaggio, whom I had recently made head of the
political work of UNA-USA, where I was president. Suzanne had
been working with Zarif and proposed that UNA-USA take the
lead in an informal "track two," or back-channel, discussion with
Iranian officials, with the assumption that the tense standoff with
Iran and the US could not go on indefinitely: the issues were
too pressing, the Middle East too volatile, and America's physical presence in Iran's neighborhood was too formidable to allow
stagnation.

Indeed, the US-Iranian relationship presented perhaps the
most important and troubling foreign-policy challenge facing
both countries. In the near-term, change seemed inevitable.
Whether the change was in a positive or negative direction was

yet to be determined. UNA-USA and its Iranian counterpart set out to devise some mutually acceptable strategy before having to head off a destructive confrontation between the US and Iran. Over many hours of track-two dialogue with Iranian officials, we began to understand that while the issues were extremely difficult, they revealed that the interests of Iran and the US could well overlap and provide grounds for cooperation toward common objectives. Both sides concluded that an escalation of the conflict between Iran and the US was not inevitable. Our dialogue process also demonstrated that face-to-face discussions between diverse experts and policy analysts, hearsay, guess work, and even educated guesses are no substitute for the understanding that can derive from direct discussions.

At that time, in the year 2000, immediately following the American invasion of Iraq, the Iranians were concerned about potential US military action against Iran, Iraq's neighbor. This contributed to both countries persisting in the failed policy of hostility toward one another. The difference of opinion over Iran's nuclear program, the intentions of each country in Iraq, and the failure to articulate a common purpose in the struggle against global terrorism all contributed to misunderstanding and mutual hostility between governments. There were also the deeply entrenched differences over the Israeli-Palestinian conflict.

Drawing on these sources of impasse, our track-two dialogue tried to develop mutually agreed-upon approaches to managing these crucial areas of dispute. Our track-two dialogue contributed to an eventual official dialogue between the Iranian and US governments that would go on to produce the Joint Comprehensive Plan of Action (JCPOA), which was finally reached between the US, Iran, and other governments in 2015. To explain to the public the progress on this track-two dialogue, ambassador Tom Pickering and nuclear analyst at MIT James Walsh, and I wrote a series of long articles in the *New York Review of Books* with the help of the enthusiastic editor, Robert Silvers.

The first article in the *New York Review of Books* ("How to Deal with Iran" by Pickering, Walsh, and Luers) was highly recommended by Lee Hamilton, the chairman of the House Foreign Affairs Committee and cochair of the Iran Study Group, and by the former national security advisor to President Carter, Zbigniew Brzezinski. This active pursuit of track-two dialogue continued, with the full approval of UNA-USA, between 2002 and 2009, when I left as president, under the title the Iran Project, which became a project of the Foundation for a Civil Society, a New York–based NGO.

The initiative that became the Iran Project was strongly endorsed by Stephen Heintz and the board of the Rockefeller

THE WHITE HOUSE
WASHINGTON

Bill —

Thanks to you and the Iran Project on your leadership on the nuclear deal. It made a huge difference, and the world will be safer for it.

Obama Letter

Brothers Fund (RBF), on which I served as a member for many years. The RBF was a consistent supporter of the work with Iran and remained a firm believer in track-two diplomacy. However, the board of UNA-USA was not easily convinced of the wisdom of pursuing this track-two diplomacy. My colleague Tom Pickering was then the chairman of the UNA-USA board, and he managed to convince a skeptical UNA-USA board that this type of diplomacy must be pursued whenever possible.

Obama's ambition to turn JCPOA, otherwise known as the Iran Nuclear Deal, into a diplomatic framework for resolving some of the differences between the US and Iran failed when Donald Trump became president of the United States and essentially killed the JCPOA. Nevertheless, the Iran Project has persisted in its track-two efforts with Iranian officials.

As relations between the US and Iran deteriorated over the

Bill, Wendy, Karel Schwarzenberg, Patty Cisneros,
Count Riprand Arco, Czech Republic.

next couple of years, it became clear that diplomacy had failed, for now. Nevertheless, our back-channel dialogue and, hopefully, official exchanges will move forward.

Our time in New York and Connecticut since 1986 has been blessed with great friendships, fascinating trips, and enriching cultural experiences. And so it continues.

CHAPTER 19

Uncommon Company

In 1957, I was in the queue with hundreds of aspiring young diplomats who had successfully passed the formidable Foreign Service exam and had been through the oral examination. Like the others, I was waiting to be invited to a class of Foreign Service Officers and a training program at the Foreign Service Institute. Most of us knew little about the practice of diplomacy—many, like I, were newly released from the military. We were waiting in that line because it seemed to be an auspicious moment for American diplomacy.

After World War II, the United States was the strongest superpower, economically and politically. The strengths of the US were compounded by the prestige of having a democratic and open political system at a moment when world colonialism was receding and giving way to new nations in Asia and Africa. Determined to prevent the catastrophic devastation caused by another world war, the international community had created a new structure (the United Nations) to preserve peace and maintain a world order.

It was also during this time that cross-cultural diplomatic exchanges began. Soviet and American artists and writers and painters and playwrights flowed across borders and talked and shared and inspired one another. Despite the antagonism and posturing and conflicts—these were some of the darkest years of the Cold War—Moscow and Washington's diplomatic communications stayed open. And though tensions between the US and the USSR remained high, sometimes perilously high, nuclear war did not happen. Diplomacy worked.

I believe there are grave lessons to be found during that time of tense peace—a period in which the United States learned to work with our adversaries . . . not go to war with them. These lessons should not be lost or discounted. The first is that we should never resort to military force first. Diplomacy must lead. Second, we must not leave open the question of what would be a win for us in the event we do find ourselves in a military confrontation. Third, we must have an attainable objective short of total victory or unconditional surrender, which are *unobtainable in the nuclear age.* And fourth, I have become convinced that when diplomacy leads with culture, our shared goals can be better understood and more readily heard by the adversary.

I have come to share President Kennedy's view that art is the common language among all people: "Art is not a form of propaganda it is a form of truth," Kennedy said in his eulogy for Robert Frost. "In a democratic society, the highest duty of the writer, the composer, the artist is to remain true to himself and to let the chips fall where they may. In serving his vision of the truth the artist best serves his nation."

Over the many years I have worked with artists—and in the arts—I, too, have concluded that truth is the driving motivator of artists in every society, even when suppressed by autocratic ideologies. Autocrats fear artists because they understand that artists form the basis of a civil society—something they mightily reject. Communications among artists across cultures, if allowed, can form unique bonds between states and nations; such communications are largely devoid of the sources of conflicts that divide states. I have learned, too, how artists help illuminate for diplomats the true rub or strain between inimical societies. It has been a universal truth across time that every society, whether autocratic or democratic, finds its soul and its voice in the arts. Seeking to understand a country's culture in all its dimensions allows the diplomat a deeper understanding of the other, even an adversary. The arts and artists should be a core component of diplomacy—for America, for everyone.

There are a number of challenges America faces today that do not involve a foreign enemy. I believe the biggest enemy we face is ourselves. Just as in the Cold War, communication is the key to peace. Let us begin there. Yes, America has let herself become rife with political and social animosities that imperil the magnificent constitutional experiment that makes this country what it is. But too often these days, we are siloed; we talk to our group and no one else. We listen to our group and no one else. I strongly suggest we address this problem by becoming diplomats. I believe America could more quickly achieve a new stability if it were to adapt the rules of diplomacy in the conduct of its politics. The rules are simple. Listening is better than talking. Asking questions is better than confrontation. Total long-term victory in verbal or actual combat is not possible, nor should it be sought. The best and most durable agreements are those in which all sides believe they have won something. Talking with your adversary is better than warring. Negotiated agreements are not "appeasements." Compromise is not a four-letter word. Humor is the great mediator.

There is one more rule. It may be the most important: keeping uncommon company should always be the goal. In the Soviet

Union, I learned how effective it was to mix up the community to include unlikely participants. I found that including in the discourse those who opposed the US involvement usually enriched the level of candor and the options for solutions. Doing so via culture and the arts just made it that much easier and more effective. I learned that celebrating the beauty of Russian literature and music, the richness of Latin American visual arts, and the theater and literature in Czechoslovakia broke down barriers and allowed relationships to flourish. I also found that in difficult conversations, finding common ground among uncommon company softens the communications and eases the confrontations. I became convinced that when I could talk to my adversary and identify their goals, doing so moved the conversation forward. When I took pains to respect the concerns of my adversary, even if they were not my own concerns (or America's concerns), progress was made; we lived to talk some more. In conventional diplomatic ventures, it is often difficult to incorporate confrontational points of view, but I became convinced that it is essential to force candor in the conversation with enemies. Such is an essential component of diplomatic behavior. The fact is that the US and the Soviet Union maintained diplomatic relations and civil dialogue during the entire Cold War.

Let us not fool ourselves: the political and social climate in the United States is not good, and it is impinging on our capacity to impact and shape the world and keep our country at peace. The US *must* find a way to resolve our domestic tensions before we can solve the hard international tensions that we face today and will face in the future. Communication is key. For all the trouble of the Cold War diplomacy, no nuclear war was waged. President Kennedy deployed back-channel contacts and hotline and joint communications to avoid nuclear war. Back channels and hotlines and joint communications—they're all avenues of dialogue.

As we look more broadly to the world today, there are international situations that won't wait. With an unflinching belief in the fundamental principle of talking to the other in uncommon company, I am persuaded that we must talk even with Putin or his closest advisors to see when and whether he would be prepared to share his own thoughts on how to organize an end to the war with Ukraine. Some way must be found to seek back-channel communications with the Kremlin, with friends and associates of Putin, to determine whether there is an inclination to address our differences and explore ways to end this conflict with Ukraine. The demonization of Putin is fully understandable given the inhumanity of this war between Russia and Ukraine, but the need to converse with uncommon company, including your enemies, should override the hatred and hostility of the enemy. If the US is engaged in supporting a military conflict or conducting a military conflict, it must set objectives short of total victory. Incidentally, wins that are achievable allow the US to sustain conflicts without having to face up to humiliating defeat or endless wars.

ACKNOWLEDGMENTS

Since virtually everyone I have listened to and heard during my life has informed my thinking, it is impossible for me in this space to single out the key individuals who have helped shape this book. I remember, with gratitude, my nanny after my birth, Emma, who was a German American grandmother living in Springfield, Illinois, in 1930. My mother needed a kidney operation after my birth, so she hired Emma to take care of me during that first year or so. To my caretaker today, Emilia Kozakova, a very young, lively, and smart Slovak grandmother living in nearby New Milford, Connecticut, who has helped Wendy keep me healthy and alert for the past two years into my nineties. I want to add two additional names who are co-partners of the team we have had in Connecticut during the last many years. The first is Dave Boccuzzi, who was our caretaker and valuable supporter in all matters that deal with our house and wellbeing, and the other is Ginny Hallock, who helped Wendy keep an ordered environment in the house for thirty years. She is a valuable backup to us all. In addition to the staff in Connecticut, the loyal and hardworking Raquel Vattuone has taken care of our New York apartment since 1986.

To those who made possible the publication of the book:

I want to first thank the generosity of the Phelps family for their friendship and support of this publication. The friendship I have with Bill Phelps has grown closer as our lives have grown into each other's. Bill's sister Ann Phelps Jacobs has graciously joined the Phelps family in the support of this venture. My friendship with my nephew William Luers Phelps, the son of my sister Lynd Phelps and Dick, helped encourage the generosity of the Phelps family. Dick Phelps, who was my former brother-in-law, has generated in his children his own instinct for altruism. Bill Phelps was greatly admired by my eldest son, Mark, who worked for Bill's company. Bill helped Mark build a new life for himself. Dick Phelps also made it possible for my son William to attend Andover.

I thank Wendy's brother, Ward Woods, for his generosity once again. After I almost died in Punta del Este, Uruguay, from a bacterial infection known as *Vibrio vulnificus*, Woody sent his plane to bring me back to New York, so that I could recover under the care of Dr. Valentin Fuster at Mt. Sinai Hospital in New York.

Woody, who had been very successful at Lazard Frères and later as the head of Bessemer Securities, established the Woods Institute for the Environment at his alma mater, Stanford University. Woody has been a generous and hands-on philanthropist for over a decade. He has claimed to respect my interesting life and I have been dazzled by his financial success.

A special thanks goes to Alex and Patricia Farman Farmaian who initially convinced me that I should write a memoir. Alex and his sister, Roxane, had been pleased by the memoir they had published on their father, Manucher Mirza Farman Farmaian, entitled *Blood and Oil: Memoirs of A Persian Prince,* which is a big history of Iran and one of its most fascinating families over the past hundred years. I came to know Alex's sister when she cooperated as a scholar at Cambridge University with the Iran Project. I hardly could imagine how a book by Bill Luers from

Springfield, Illinois, could find a place in a reader's interest that would be comparable for the curious reader to the book they had just published about their father.

I also thank our close friends Ben and Cris Heineman, with whom we have discussed for hours the big and small issues I deal with in this book, during our marathon lunches on Martha's Vineyard and in Connecticut. There are few couples in Wendy's and my life with whom we are more attuned than the Heinemans and we have many hours of conversation that confirm that fact.

Ken and Susan Wallach are especially close friends from Marth's Vineyard and New York. I knew Ken's father, Ira Wallach, well and he supported much of my work in international affairs, particularly my work as president of UNA-USA. Ira was a close associate of one of my great and strongest New York patrons, Arthur Ross. Ken and Susan have taken up an interest in Wendy's and my life interests that is most reassuring and comforting.

Our newest friends are Ilaria Vigano and Gerard Francis. They are new to our community and large contributors to its vitality and creativity. Ilaria is from Naples, Italy, which assured me that I would be drawn to her; Gerard is a highly intelligent systems professional and authority on AI, who is overseeing the installation of a new system for JP Morgan Chase Bank.

Finally, Geoffrey Cowan and Aileen Adams are both poly-maths who have played their traditional role of permanent boosters for Wendy and me. Geoff led Voice of America and was the dean of the Annenberg School of Communications at USC. Geoff also wrote several books, including *The People v. Clarence Darrow: The Bribery Trial of America's Greatest Lawyer.* He also wrote a play called *Top Secret: The Battle for the Pentagon Papers.*

Geoff and Aileen adopted me as an honorary friend because I married their pal. As soon as Geoff heard I intended to write this memoir, he called me enthusiastically to offer the support of two of his most brilliant staff members for the course he teaches at USC. Demme Durrett is employed part-time by USC and part-time by the US government. Demme was great at identifying sources and individuals to help me write my biography. The other is Grace Huang, a brilliant Chinese student who was superb at doing impossible searches and finding the answers. I got to know both Demme and Grace well; they became real collaborators in this effort.

Also, there are several people without whom the book would have never been finished. Anyone who knows my life, knows that Wendy is the person who makes things happen, including encouraging me to write this book and contributing valuable insights, since this book is about Wendy and me in action and in love.

The second person who was invaluable was Katie Hall, who began working with me as my editor five years ago. I found her by speaking to other editors. She was recommended to me by a former editor who knew of her work in pulling together the final manuscript of *DeKooning: An American Master*, published by Knopf and written by Mark Stevens and Annalyn Swan. Katie has been both a cheerleader and a wise guide to writing a book, as opposed to a long article, which is what I am used to writing. She encouraged me to have my own voice throughout and guided me wisely. I am eternally grateful and strongly recommend her to anyone writing a book—especially a first one.

The third person who made this book possible is Oscar Cespedes Medina, a brilliant student of political science, who stood and sat with me for hours transcribing my thoughts and making sense of them and worked closely with Wendy in assembling and positioning the photos in this book.

I also must acknowledge and thank Harry Woolf who was the director of the Institute for Advanced Studies and who gave me the job of Director's Visitor at the Institute after I left Venezuela. The year I spent at the Institute in Princeton allowed me to write an article on the Falklands War and talk about writing with George Kennan, who sat on the floor directly under mine and who also encouraged my writing.

I also acknowledge Lee Hamilton, a former congressman from Indiana, who invited me to become a Senior Fellow at the Woodrow Wilson Center when he was director there and who was followed by Jane Harman. I prepared much of the work in this volume on talking with the enemy while at the Wilson Center, which proved to become an invaluable environment for me to write this book.

I also want to thank multiple colleagues from the Foreign Service—diplomats who are worthy of the title of diplomat. Standing tall among this group is Tom Pickering, who is generally acknowledged as the outstanding professional diplomat of his generation and who asked me to be a deputy in the Executive Secretariat when Henry Kissinger became secretary of state. Tom later became ambassador to Russia. Tom was ambassador to many countries including Jordan, Israel, India, and El Salvador. His role as the US ambassador to the UN prepared him brilliantly to become chairman of my board when I was the head of UNA-USA. Tom has been an invaluable friend for most of my foreign service career and afterward.

I want to thank Frank Wisner, whom I had known professionally for decades. Frank, like Tom Pickering, is one of the most distinguished Foreign Service professionals and a career diplomat who is perhaps the most adept of us all at describing the art of diplomacy, as he is the premier artist of diplomacy. His memory and wit and constructive approach to diplomacy is unequaled. If there is a major ambassador whom I know well, it is Frank Wisner.

Finally, I wish to thank Stephen Heintz who is president of the Rockefeller Brothers Fund, on which board I served on for many years. He is a close friend with a penetrating mind and admirable discipline. Stephen, while not a professional diplomat, might as well be, because of his great skill in dealing with our work. I learned as much informally from him about diplomacy as I have from my formerly mentioned, two remarkable colleagues in the foreign service.

Tom Pickering, Frank Wisner, and Stephen Heintz formed the core group that made up the leadership of the Iran Project, which further convinced me of the value of talking with the enemy. In many hours of discussion over decades, with the three of them and others, I became even more convinced of the wisdom of our back-channel discussions with Iranian officials. A key element in these discussions was Suzanne DiMaggio, whom I hired when I was president of the UNA-USA to take over politics for our small NGO. Suzanne developed unusually strong and unique skills in her role as key communicator of the back channel between Iran and the US. Suzanne replaced me as head of the Iran Project and has succeeded brilliantly in moving it forward. The Rockefeller Brothers Fund under Stephen Heintz became the principal funder and supporter of our work and continued to be so for two decades, as we tried to establish a conversation with Iranian officials who had a desire to establish a regular channel to Iran to encourage official interaction between our two governments. President Obama recognized the role of the Iran Project in a note he wrote to me in 2012.

I want to recognize the work of so many friends in Connecticut who have boosted me up during the writing of this book. First are Woody and Maria Campbell. Maria has been a very successful agent and scout within the publishing industry and provided excellent ideas and suggestions as I sought the publisher who would take on this project. Maria was able to find Kim Schefler who negotiated our deal with Rodin Books. I also want to mention Barbara Kohn, who recommended the publisher Arthur Klebanoff of Rodin Books, who has been a most creative and energetic partner in taking on this publication. Arthur had published the book of Jan Vilček a Slovak scientist friend of ours, who strongly recommended him as the publisher of this book.

I send a special thanks to Dr. Valentín Fuster, who saved my life at least twice; once when he talked almost daily on the phone in Spanish from Mt. Sinai Hospital in New York with Wendy and with doctors in a small clinic in Punta del Este, Uruguay, where I was close to death after the infection from *Vibrio vulnificus* several years before I started on this book. Dr. Fuster, who is the chief of Cardiology at Mt. Sinai Hospital, is unquestionably the best cardiologist in New York City. He is kind and supportive of all of his patients. He is a unique medical asset to New York. Dr. Fuster saved me from death a second time when I came down with a pneumonia that was difficult to diagnose.

In addition to Dr. Fuster, I was taken care of by the excellent concierge doctor in Washington, CT: Alfonse Altorelli, whose office is ten minutes from our house. Dr. Altorelli is an unusually attentive doctor who is practical, not given to exaggerations or frightening scenarios. His calm and thorough approach is matched by his nurse who is also his wife, Deborah Altorelli. Together they are an extremely valuable asset for our community. He has pulled me through a number of difficult moments and works well and closely with Dr. Fuster.

I want to thank and acknowledge my special assistant during my years at the State Department. Marie Campello was my pal and close advisor when I was Ambassador to Venezuela and Czechoslovakia. If my former records and calendars are clear and organized, which they are, it is due to the attention given to them by Marie, who spent two weekends with us preparing me to write this book and organizing my files. I could not persuade Marie to join me at the Met because she was intimidated by New York City and my job, which was certain to be a challenge for both of us. Marie was an exceptional Foreign Service professional who ordered my schedule and my life for nearly eight years in three different locations. Hats off to Marie and the other professionals I was lucky to know in the Foreign Service. This includes Marjorie Jackson, who was my special assistant when I was the Guyana Desk Officer when she had her first assignment as a professional in the State Department. Marjorie Jackson served with me at a very low level and proved exceptionally talented. She ended her career at the top of the State Department as the executive assistant to Secretary of State Colin Powell.

I must acknowledge all the staff of the American Embassy in Prague that worked to prepare Wendy and me during those exciting years between 1983 and 1986. I particularly praise Carl Schmidt, who was a Czech-speaking expert on Central Europe and served as my Deputy Chief of Mission. He and his wife, Rika, were good friends of Václav and Olga Havel. His feel for the country was invaluable to me.

I also want to single out William Kiehl who represented USIS and is a model for the talent that is needed today in every American embassy around the world. He spoke the language, loved the arts, was outgoing and affable with all the Czechs that knew him. Most of the programs that were organized for visiting artists and painters were accomplished by Bill working closely with his wife Pam.

I would like to single out for thanks two senior staff members of the United Nations Association without whom UNA-USA would not have been nearly so creative. First is Nahela Hadi who was a refugee from Afghanistan and whom I appointed as the director of Adopt-A-Minefield. Nahela was unusually creative in organizing and working with Paul McCartney on our annual dinners in Los Angeles. Nahela had and has big abilities and she helped me manage UNA-USA during the end of my tenure.

Secondly, I must single out Lucia Rodriguez who was the Afro-Cuban American who developed and led our Global Classrooms programs with a budget of nearly 10 million dollars. Over a decade, she developed this particular and unique program and curriculum for the public high school students to learn about the world, the UN, and diplomacy. She organized a worldwide Model United Nations program annually in the UN General Assembly Hall with great success. She was completely bilingual which greatly enabled her leadership and communications with our Global Classrooms high school students in ten of the largest public-school systems in the United States.

I've already mentioned on several occasions the special relationship with the Cisneros family. This book is weaker because Gustavo died before he was able to provide me his final thoughts on these various chapters.

There are at least three families that were important during our lives in Czechoslovakia. The first were the Svejda family with whom we spent many weekends in Northern Bohemia. Wendy is godmother to Amalka, the eldest daughter of Marian and Lisa Svejda. Lisa was a student activist during the Velvet Revolution and became a partner with Wendy's foundation, running her first program called the Masaryk Fellows, which placed hundreds of Americans in schools in Czechoslovakia to teach English. Their sons Adam and Josef are very special to us. The second family was Daniel and Victoria Spicka. Daniel is an accomplished preservationist who also led a chamber group that played baroque music with old instruments from the baroque era. He had a small quartet that played regularly at our dinners at the Residence. Finally, there was Prince Karel Schwarzenberg, who was Havel's foreign minister and trusted partner. Karel Schwarzenberg had been a unique leader of European movements for human rights prior to the Velvet Revolution in 1989.

Two other friends I want to thank are Riprand Arco and his wife, Maria Beatrice Arco, who were invaluable in introducing us to Austria and Central Europe.

Finally, I want to thank our five children, plus a sixth who died during the writing of this book, for the love and understanding they have given to me through many years of absence at work and the travails that have been caused by traveling and having to live in so many different places. David, William, and Amy endured particular stress after my divorce from their mother and the loss of their brother. They've all been unusually caring during my years of immobility. David, now my eldest, and his wife, Kate, are the center of Sandpoint, Idaho where they run Foster's Crossing Antiques and enjoy the beauty of nature. His daughters

Riley and Erin are our eldest grandchildren. Erin is married to Cory Abbott. My son, William "Will" Luers, an assistant professor of New Media at Washington State University, and his wife Katie, an accomplished nurse, have been enormously attentive and caring, spending many weeks with us during crucial times in my recovery. Their daughter, Arden, graduated from college summa cum laude in neuroscience in 2023 and their son, Carl (named after my father), is in his second year at university. My daughter Amy, a brilliant climate scientist, is senior global director of Sustainability, Science and Innovation at Microsoft. She and her husband, Leonard Sklar, a geomorphologist with a PhD from Berkeley live in Seattle. Their son, Cedar Sklar Luers, just graduated from NYU in 2024.

I also want to acknowledge the extraordinary role played by Ramsay and Connor Turnbull, who joined our family when Wendy and I married in 1979. They were raised in Caracas and came to know well David, William, and Amy during their visits to Caracas, where they had lived four years before. Ramsay has been particularly helpful in assembling our family's photos for this book, since she lived with us during both of my foreign assignments as ambassador. She is also an accomplished photographer. Connor is the ever-present and forceful creative player in this clan and a talented professional preservation architect. Ramsay's husband is Sergio Missana, a Chilean novelist who now heads Climate Parliament, which works with the Parliaments of Africa and Europe to promote knowledge of climate change. Sergio's primary trade is as a Chilean novelist who has provided invaluable insights into the role of Pinochet in Chile and into the chapter on Operation Condor. They have three children, Maya, Luis, and Sofia, who spent seven years living near us in Washington, Connecticut, as they finished middle school and high school. All three are now in college. Connor is married to Ken Ishiguro, a Japanese architect who was headed for the professional golf circuits before he graduated from Berkley in architecture. Since then, he's become a star architect for a series of architectural firms dealing with leisure hotels and housing. Ken and Connor have two children, Seiji and Mika.

Like Fabrizio, the hero and author of my favorite novel, *The Leopard*, I feel like the patriarch who has benefited from so many joys with my children and grandchildren, each of whom has kept trying to educate me on how their generation thinks differently from mine. I treasure the role of patriarch, particularly of this clan.

ABOUT THE AUTHOR

William Luers, a career Foreign Service Officer for thirty years and an officer in the Navy for five years, has served as ambassador to Venezuela and Prague, president of the Metropolitan Museum of Art for thirteen years, president and CEO of UNA-USA, director of the Iran Project, and adjunct professor at Columbia University. He has written articles for various publications, including *Foreign Affairs,* and op-eds in the *New York Times,* the *Washington Post,* the *Wall Street Journal, Newsweek, Christian Science Monitor,* and the *Philadelphia Inquirer.* He is a member of the Council on Foreign Relations, and the Academy of Arts and Sciences, and for fourteen years was the American advisor of the Praemium Imperiale, an international arts prize. He has served on many corporate and nonprofit boards of directors.

He lives in Connecticut and New York City with his wife, Wendy.

PHOTO CREDITS

Photos not listed here are courtesy of William and Wendy Luers.

Introduction
Page xiii: Duke Ellington and Paul Gonsalves jam session in
    Leningrad with Soviet musicians, 1971. *Naum Kazhdan.*

Chapter 1
Page 2: Bill at six years old. *Blanche, Inc.*

Chapter 2:
Page 42: Baby carriage on steps in Odessa from the film *Battleship
    Potemkin* by Sergei Eisenstein. *Encyclopedia Britannica.*

Chapter 4
Page 63: Zverev Self Portrait. *Copyright Woody Campbell.*

Chapter 6
Page 111: Averell and Pamela Harriman in Washington, D.C.
Copyright Diana Walker.

Chapter 7
Page 128: Ambassador Robert McClintock Caracas, 1970. *State
    Department.*
Page 130: Nixon, Ambassador McClintock greeting Bill in the
    Ambassador's Residence *White House.*

Chapter 8
Page 138: Pinochet and Kissinger, 1976. *Copyright Creative Commons.*
Page 158: *The Condor Years: How Pinochet And His Allies Brought
    Terrorism To Three Continents* by John Dinges. © *The New Press.*

Page 159: *The Pinochet File A Declassified Dossier on Atrocity and Accountability. A National Security Archive Book* by Peter Kornbluh. © *The New Press.*

Chapter 9

Page 161: Looking over Caracas. *Photo by Inge Morath.*

Page 161: Connor, Tomales, Ramsay arrival in Caracas. *From* The Daily Journal, *Caracas.*

Page 162: Bill with Connor and Wendy. *Photo by Inge Morath.*

Page 185: Carlos Rangel and Bill with model of *Museo de Arte Contemporaneo,* Caracas.

Page 185: Bill Styron and Peter Matthiessen in Venezuela. *Photo by Inge Morath.*

Page 186: Vice President Bush greeting Marines at the Embassy. *The White House.*

Page 186: Bill, Wendy, and Jeane Kirkpatrick. *The State Department.*

Chapter 10

Page 196: George Kennan at IAS, 1982. *Copyright Grace Warnecke.*

Page 203: Vice President Bush and Bill discussing ambassadorship. *The White House.*

Page 209: Swearing in, Prague, 1983. Connor, Ramsay, Amy, William, David, Mark, Chief of Protocol Tim Towell, Wendy, Bill, and Larry Eagleburger. *The State Department.*

Chapter 11

Page 226: Wendy after the party. *Photo by Inge Morath.*

Chapter 12

Page 251: Wendy and Bill in the American Wing. *Copyright Horst.*

Page 273: Kevin Roche the architect of the Met, Bill, Diane Coffey, Ed Koch, Philippe de Montebello, Punch Sulzberger, looking at a new wing of the Met. *Courtesy Joan Vitale Strong, Office of the Mayor.*

Chapter 13

Page 275: Ronald Reagan and Bill, 1983. *The White House.*

Page 279: Bill with Gorbachev. *Photo by Joe Veriker/PhotoBureau.*

Page 285: Bill escorting Andrei Sakharov at the Met *Photograph by Richard Lombard.*

Chapter 14

Page 302: Wendy, President Havel, Bill, and Michael Žantovský on Fifth Avenue, February 22, 1990. *Courtesy* The New York Times.

Page 308: Michael Žantovský, Bill, and President Havel on steps of the Metropolitan Museum of Art, 1990. *Courtesy Mary Hilliard.*

Chapter 16

Page 334: Wendy, President Clinton, and Bill at Styron dinner. *The White House.*

Chapter 17

Page 347: Gabe, Inge, Bill, Linda, and Arthur. *AP/Jose Gotia.*

Chapter 18

Page 286: Bill speaking in Tokyo at the Praemium Imperiale, 2018. ©*The Japan Art Association/The Sankei Shimbun.*

NOTES

1. Louis Menand, *The Free World: Art and Thought in the Cold War* (New York: Farrar, Straus and Giroux, 2021), xi–xii.

2. Mel Gussow, *Edward Albee: A Singular Journey: A Biography* (Applause Theater Books, 1999), 208.

3. Gussow, 208.

4. United States Department of State, *Department of State Bulletin* XXIX, no. 732, publication 5114 (July 6, 1953): 125.

5. Yevgeny Yevtushenko, "Babi Yar," *The Collected Poems, 1952–1990* (New York: Henry Holt & Co., 1991).

6. Yevgeny Yevtushenko, "The Heirs of Stalin," *The Collected Poems, 1952–1990* (New York: Henry Holt & Co., 1991).

7. Raymond H. Anderson, "Andrei Voznesensky, Russian Poet, Dies at 77," *New York Times*, June 1, 2010, https://www.nytimes.com/2010/06/02/books/02voznesensky.html.

8. Andrei Voznesensky, "The Ditch: A Spiritual Trial," 1986.

9. Taru Spiegel, "'In Search of Melancholy Baby': Vasilii Aksenov and Soviet Émigré Life in Washington, DC," Library of Congress blog, August 18, 2021, https://blogs.loc.gov/international-collections/2021/08/in-search-of-melancholy-baby-vasilii-aksenov-and-soviet-migr-life-in-washington-dc/.

10. Mark Yoffe, "Vasily Aksyonov, Libertarian Russian writer and leading light in 'youth prose', fell foul of the KGB," *Guardian*, July 15, 2009, https://www.theguardian.com/books/2009/jul/16/vasily-aksyonov-obituary.

11. Mihajlo Mihajlov, as cited in the CIA FPOA (foia.cia.gov). Document publication date, April 12, 1965. Released on July 27, 1998, (https://www.cia.gov/readingroom/print/1358899).

12. Boris Schwarz, *Music and Musical Life in Soviet Russia: Enlarged Edition, 1917-1981* (Bloomington: Indiana University Press, 1972).

13. Timothy McClure, "The Politics of Soviet Culture 1961–1967," *Problems of Communism*, (1967), 43.

14. A. Fadeev, *Molodaia g`vardiia*, no. 10 (1965): 121.

15. Ilya Glazunov, *Molodaia g`vardiia*, no. 6 (June 3, 1966): 257.

16. V. Lakshin "The Writer, the Reader and the Critic," *Novyi Mir*, no. 8 (1966), Moscow, Russia.

17. "Anatoly Zverev," AZ Museum, https://museum-az.com/en/az/#:~:text=Anatoly%20Zverev%20(1931%20%2D%201986).

18. Joseph Backstein, letter to the author, 1995. William Luers archives.

19. Glazunov, *Molodaia g`vardiia*, 257.

20. Isaiah Berlin, "Anna Akhmatova: A Memoir," in *The Complete Poems of Anna Akhmatova*, ed. Roberta Reeder, trans. by Judith Hemschemeyer (Boston: Zephyr Press, 1997), 35–55.

21. "Text of Pravda Editorial on Ouster of Khrushchev," *New York Times*, October 17, 1964, www.nytimes.com/1964/10/17/archives/text-of-pravda-editorial-on-ouster-of-khrushchev.html.

22. Henri Neuendorf, "Shchukin Collection at Fondation Louis Vuitton," *artnet*, February 12, 2016, https://news.artnet.com/art-world/foundation-louis-vuitton-shchukin-collection-425546.

23. *Pravda*, October 15, 1964.

24. Susan Emily Reid, "In the Name of the People: The Manege Affair Revisited," *Kritika: Explorations in Russian and Eurasian History* 6, no. 4 (2005): 673–716, https://doi.org/10.1353/kri.2005.0058.

25. Sergey, "Manege Scandal of Khrushchev," subscribe.ru/archive/history.sezik/200202/03135229.html.

26. "Biography—Ernst Neizvestny," personal website, www.enstudio.com/about_artist/.

27. "Biography—Ernst Neizvestny."

28. "Biography—Ernst Neizvestny."

29. J. Hoberman, "Social Realism from Stalin to Sots," *Artforum*, September 26, 2023, www.artforum.com/features/social-realism-from-stalin-to-sots-204159/.

30. Hoberman, "Social Realism."

31. Timothy Snyder, *Bloodlands: Europe between Hitler and Stalin*, 2nd paperback ed. (New York: Basic Books, 2022), xiii.

32. Robert Hughes, "Art: California in Eupeptic Color," *Time*, June 27, 1977, content.time.com/time/subscriber/article/0,33009,915092,00.html.

33. John Ruskin, "Preface," *St. Mark's Rest: The History of Venice* (New York: J. Wiley & Sons, 1877), 1.

34. Benedict Cross, "Marxism in Venezuela," Problems of Communism (November 1973).

35. Tim Weiner, *Legacy of Ashes: The History of the CIA* (New York: Doubleday, 2007), 222.

36. Weiner, *Legacy of Ashes*, 209.

37. Weiner, *Legacy of Ashes*, 222.

38. William Styron, *My Generation: Collected Nonfiction* (New York: Random House, 2015) 447–448.

39. Teodoro Petkoff, *Checoeslovaquia: El Socialismo Como Problema* (Caracas: Monte Ávila, 1990), i.

40. Glenn Lowry, personal letter to the author, October 2023. William Luers Archives.

41. Nicanor Costa Mendez, Presentation on the Falklands to the OAS, Organization of the American States, 1982.

42. Costa Mendez, Speech.

43. "Mission & History," Institute for Advanced Study, https://www.ias.edu/about/mission-history.

44. Charles Stuart Kennedy, interview, Foreign Affairs Oral History Project, The Association for Diplomatic Studies and Training, May 11, 2011. Copyright 2020 ADST.

45. Kennedy, interview, Foreign Affairs Oral History Project.

46. Mitchell Lerner, "'Trying to Find the Guy Who Invited Them': Lyndon Johnson, Bridge Building, and the End of the Prague Spring," *Diplomatic History* 32, no. 1 (2008), 77, http://www.jstor.org/stable/24916056.

47. Lerner, "'Trying to Find,'" 77.

48. Ronald Reagan, "Letter From President Reagan to Soviet General Secretary Brezhnev," US Department of State, April 21, 1981, history.state.gov/historicaldocuments/frus1981-88v03/d46.

49. Jan Hamara, "Warsaw Pact Invasion of Czechoslovakia," *The History of Czechoslovakia*, https://scalar.usc.edu/works/dissolution-of-czechoslovakia/warsaw-pact-invasion-of-czechoslovakia#:~:.

50. Jan Palmowski, *A Dictionary of Contemporary World History: From 1900 to the Present Day* (Oxford: Oxford University Press, 2008).

51. Ed Vulliamy, "1989 and All That: Plastic People of the Universe and the Velvet Revolution," *The Guardian*, September 5, 2009, https://www.theguardian.com/music/2009/sep/06/plastic-people-velvet-revolution-1989.

52. Václav Havel, *To the Castle and Back, translated by Paul Wilson* (Edinburgh: Portobello Books, 2009), 20.

53. Michael Žantovský, *Havel: A Life* (New York: Grove Press, 2015), 250.

54. Walter Annenberg, press release, March 12, 1991.

55. Philippe de Montebello, letter to the editor, *Wall Street Journal*, March 14, 1991.

56. Anatoly Dobrynin, *In Confidence,* Random House, 1995, 484.

57. Dobrynin, 484.

58. Jack F. Matlock Jr., *Reagan and Gorbachev: How the Cold War Ended* (New York: Random House, 2004), 92–93.

59. Suzanne Massie, *Trust but Verify: Reagan, Russia and Me* (Blue Hill, Maine: Hearttree Press, 2013).

60. Dobrynin, *In Confidence*.

61. Dobrynin, *In Confidence*, 606.

62. Thomas Blanton and Svetlana Savranskaya, "The Moscow Summit 20 Years Later," National Security Archive, *National Security Archive Electronic Briefing Book*, no. 251.

63. Václav Havel, "Text of Havel's Speech to Congress," Reuter, published in *Washington Post*, February 21, 1990, https://www.washingtonpost.com/archive/politics/1990/02/22/text-of-havels-speech-to-congress/df98e177-778e-4c26-bd96-980089c4fcb2/.

64. Havel, "Havel's Speech to Congress."

65. Havel, "Havel's Speech to Congress."

66. "Havel, Walesa, Ex-Dissidents to Meet at Border Hideaway," Reuter, published in *Washington Post*, March 16, 1990, https://www.washingtonpost.com/archive/politics/1990/03/17/havel-walesa-ex-dissidents-to-meet-at-border-hideaway/3a29e1fe-07e8-4b66-9519-bfa0dbdc873c/.

67. "Helsinki Final Act, 1975," Office of the Historian, US Department of State.

68. Seymour Hersh, *The Price of Power: Kissinger in the Nixon White House*, Summit Books, 1983.

69. "Charter 77," *Economic and Political Weekly* 12, no. 21 (1977): 831–33, http://www.jstor.org/stable/4365612.

70. Brian K. Goodman, *The Nonconformists: American and Czech Writers across the Iron Curtain* (Cambridge: Harvard University Press, 2023), 231.

71. Goodman, *The Nonconformists*, 20–21.

72. William H. Luers, "Czechoslovakia: Road to Revolution," *Foreign Affairs*, March 1, 1990.

73. Luers, "Czechoslovakia: Road to Revolution."

74. Ian Willoughby, "A Few Sentences: 'One of the most important

steps before November 1989,'" Radio Prague International, June 27, 2019.

75. Michael Kimmelman, "Annenberg Donates a van Gogh to the Met," *The New York Times*, May 25, 1993, www.nytimes.com/1993/05/25/arts/annenberg-donates-a-van-gogh-to-the-met.html.

76. Sharon Waxman, "Chasing the Lydian Hoard," *Smithsonian Magazine*, November 14, 2008, www.smithsonianmag.com/history/chasing-the-lydian-hoard-93685665/. Excerpted from Sharon Waxman, *Loot: The Battle over the Stolen Treasures of the Ancient World* (New York: Times Books, 2008).

77. Waxman, "Chasing the Lydian Hoard."

78. William Luers, personal conversation with Helen Frankenthaler, 1987.

79. "Outline," Praemium Imperiale, accessed April 16, 2024, www.praemiumimperiale.org/en/aboutus-en/about-en.

80. Arthur Miller, "A Visit with Castro," *Nation*, December 24, 2003, https://www.thenation.com/article/archive/visit-castro/.

81. Miller, "A Visit With Castro."

82. Miller, "A Visit With Castro."

83. Miller, "A Visit With Castro."

84. Miller, "A Visit With Castro."

85. Miller, "A Visit With Castro."

86. Ángel Esteban and Stéphanie Panichelli, *Fidel & Gabo: A Portrait of the Legendary Friendship Between Fidel Castro and Gabriel García Márquez* (New York: Pegasus, 2009), viii.

87. Alan Gomez, "Fidel Castro to Obama: 'We don't need the empire to give us anything,'" *USA Today*, March 28, 2016, https://www.usatoday.com/story/news/2016/03/28/fidel-castro-president-obama-cuba-trip/82347680/.

BIBLIOGRAPHY

Adelman, Kenneth L. *Reagan at Reykjavik: Forty-Eight Hours That Ended the Cold War*. Broadside Books, 2014.

Alcántara, Tomás Polanco, et al. *Venezuela y Estados Unidos a Través de 2 Siglos*. VenAmCham, Cámara Venezolano-Americana de Comercio e Industria, 2000.

Algeo, Matthew. *When Harry Met Pablo: Truman, Picasso, and the Cold War Politics of Modern Art*. Chicago Review Press, 2024.

Allison, Graham T. *Destined for War: Can America and China Escape Thucydides's Trap?* Houghton Mifflin Harcourt, 2018.

Arendt, Hannah. *The Origins of Totalitarianism*. Harcourt, 2005.

Begley, Adam. *Updike*. HarperCollins, 2014.

Blumay, Carl, and Henry Edwards. *The Dark Side of Power: The Real Armand Hammer*. Simon & Schuster, 1992.

Boutros-Ghali, Boutros. *Egypt's Road to Jerusalem: A Diplomat's Story of the Struggle for Peace in the Middle East*. Random House, 1997.

Bradley, James. *The Imperial Cruise: A Secret History of Empire and War*. Back Bay Books, 2010.

Brodsky, Joseph. *Flucht Aus Byzanz: Essays*. Fisher Taschenbuch Verlag, 1991.

Byrne, Malcolm, and Kian Byrne. *Worlds Apart a Documentary History of US-Iranian*
Relations, 1978-2018. Cambridge University Press, 2022.

Catto, Henry E, Jr.. *Ambassadors at Sea: The High and Low Adventures of a Diplomat*. University of Texas Press, 1999.

Cerf, Christopher, and Victor S. Navasky. *Experts Speak: Definitive Compendium of Authoritative Misinformation*. Pantheon Books, 1984.

Chernow, Ron. *Titan: The Life of John D. Rockefeller, Sr.* Vintage, 2004.

Cork, Richard. *Encounters with Artists.* Thames & Hudson, 2023.

Corsini, Ray Pierre. *Caviar for Breakfast: An American Woman's Adventures in Russia.* Harvill, 1965.

Dallek, Robert. *Nixon and Kissinger: Partners in Power.* Harper Collins, 2007.

Dinges, John. *The Condor Years: How Pinochet and His Allies Brought Terrorism to Three Continents.* New Press, 2005.

Dirscherl, Denis. *The New Russia: Communism in Evolution.* Pflaum Press, 1968.

Djilas, Milovan. *Conversations with Stalin.* Translated by Michael B. Petrovich, Harcourt Brace & Co., 1992.

Djilas, Milovan. *The New Class: An Analysis of the Communist System.* Unwin Books, 1966.

Dobrynin, Anatolij Fedorovič. *In Confidence: Moscow's Ambasador to American's Six Cold War Presidents (1962–1986).* Time Books, 1995.

Donaldson, Scott. *John Cheever: A Biography.* Random House, 1988.

Ehrenburg, Ilya. *Memoirs: 1921–1941.* Translated by Tatania Shebunina. Grosset & Dunlap, 1966.

Epstein, Edward Jay. *Dossier: The Secret History of Armand Hammer.* Random House, 1996.

Feifer, Gregory. *Russians: The People behind the Power.* Twelve, 2015.

Figes, Orlando. *The Story of Russia.* Bloomsbury Publishing, 2022.

Goldberger, Paul. *Building Art: The Life and Work of Frank Gehry.* Alfred A. Knopf, 2015.

Goodman, Brian K. *Nonconformists: American and Czech Writers across the Iron Curtain.* Harvard University Press, 2023.

Goodwin, Doris Kearns. *Leadership in Turbulent Times.* Simon & Schuster, 2019.

Graham, Thomas, Jr. *Getting Russia Right.* Polity Press, 2023.

Greenfield, Meg. *Washington*. Public Affairs, 2001.

Gross, Michael. *Rogues' Gallery: The Secret Story of the Lust, Lies, Greed and Betrayals That Made the Metropolitan Museum*. Broadway Books, 2010.

Gussow, Mel. *Edward Albee: A Singular Journey*. Simon & Schuster, 1999.

Haraszti, Miklós. *The Velvet Prison: Artists under State Socialism*. Basic Books, 1987.

Havel, Václav. *Disturbing for Peace*. Translated by Paul Wilson. Vintage Books, 1991.

Vaclav Have. *To the Castle and Back*. Translated by Paul R. Wilson, Alfred A. Knopf, 2009.

Homans, Jennifer. *Apollo's Angels: A History of Ballet*. Random House Trade Paperbacks, 2011.

Homans, Jennifer. *Mr. B: George Balanchine's 20th Century*. Random House, 2022.

Hughes, Robert. *The Shock of the New: The Hundred-Year History of Modern Art—Its Rise, Its Dazzling Achievement, Its Fall*. Knopf, 1991.

Inboden, William. *The Peacemaker: Ronald Reagan, the Cold War, and the World on the Brink*. Dutton, 2022.

Indyk, Martin. *Master of the Game: Henry Kissinger and the Art of Middle East Diplomacy*. Alfred A. Knopf, 2022.

Isaacson, Walter, and Evan Thomas. *The Wise Men: Six Friends and the World They Made*. Simon and Schuster, 1988.

Judt, Tony. *Postwar: A History of Europe since 1945*. Penguin Books, 2006.

Kagan, Donald. *On the Origins of War: And the Preservation of Peace*. Anchor, 1995.

Kapuściński, Ryszard. *Imperium*. Translated by Klara Glowczewska, Vintage International, 1995.

Kennan, George F. *Around the Cragged Hill: A Personal and Political Philosophy*. W. W. Norton & Company, 1993.

Khodorkovsky, Mikhail. *The Russia Conundrum: How the West Fell for Putin's Power Gambit—and How Fix It*. St Martin's Press, 2022.

Klíma, Ivan. *My Crazy Century*. Translated by Craig Stephen Cravens. Grove Press, 2014.

Kopelev, Lev. *Ease My Sorrows*. Random House, 1983.

Kopelev, Lev *No Jail for Thought*. Translated by Anthony Austin, Penguin Books, 1979.

Kopelev, Lev *The Education of a True Believer*, Translated by Gary Kern. Harper & Row, 1980

Kornbluh, Peter. *The Pinochet File: A Declassified Dossier on Atrocity and Accountability*. New Press, 2004.

Levitsky, Steven, and Daniel Ziblatt. *How Democracies Die*. Broadway Books, 2019.

Llosa, Vargas Mario. *Notes on the Death of Culture: Essays on Spectacle and Society*. Translated by John King. Farrar, Straus and Giroux, 2015.

Lord, Winston. Kissinger on Kissinger. Reflections on Diplomacy, Grand Strategy, and Leadership. All Points Books, 2019.

Macomber, William. *The Angel's Game: A Handbook of Modern Diplomacy*. Stein and Day, 1977.

Mandelbaum, Michael, and Strobe Talbott. *Reagan and Gorbachev*. Vintage Books, 1987.

Mandelshtam, Nadezhda. *Hope against Hope: A Memoir*. Atheneum, 1987.

Massie, Suzanne. *Land of the Firebird: The Beauty of Old Russia*. HeartTree Press, 2002.

Matlock, Jack F., Jr. *Reagan and Gorbachev: How the Cold War Ended*. Random House, 2005.

McDonell, Terry. *Irma: The Education of a Mother's Son*. Harper, 2023.

McNamara, Craig. *Because Our Fathers Lied: A Memoir of Truth and Family, from Vietnam to Today.* Little Brown and Company, 2022.

Meacham, Jon. *And There Was Light: Abraham Lincoln and the American Struggle.* Random House, 2022.

Miller, Arthur. *Echoes down the Corridor: Collected Essays, 1944–2000.* Edited by Steve Centola, Penguin Books, 2001.

Miller, Chris. *The Struggle to Save the Soviet Economy: Mikhail Gorbachev and the Collapse of the USSR.* University of North Carolina Press, 2020.

Morgan, C. Lloyd. *Cold War Confrontations: US Exhibitions and T heir Role in the Cultural Cold War, 1950–1980.* Lars Müller Publishers, 2008.

Morris, Edmund. *Dutch: A Memoir of Ronald Reagan.* Modern Library, 1999.

Neuman, William. *Things Are Never So Bad That They Can't Get Worse: Inside the Collapse of Venezuela.* St. Martin's Press, 2022.

Neumann, Ariana. *When Time Stopped: A Memoir of My Father's War and What Remains.* Scribner, 2020.

Nye, Joseph S. Soft Power : the Means to Success in World Politics. New York :Public Affairs, 2004

Ogden, Chris. *Legacy: A Biography of Moses and Walter Annenberg.* Little, Brown and Company, 1999.

Osnos, Evan. *Wildland: The Making of America's Fury.* Farrar, Straus and Giroux, 2021.

Padura, Leonardo. *Havana Black.* Translated by Peter R. Bush. Bitter Lemon Press, 2008.

Patterson, Richard North. *Trial.* Post Hill Press, 2023.

Petkoff, Teodoro. *Checoeslovaquia: El Socialismo Como Problema.* Editorial Domingo Fuentes, 1969.

Plessix Gray, Francine du. *At Home with the Marquis de Sade: A Life.* Penguin Group, 1999.

Rangel, Carlos. *The Latin Americans: Their Love-Hate Relationship with the United States.* Harcourt Brace Jovanovich, 1977.

Reardon, Robert J. *Containing Iran: Strategies for Addressing the Iranian Nuclear Challenge.* RAND, 2012.

Remnick, David. *The Devil Problem and Other True Stories.* Random House, 1996.

Remnick, David, Lenin's Tomb: *The Last Days of the Soviet Empire.* New York, Random House, 1993.

Risen, James and Tom Risen. *The Last Honest Man: The CIA, the FBI, the Mafia, and the Kennedys—and One Senator's Fight to Save Democracy.* Thorndike Press, a part of Gale, a Cengage Company, 2023.

Rodgers, Mary, and Jesse Green. *Shy: The Alarmingly Outspoken Memoirs of Mary Rodgers.* Farrar, Straus and Giroux, 2022.

Rogoff, Natasha Lance. *Muppets in Moscow: The Unexpected Crazy True Story of Making Sesame Street in Russia.* Rowman & Littlefield Publishers, 2023.

Roth, Philip. *American Pastoral.* Vintage International, 2006.

Roth, Phillip *The Human Stain.* Vintage Books, 2001.

Saharov, Andrej Dmitrievič, and Harrison E. Salisbury. *Progress, Coexistence, and Intellectual Freedom.* W. W. Norton & Company, 1968.

Saito, Yoshiomi. *The Global Politics of Jazz in the Twentieth Century: Cultural Diplomacy and "American Music".* Routledge, 2021.

Sakharov, Andrei. *Memoirs.* Alfred A. Knopf, 1990.

Sakwa, Richard. *The Lost Peace: How the West Failed to Prevent a Second Cold War.* Yale University Press, 2023.

Salcedo-Bastardo, J. L., and Annella McDermott. *Bolivar: A Continent and Its Destiny.* Humanities Press, 1986.

Stevens, Norma and Steven M. L. Aronson. 2017. *Avedon: Something Personal.* Spiegel & Grau.

Salisbury, Harrison Evans. *The Soviet Union: The Fifty Years*. New York Times, 1968.

Schlesinger, Arthur M, Jr. *Journals, 1952–2000*. Penguin Press, 2008.

Schlesinger, Arthur. *The Disuniting of America*. Norton, 1993.

Schoultz, Lars. *In Their Own Best Interest: A History of the US Effort to Improve Latin Americans*. Harvard University Press, 2020.

Shear, Jack, et al. *Ways of Seeing*. The Drawing Center, 2022.

Shields, Charles J. *And So It Goes: Kurt Vonnegut, a Life*. St. Martin's Griffin, 2012.

Smith, Bruce L.R. *The Last Gentleman: Thomas Hughes and the End of the American Century*. Brookings Institution Press, 2021.

Solomon, Andrew. *The Irony Tower: Soviet Artists in a Time of Glasnost*. Knopf, 1991.

Solzhenitsyn, Aleksandr Isaevich. *One Day in the Life of Ivan Denisovich*. New American Library, 2009.

Steel, Ronald. *Pax Americana: Ronald Steel*. Viking Press, 1967.

Styron, William. *Darkness Visible: A Memoir of Madness*. Random House, 1999.

Styron, William *My Generation: Collected Nonfiction*. Edited by James L.W. West. Random House, 2015.

Styron, William, 1925–2006. 2008. Havanas in Camelot: Personal Essays. Random House.

Taubman, William. *Gorbachev: His Life and Times*. W. W. Norton & Company, 2017.

Thomas, Evan. *Ike's Bluff: President Eisenhower's Secret Battle to Save the World*. Little, Brown and Company, 2012.

Thomas, Evan *Road to Surrender: Three Men and the Countdown to the End of World War II*. Random House, 2023.

Thomas, Evan. *The War Lovers: Roosevelt, Lodge, Hearst, and the Rush to Empire, 1898*. Little, Brown and Company, 2010.

Tyler, Patrick. *A Great Wall: Six Presidents and China: An Investigative History*. Public Affairs, 2000.

Updike, John. *Beck a Book*, Fawcett Books, 1998.

Updike, John. *Bech at Bay: A Quasi-Novel*. Penguin, 1999.

Updike, John. *Bech Is Back*. Alfred A. Knopf, 1982.

Updike, John. *Bech: A Book*. Alfred A. Knopf, 1970.

Updike, John. *Museums & Women and Other Stories*. Alfred A. Knopf, 1972.

Updike, John. *Self-Consciousness: Memoirs*. Random House Trade Paperbacks, 2012.

Updike, John. *The Afterlife and Other Stories*. Alfred A. Knopf, 1994.

Updike, John. *The Early Stories, 1953–1975*. Alfred A. Knopf, 2004.

Waal, Edmund de. *The Hare with Amber Eyes: A Hidden Inheritance*. Picador, 2021.

Wallach, Janet. *Flirting with Danger: The Mysterious Life of Marguerite Harrison, Socialite Spy*. Doubleday, 2023.

Walter, Barbara F. *How Civil Wars Start: And How to Stop Them*. Crown, 2022.

Wasik, John F. *Lincolnomics How President Lincoln Constructed the Great American Economy*. Diversion Books, 2021.

Weintraub, Sidney. *A Marriage of Convenience: Relations between Mexico and the United States*. Oxford University Press, 1991.

Wellerstein, Alex. *Restricted Data: The History of Nuclear Secrecy in the United States*. The University of Chicago Press, 2021.

West, James L.W. *William Styron: a Life*. Random House, 1998.

Zimmermann, Warren. *First Great Triumph: How Five Americans Made Their Country a World Power*. Farrar, Straus and Giroux, 2004.

INDEX